P9-ELI-038

BUTLER TO THE WORLD

Also by Oliver Bullough

Moneyland

The Last Man in Russia

Let Our Fame Be Great

BUTLER TO THE WORLD

How Britain Helps the World's Worst People
Launder Money, Commit Crimes,
and Get Away with Anything

OLIVER BULLOUGH

ST. MARTIN'S PRESS
NEW YORK

CARLSBAD CITY LIBRARY
CARLSBAD, CA 92011

DISCARD

First published in the United States by St. Martin's Press,
an imprint of St. Martin's Publishing Group

BUTLER TO THE WORLD. Copyright © 2022 by Oliver Bullough. All rights
reserved. Printed in the United States of America. For information, address
St. Martin's Publishing Group, 120 Broadway, New York, NY 10271.

www.stmartins.com

The Library of Congress Cataloging-in-Publication Data
is available upon request.

ISBN 978-1-250-28192-0 (hardcover)
ISBN 978-1-250-28193-7 (ebook)

Our books may be purchased in bulk for promotional, educational,
or business use. Please contact your local bookseller or the Macmillan
Corporate and Premium Sales Department at 1-800-221-7945, extension
5442, or by email at MacmillanSpecialMarkets@macmillan.com.

Originally published in Great Britain by Profile Books Ltd

First U.S. Edition: 2022

10 9 8 7 6 5 4 3 2 1

AUG 2 6 2022

Contents

BUTLER TO THE WORLD

1

THE BUTLER BUSINESS

In June 2021, President Joe Biden and Prime Minister Boris Johnson marked eight decades since the birth of Britain and America's wartime alliance by issuing what they called the New Atlantic Charter. Divided into eight points, like the original document—which set out the two countries' approach to the Second World War—the new charter laid out how they should tackle challenges from climate to China and from pandemics to Putin.

Much has changed since Winston Churchill and Franklin D. Roosevelt agreed on their own vision in 1941, but one thing clearly remained constant: the strength of the bond between the two English-speaking nations.

The connections between Britain and America are profound—in foreign policy, in investment, in literature, in pop music, in the sharing of each other's celebrities. Sometimes, the closeness leads the two countries into terrible mistakes, as with the Iraq War; sometimes, as with defeating the Nazis or filming *This Is Spinal Tap,* the exchange leads to something magnificent. The term Special Relationship—which was popularized, if not invented, by Churchill—has become a cliché, invoked increasingly dutifully by American politicians and increasingly needi-fully by British ones, but it still reflects a deep and

enduring connection that goes far beyond what the two countries have with anyone else.

Perhaps the most remarkable demonstration of the closeness of these ties was revealed by General Michael Hayden,
the former director of the National Security Agency, in his
2016 memoir *Playing to the Edge*. In December 2003, American intelligence operatives became concerned that terrorists
armed with a nuclear bomb could attack Fort Meade, from
where the NSA controls its vast data-gathering operation.
Operatives were out scouring the country, looking for an Al-
Qaeda cell, and their managers were in the office at all hours,
despite the holiday season. They were being as thorough as they
could be, but there was still a chance the terrorists would
escape detection, and Hayden needed to prepare for the
worst. He had to be sure his agency could continue to defend
America even if the terrorists reached their target, detonated
their device, killed Hayden, and decapitated the NSA. So, what
did he do? He rang up his British counterpart—David Pepper,
director of GCHQ, the UK's signals intelligence (SIGINT)
agency.

"Happy Christmas, David," he said, before getting down to
business. "We feel a bit under threat here, so I've told my liaison to
your office that should there be catastrophic loss at Fort Meade,
we are turning the functioning of the American SIGINT system
over to GCHQ . . . it's just a precaution, but if we go down, you
run the show." There was then, according to an account he later
gave in a book promotional event, "a long pause."

It is not surprising that Pepper was taken aback. The NSA is
possibly the most potent intelligence agency in the world, and
it is remarkable testimony to the closeness of their relationship
that Hayden would be prepared to hand over such a weapon
to a foreign country, to trust a foreign national to defend the

United States on his behalf. We could all do with friends as reliable as that.

Or could we?

In this book, I reveal a less-known side to Britain, how it has spent decades not helping America but picking its pocket, undermining its government, and making the world poorer and less safe. While the British government's foreign policy has been built on the bedrock of its alliance with Washington, there has always been a separate dynamic, which has treated the United States and other allies not as partners to support but as opportunities to exploit. And, fundamentally, over the last eighty years, that secret side of Britain has had a far more significant impact on the world than its avowed public policies.

In this book, I reveal that hidden side of Britain, which I fear the vast majority of people have no idea exists and which will shake anyone's confidence in its worth as a close ally. The country's public image is as the home of Harry Potter, Queen Elizabeth II, top flight soccer, and socialized healthcare; as an exporter of whiskey, Hollywood baddies, late-night television personalities, and endless costume dramas. But behind the scenes, there is an entirely different country, one which—in a career of writing about corruption, money laundering, and financial crime—I have gradually come to glimpse, understand, and grow alarmed by. It was an understanding that crystallized during a conversation that took place a couple of years ago, with an American academic called Andrew.

Andrew got in touch with me because he was researching Chinese money, and he knew that I act as a guide on the London Kleptocracy Tours, in which we show our guests around the British capital, point out which luxury properties belong to oligarchs, and tell the story of those oligarchs' money. Most of the mansions that we highlight belong to Russians, Arabs, or Nigerians, but he was keen to know if any Chinese tycoons had bought hidey-holes in London, too, and what the British government was doing to make sure their wealth had been acquired legally.

We met at a café on the first floor of a bookshop in a rather grand building on Trafalgar Square—a building that, funnily enough, considering the topic we had met to discuss, Ukrainian oligarchs had swapped between them in 2016 to settle an argument in the way that my son might give a small gift to a friend after they've fallen out on the playground.

Andrew had come well prepared for the meeting and had a checklist to work through, which was clearly designed to generate a list of names of other people he could speak to. Which law enforcement agency was doing the most to tackle the threat of Chinese money laundering? Who was the best person to talk to at that agency? Which prosecutors had brought the best cases? Who had done the most robust research on the volume of Chinese-owned money in the UK, and what assets did that money tend to buy? Which politicians were most alert to the question, and how did they organize themselves?

Because of the shared language, Americans and Brits often think their countries are more similar than they actually are, which is something I am as guilty of as anyone. When I do research in the United States, I am consistently amazed by the willingness of officials to sit down with me and talk through their work. I call them without an introduction, and yet time and again they trust me to keep specific details of our discussions off the record. Court documents are easy to obtain, and prosecutors are willing to talk about them. Politicians, meanwhile, seem to have a genuine belief in the importance of communicating their work to a wider public, which means they're happy to talk to writers like me. American journalists complain about their working conditions, just like everyone does everywhere, but, for a European, doing research into financial crime in the US is as heady an experience as letting my sons loose in a Lego shop.

Andrew, however, was discovering that the pleasant surprise sadly does not work in the opposite direction. I think he had been hoping that I would share a few contacts for British equivalents of the kind of people I have always found without too much trouble when I've visited Miami; Washington, DC; San Francisco; or New York. It's possible that he had been concerned I would refuse to open my address book to him, but it seemed not to have occurred to him that I would have no address book to open; that, essentially, the people he was looking for would not exist.

There was no concerted law enforcement effort against Chinese money laundering, I told him, so there was no investigator who could talk to him about it. There have been essentially no prosecutions for him to look into, and there is almost no research into where the money has been going, how it's been getting there, or indeed how much of it there is.

He kept coming at the questions from different angles, as if he thought that he just needed to find the right password to unlock the door hiding Britain's enforcement mechanism. Where was the equivalent of the Federal Bureau of Investigation's international corruption squad? Who was doing the work of the kleptocracy team at the Department of Justice? What about Homeland Security Investigations; did Britain have something like them? Were prosecutors building cases in a British version of the Southern District of New York? Was bringing down a big Chinese money-laundering ring the kind of case that would make their careers? Which parliamentary commissions were forensically probing this? Surely, someone was? As he talked, I began to see the situation through his eyes, which gave me a perspective I'd never had before.

The problem was that he could keep trying different passwords until the rocks rotted away, but it wouldn't help: there was no cave of treasures for him to open. If he wanted to find out how much Chinese money was entering the UK, who was moving it, and what it was buying, he was going to have to start from scratch and do all the work himself. Andrew had come to London expecting to discover how Britain was helping to fight illicit finance, and he was discovering that this was not happening at all. Quite the reverse, in fact.

It is, of course, not just Britain that helps Chinese kleptocrats and criminals to launder money. The shadow financial system used by the Chinese criminals he was investigating is transnational by its nature. It transcends any one jurisdiction and derives its power and its resilience from the fact it does not rely on any one place: if one jurisdiction becomes hostile, money effortlessly relocates to somewhere that isn't. And it grows all the time as lawyers, accountants, and others persuade politicians to give them access to the kind of fees they can generate by moving money around. You can find it as much in Dubai, Sydney, Lichtenstein, and Curaçao as you can in Switzerland or New York. But you find it most of all in London.

And what I began to realize when talking to Andrew is how much more Britain is invested in this business than those other places are. Financial skulduggery isn't just something that happens in the UK; there has been a concerted and decades-long effort to encourage it to do so. However bad other countries are, Britain has, for decades, been worse. It operates as a gigantic loophole, undercutting other countries' rules, massaging down tax rates, neutering regulations, laundering foreign criminals' money.

It's not just that Britain isn't investigating the crooks; it's helping them, too. Moving and investing their money is, of course, central to what the UK does, but that's only the start: it's also educating their children, solving their legal disputes, easing their passage into global high society, hiding their crimes, and generally letting them dodge the consequences of their actions. I had known this before, but I had never thought of it as a single phenomenon. It was Andrew's questions that crystallized the matter in my mind.

"Britain is like a butler," I said at last as I tried to explain to both of us what was going on. "If someone's rich, whether they're Chinese or Russian or whatever, and they need something done, or something hidden, or something bought, then Britain sorts that out for them. We're not a policeman, like you guys; we're a butler, the butler to the world. That's why we don't investigate the issues that you're talking about; that's not what a butler does."

He looked at me for a few beats, perhaps trying to work out if I was being serious.

"How long has this been going on?" he asked at last, and the answer came to me without my having to think about it. It was suddenly obvious.

"It started in the 1950s. We needed a new business model after America took over as the world's superpower, and this is what we found."

Our conversation didn't last much longer, and he walked off toward Parliament perhaps hoping to find someone less depressing to speak to, but I stayed put and ordered another coffee. The idea of Britain as a butler was not one that had occurred to me before, and the more I thought about it, the more appropriate it seemed. Butlers have all the traits that Britain professes to value most—manners, resourcefulness, reserve—but they have been repurposed as the surface polish of a servant rather than the noblesse oblige of a master.

Having created this theory, however, I realized that I had not, in fact, ever met a butler, so the first thing I did was to try to see if I could find any, which led me to the thriving British export industry that is training people to serve as attendants to the world's oligarchs. British butlers are the gold standard around the world, and training up servants to the standards of the aristocracy is big business nowadays. That is how I ended up sitting in on a flower-arranging class in a basement near Covent Garden. A middle-aged and rather horsey flower expert was teaching a group of would-be butlers from as far afield as Chile, Ukraine, and Malaysia how to employ the delights of an English garden to decorate a country house, assisted by a large number of younger equivalents of herself, who scurried around with pruning shears.

Why on earth would people fly in from the other side of the world to learn how to be a butler, I wondered. How could there possibly be demand for all these people's services? "It's obvious, isn't it?" replied a dark-haired Canadian woman who was weaving stems together into a floral lattice. "Anyone who can afford it wants their own Jeeves." If I'd been a cartoon character, a lightbulb would have lit above my head at that point: she had nailed it. Britain was the geopolitical equivalent of Reginald Jeeves, fictional factotum to gormless man-about-town Bertie Wooster in the comic novels of P. G. Wodehouse. As Jeeves does for Bertie Wooster, Britain's leading industry lies in solving problems for its clients, discreetly and profitably. If I could follow this group of trainees as they moved into the homes of the very wealthy, it struck me I'd be able to see what exactly this entailed.

Sadly, however, it was at this point that the manager of the butler training center appears to have researched my previous work and discovered that I write about financial crime rather than about domestic employment, and he became markedly less enthusiastic about helping me research his trade. Unable, therefore, to base my book on real-life butlers, I took inspiration from the words of that Canadian trainee and turned to the work of Wodehouse, author of the many stories about Wooster and Jeeves, his "gentleman's personal gentleman."

The way Wodehouse describes Jeeves, he's an amusing and reassuring presence, a man of infinite resource who helps Wooster and his friends out of scrapes, whether that's an unwise engagement to an inappropriate girl, an elderly relative withdrawing an allowance, an attempt by a rival family to poach a chef, or stealing a diamond pendant to settle a gambling debt run up while operating as an illegal bookmaker. It's all very amusing, thanks to Wodehouse's featherlight command of his distinctive prose style, but it can also be surprisingly sordid.

In "Without the Option," for example, one of Bertie's friends has been jailed for punching a policeman and risks falling out of his wealthy aunt's favor if she finds out about it. After a tortuous series of mishaps, Jeeves solves everything, owing to his access to police secrets. It's jolly funny when written the way Wodehouse writes it, but it wouldn't be hard to rewrite it so as to end up with a very different impression of Bertie Wooster's valet.

"Good Lord, Jeeves! You didn't bribe him?"

"Oh, no, sir. But it was his birthday last week, and I gave him a little present."

I've heard Ukrainian lawyers talk about how they've settled tricky legal disputes with the help of "a little present," and it never sounded funny the way they said it. If you focus on Jeeves's actions rather than on his appearance as a smooth-talking, soft-shoed valet, you end up with something extremely dark: a mercenary, a fixer for hire. Behind his polished exterior, he helps anyone who can pay him. Take away his immaculate appearance, his educated accent, and his ability to quote Marcus Aurelius, and you have not a butler but a consigliere. Paying off police officers is just the start of his talents; on one occasion, he beats a policeman unconscious; on another, he terrifies a fascist into silence by threatening to reveal the source of his secret wealth. With brains like his, he could succeed at almost anything but devotes himself exclusively to helping the very rich to escape the consequences of their actions while earning a nice living from their tips.

Over the last few years, Britons have taken to arguing about what figures represent us and, by extension, who we should be proud of. Cecil Rhodes, an imperialist who conquered much of southern Africa and built a diamond-mining empire, has attracted a lot of attention, thanks to his statue on a building at Oxford University. After a statue of the slave trader Edward Colston ended up at the bottom of Bristol Harbor thanks to Black Lives Matter protesters, far-right activists mounted guards around statues of Winston Churchill, Robert Peel, and other long-dead politicians. The BBC has erected a statue to George Orwell outside its headquarters to commemorate a different kind of Britain, one of skepticism and progressive values, although that provoked an argument over whether he was too left-wing. Similarly, when the suffragist Millicent Fawcett became the first woman to be commemorated in Parliament Square, rival columnists had a row over whether she deserved to be there. And it's not just statues: every couple of years, the Bank of England puts someone new on the bank notes, which provides a fresh reason to row about who we are, as—occasionally—do the figures chosen for commemoration on stamps. It all gets rather exhausting, to be honest.

But while Britons appear to disagree profoundly about which of their ancestors to commemorate, they clearly agree on one thing: the kind of people worth remembering. All these people—whether suffragist or suffragette, imperialist, or socialist—made a mark on the world, whether they conquered a new continent or campaigned to end slavery. The country likes to see itself as somewhere that knows what it is, what it wants, and which isn't afraid to stand alone to achieve it.

But that self-image increasingly doesn't fit with how Britain has behaved in the last few decades, when it has been far more focused on helping others achieve what they want and earning a good living from doing so than on proposing its own vision for how the world should be. When dictators want somewhere to hide their money, they turn to Britain. When oligarchs want someone to launder their reputation, they come to Britain.

That is what I mean when I say Britain behaves like a butler. It's an amoral enabler for hire, an enforcer for cash, which hides the reality of what it's doing behind quaint traditions, literary allusions, immaculate tailoring, references to World War Two, and a supercilious manner. But if Britain is a butler, who is its employer? Who is it working for? Who are the equivalents of the Edwardian flaneurs on whose behalf Jeeves assaulted policemen, stole novelty items of silverware, and provided immaculate evening dress on time for dinner? That is the question I intend to answer in this book.

There is one thing we can establish in advance, however. While Jeeves's clients were young men with more money than brains, Britain's clients are some of the worst people in existence, and the scrapes they need extricating from are very far from being amusing. They have real-life victims whose loss is far greater than Britain's gain. The butler earns only a tip, after all. As a result, the stories I'm about to tell will not be anything near as funny as those of Mr. Wodehouse. On the contrary, this couldn't be much more serious.

Some of the numbers I will quote in the chapters ahead are so huge that it's hard to understand them, such as the fact that hundreds of billions of pounds are laundered through the British banking system every year. That is money that has been stolen from people that desperately need it, that was intended to pay the wages of nurses or teachers or to build roads or power lines, but instead ended up owned by dishonest politicians or crooked businessmen, thanks to the discretion and skills of Butler Britain. If you sat down to count a hundred billion pounds, a pound a second till you were done, it would take you more than three thousand years. You'd have had to have started counting at the time of the Trojan War in order to get to a hundred billion around now.

And Britain doesn't just help kleptocrats steal that money; it provides them with a place to spend it, too. At the start of the COVID-19 crisis, when international travel froze, a major problem for wealthy Nigerians was that they suddenly couldn't visit their doctors, who were all based in London.

In 2019, the Nigerian government's health spending came to just $11 per person, which is barely an eighth of what the World Bank recommends it spend in order to cover basic needs. With spending so low, its medical facilities are in disrepair, drugs are unavailable, and newly qualified doctors often prefer to leave to work in Britain, Saudi Arabia, or the United States. Politicians promise to do something about this when they seek election, then consistently fail to do so, preferring instead to fly abroad. In healthcare, as in legal services, banking, and so much else, Britain has provided a luxury alternative that the elites of other countries can enjoy while they ruin their own systems, turning them into tools of theft rather than governance.

"Nigeria has two medical systems. If you don't have money, you go to pastors and imams to prospect for miracles," the

Nigerian novelist and essayist Okey Ndibe told me. "If you have a ton of money or political connections, you are flown abroad where you receive good treatment. When they fall sick they like to be airlifted to Britain."

When I say Britain, I'm referring not just to the United Kingdom but also to its archipelago of offshore territories, the last fragments of the British empire, which have their own parliaments but which are overseen by the government in London. Thanks to them, Britain is able to provide butlering services not just to wealthy foreigners but to wealthy Britons and their companies, too. The same tricks that allow wealthy Nigerians to exploit their compatriots have allowed—for example—gambling companies to base themselves in Gibraltar and suck money out of the UK. That means there are victims in Britain, too, like the hundreds of young men and women who have killed themselves thanks to being addicted to the products offered freely by the problem companies that Britain allows to offer gambling services to anyone that wants them.

Britain has been going through a crisis of confidence for much of the past decade with the stresses of the Brexit vote and the pandemic exacerbated by the antics of increasingly incompetent political leaders on all sides of the debate. I believe Britain's role as the world's butler is at least partly to blame for this crisis: thinking as a butler precludes sympathy for those less fortunate than yourself. There is no solidarity in P. G. Wodehouse's world; Jeeves helps those who can afford to pay him, and everyone else must manage on their own. Wodehouse clearly recognizes the irony of this, even making a joke out of Jeeves serving a substantial meal to a family of revolutionaries that—through a series of improbable plot twists—ends up dining at Wooster's luxurious flat.

"Don't call me 'sir.' Call me Comrade. Do you know what

you are, my lad? You're an absolute relic of an exploded feudal system," one revolutionary tells Jeeves.

"Very good, sir," Jeeves replies.

I also believe Britain is only at the start of this crisis; there are many more wealthy clients out there for the UK to advise and many more bright young graduates to be lured into serving them—as lawyers, as accountants, as family office managers, as reputation protection consultants, and as any other role that can earn fees from people able to pay them—which will inevitably undermine the quality of services available to the rest of the country. It is now so profitable for intelligent and well-connected Brits to act as butlers that ever more of the country's most gifted children have chosen to go into the family business rather than into something more constructive or more generous.

Already, judges are warning that British courts are suffering from the reluctance of the best barristers to forego their fees and become judges. "If the profession stops producing the brightest and the best for appointment to the bench, the reputation of our jurisdiction for superlative quality in decision-making will quickly fade. It will become a self-fulfilling prophecy," said one judge in a speech in 2018. It's a strong argument, but it applies only if barristers think of themselves as part of a larger community. If they think of themselves as individuals out to do the best that they can for the people that pay them—as butlers, in short—then there is no reason why they should care about the long-term prospects of the country's institutions at all. They don't even have to be reliant on Britain for a job anymore. Entrepreneurial lawyers have opened tribunals in Dubai and in Kazakhstan, working on English law, employing British lawyers, to support the efforts of local governments keen to develop their financial systems.

Many British people may be reading this and bristling

at the criticism. Of course, not everything about Britain is pernicious—Welsh rugby, Scottish literature, English universities are all stellar contributions to making the world a better place. A country that invented pubs quite obviously cannot be all bad. Not all of the country's people are so amoral as to take money from anyone; and, of course, the country has lots going for it beyond its butlering industry. But, when you read the chapters that follow, I hope two things will become abundantly clear: firstly, that the tendency is alarmingly widespread, far more widespread than you will have realized; and secondly, that much of the national elite is devoted to serving the interests of the rich and powerful, whatever those interests are. So much of what makes Britain British and that Britons take so much pride in—their history, their traditions, their humor, their institutions—has become a costume for the country's elites to wear as they scour the world for fresh clients.

What does this mean for the world? Thanks to the City of London, Russian oligarchs who know how to steal an oil company but not how to raise capital have had access to all the money they need. Thanks to Britain's offshore archipelago, American companies that love the US government's protection but not having to pay for it can avoid taxes with ease. Thanks to London's law courts, kleptocrats that have gotten rich by abusing the law in their own countries have access to the best justice money can buy when they need to protect their fortunes from others. And other countries have had to lower their standards, too, so as to prevent Britain stealing all their business. Britain has become a huge loophole through which anyone able to afford its services can slip themselves, their fortunes, or their businesses whenever they like. This is not just bad for the world but, in the long run, is also bad for Britain. If the country's richest and most powerful citizens are focused on serving the needs of their clients, it leaves them scant time to consider their fellow citizens.

This is, quite naturally, a huge topic to try to address in one book: an exhaustive account would fill dozens of volumes the size of this one. I have chosen to focus on small parts of the situation and describe them closely. These detailed accounts of specific aspects of Britain's behavior over the last seventy years are representative of a far larger whole without, I hope, being too overwhelming.

One of the reasons I wanted to write this book was because, in the months and years after the UK's decision to leave the European Union, there was so much anguish about what kind of country Britain should be without—as far as I could tell— much public discussion of what kind of country it actually was. Brexit felt, at the time, like a crisis that required a response, but it has since been eclipsed by the far more serious crisis brought by COVID-19. The urgency to diagnose what's wrong with Britain has been heightened by the pandemic, which has exposed the existing tensions in all the world's countries, particularly in Britain—with its terrible and world-beating death toll and stumbling governmental response. I hope that when the crisis passes, British people can heed its lessons and forge a new kind of country that does not see every moment as an opportunity to earn a fee, and does not engage quite so readily in enabling the kind of activities I describe in this book, but acts more like the heroes they claim to admire.

This is not an unrealistic hope. There are some years when history speeds up and societies change in ways they normally cannot manage in decades: we know this, because it was just such a crisis that gave birth to Britain's butlering career back in the years when my parents were young and I was unthought of. The story begins with a visit to someone who lived through it.

2

SUN, SAND, CANAL

In spring 2020, the one trip I tried hardest not to cancel—and the one I was eventually sorriest to miss out on when COVID-19 became too huge to ignore—was one to Sunderland, in the northeast of England, scheduled for March 29.

That was when the Suez Veterans' Association was due to lay up its standard—that is, to finally fold up its flag, because there were too few veterans to fly it anymore—and to close for good. It would have been the final act in the history of this overlooked, determinedly narky and generous group of ex-servicemen, who had all served in British bases along the Suez Canal. Sadly, with two weeks to go, and the rapid spread of COVID-19 making total lockdown inevitable, the membership secretary was forced to contact the handful of surviving veterans (and me), and inform them the event had been postponed indefinitely owing to the risk to the attendees posed by the coronavirus. As far as I could tell, no one outside the SVA noticed, which, considering how little attention anyone in power had paid to the group before, was entirely appropriate.

The general indifference to the organization's end is curious considering how important these troops had once been to the United Kingdom, and for how long. The engineers who built the Suez Canal in the mid-nineteenth century were French, but this thread of water between the Mediterranean and Red seas was always more important to the British, linking the mother country with India and its other possessions in Asia. When the Egyptian government ran out of money in 1875, the British state bought its shares and became the canal's largest shareholder. British influence grew, and the Egyptians became unsurprisingly resentful, until they rose in revolt a decade later. British troops moved in to crush the revolt, and ended up occupying the whole country. Egypt was never a formal colony, but it was the hinterland to the canal, so the empire's administrators wouldn't allow it to rule itself. The country still had a khedive—who theoretically ruled the Egypt on behalf of the Sultan of Turkey—and had ministers, but real power lay with the British consul general, Evelyn Baring, the first Earl of Cromer, scion of the banking dynasty. His power, and that of his successors, was guaranteed by the presence of the hundreds of thousands of soldiers, sailors and airmen that served the empire in Egypt over the next eighty years.

The Suez Veterans' Association represented the final generation of these men and women, those who had served in the years after the Second World War. When its members were still young enough to travel it arranged trips back to Egypt, and it published a quarterly newsletter full of the kind of sardonic humor that keeps squaddies and erks—their RAF counterparts—going during long evenings in remote bases. ("This officer should go far—and the sooner he starts, the better.")

I have a pile of the newsletters on the desk in front of me. They are illustrated with black-and-white photos of slim young men surrounded by sand and barbed wire, taken in the 1940s and 50s, grinning at the camera, all full of the cocksure carelessness of youth. And there are color pictures of the same men decades later: white-haired, stocky and blue-blazered, marching or being pushed in wheelchairs, laying poppies at memorials, weighed down now with age and memory. In one of the first bulletins, the editor requested that veterans write in with memories: "Very little has been written about what life was like in the canal zone for the ordinary squaddy and erk. Now is your chance to remedy the situation. I'm sure all of us have vivid memories of isolated events in the canal zone—humorous, frightening, incredible. Canteen food, our first guard, parades, a typical day at work etc. Put pen to paper and tell us about it."

Some of the veterans' stories were funny—one man had arrested his commanding officer, who'd climbed out of his window to "answer the call of nature," and marched him off in his underpants. Some of them were touching—another man had got married at an RAF base and wanted to know if anyone remembered the ceremony. Other letters were grim reminders of what the soldiers were really there for, with correspondence continuing on some themes for years, gradually adding details to barely remembered events—the murder of a nun, a clash with civilians, a soldier who played in goal for the regimental team getting his testicles shot off, a sentry opening fire on a rowing boat that failed to stop when challenged, then shooting the rowers as they floundered in the water.

One name that regularly features in the newsletters is that of Jeff Malone, a Yorkshireman who edited the newsletter and wrote often about his thirty-one months in Egypt as a mechanic for the RAF. Taken together, his articles are like a mini-autobiography, beginning with his departure from Liverpool docks in 1953. "I've often seen film footage of the troops going off to the Boer War and other trouble spots. Invariably there are bands playing, flags waving and crowds cheering. On that dreary October day the only people to see us go by just happened to be waiting for the bus," he wrote. From the start, the soldiers in the canal zone were under no illusions that anyone at home much cared about them.

The newsletters contain very little discussion of politics—whether the British should have been in Egypt in the first place—but the constant misery of the low-level insurgency is sign enough that the situation was unsatisfactory. The British empire in its pomp would not have tolerated such indignities as his articles describe—constant theft from the stores, Egyptian civilians throwing bricks at patrols as they passed by, collapsing infrastructure. The end of the empire was coming, and the soldiers' job was to try to make that end as dignified as possible. Malone was a first-hand witness to the fall of the mightiest empire the world has ever seen, and he hated the experience from beginning to end. He had the option of going home on leave, but he never took it, since he knew that if he ever left Egypt he could not bear to return.

"I had been in Egypt for the best part of three years and I was sick of it. The whole British military presence in the canal zone was falling apart," he wrote in his account of his final departure from Egypt by troopship. "As I watched the harbor lights disappearing I had a feeling of euphoria. I felt as if I was walking on air. I have only had this experience three or four times in my entire life."

I found his accounts fascinating, having previously known next to nothing about the British presence in Egypt. I studied history all the way up to a degree at university, and the only colony I ever studied was Ireland—and that was only because I had an Irish teacher. I doubt one in ten Brits even know their country used to rule Egypt, or own the Suez Canal, or what the British armed forces did to the Egyptians to keep things that way.

Although the recent debate over the statue of Cecil Rhodes

at Oxford University has provoked some discussion about what the empire got up to, there still seems to be a general impression that it was a more-or-less benevolent Victorian invention, dedicated to teaching English, banning slavery and making the trains run on time. The truth is different: the empire was about profit, and about eradicating anything that stood in the way of that profit. Unlike the empires of most of its European rivals, the British version made its money from trade, rather than by extorting taxes from peasant farmers, so the Brits could expand further and faster than anyone else, without having to impose complex administrative structures on the places they conquered. That's how the empire became so very large.

At its height, the British empire controlled almost a quarter of the world's land mass, and a similar proportion of its people. The "white dominions" of Australia, New Zealand and Canada, with their substantial settler populations, were self-governing but deeply loyal to the mother country and ready to help out when needed. India, ruled dictatorially, was the single most significant colony because it provided an army and a huge market for British goods. Smaller colonies were spread across every continent: Kenya, Guyana, Malaya, Cyprus. Somewhere in the British empire it was always teatime. And even this understates the extent of Britain's dominance of the globe. It was the biggest bully in class, and what it said, went. The legal, trading and financial mechanisms created to run the empire—the sterling system—became those used by the whole world. Many parts of China and South America were so dominated by British investment that they were colonies in all but name; everyone else used British ships to trade with each other, British banks to fund their business activities, and British insurance companies to manage the risk.

And all that made Britain extraordinarily rich. On the eve

of the First World War British investors owned assets overseas that were cumulatively larger than the whole home economy. But then the world wars happened, and the country spent its accumulated investments on guns and uniforms and soldiers' salaries. By the early 1950s Britain's net holdings of overseas assets had turned negative, and the country was essentially broke. Colonies, ex-colonies and dominions were owed so much money that London had to keep a tight rein on how pounds were used to prevent the currency collapsing altogether. The reversal was astonishingly quick: centuries of carefully acquired reserves spent in just a few years. The banker to the world transformed into a pauper; the global currency limping from one crisis to the next.

"We have inherited an old family business that used to be profitable and sound," said Harold Macmillan, chancellor of the exchequer, in a letter to Prime Minister Anthony Eden at the height of the crisis that was brewing. "The trouble is that the liabilities are four times the assets."

India became independent in 1947, and at a stroke Britain's position as the dominant Asian power was extinguished. Burma, Ceylon and Malaya followed over the next decade. African colonies began to agitate for freedom too. Officials in Whitehall recognized that they had no choice but to liquidate the empire in as dignified a manner as possible, but British governments became obsessed by the need not to be seen to "scuttle" out of their remaining possessions. And, in the years after Indian independence, that meant they must cling on to their sole remaining world-class geopolitical asset: the Suez Canal.

As long as Britain controlled the waterway, its strategists could dream of projecting power south into the Indian Ocean, east into the Middle East and north into the Soviet Union, and of denying the canal to its enemies and interrupting their trade. Britain could not be relegated to being a mere European power while it had such an asset in its portfolio. "If we cannot hold the Suez Canal, the jugular vein of World and Empire shipping communications, what can we hold?" asked the author of a report on the canal's future written for the government. When confronted with the prospect of handing control of the canal to the Egyptians, MPs muttered about appeasement, a dirty word since the inglorious and disastrous attempt to buy off Adolf Hitler in Munich in 1938 by offering him part of Czechoslovakia. Winston Churchill himself was overheard saying that "he never knew Munich was on the Nile."

There were many problems with this parallel, not least the fact that there was no similarity between the Egyptians' desire for their country to be free of foreign control and Hitler's annexation of the Sudetenland. If anyone was the aggressor here, it was Britain. From the military perspective, however, the primary flaw in the government's position was a more practical one and lay in the nature of a canal, which is long and thin, and thus has about as extended a defensive perimeter as is physically possible.

British bases were strung along the canal's western shore, often surrounded by desert, their communications vulnerable, their occupants demoralized. If the Egyptians did not want the British to be there, which they didn't, they had ample scope to make their opinion felt, which is why the letters written to the SVA newsletter are so full of accounts of skirmishes, riots and difficulties. The total garrison of 80,000 soldiers—that's a force slightly larger than the entire British army is today— was primarily employed in defending itself ("It is their presence there that creates the need for them to be there," quipped a foreign office official), and after the Egyptian military coup of

1952, provoked by public anger over British behavior, civilians refused to service the bases, which made the soldiers' job even harder.

"It was absolutely awful. The Egyptians had walked out of every job on the camp and the work was now being carried out by British personnel who were under-manned and stretched to the limit. Such awful jobs as cleaning latrines, removing pig swill, working in the laundry and manning the (canteen) were being done by personnel who had never been to such places before, except as customers," wrote one former airman who served in the canal zone in 1951–2. "Suez was an awful place and the Egyptians were creating hell down there."

Eventually, in 1954, after two years of this, the two countries agreed that the British would evacuate the canal zone within twenty months. Supposedly, Britain would retain the right to return to its bases in the event of "an attack by an outside power," but this was a polite fiction to preserve British dignity as it retreated from another possession. As one SVA correspondent wrote, "Even the thickest squaddy knew that as soon as we were out the Egyptians would loot the bases and that we were never coming back without a gun in our hands." Sure enough, when the evacuation was complete and there was no one left to stop him, Egypt's assertive new leader—Gamal Abdel Nasser—nationalized the Suez Canal. Britain's great strategic asset now belonged to the people whose country it ran through.

This was a monumental blow to British prestige, but it was the manner in which the government in London responded that turned defeat into disaster. The trouble was that Nasser hadn't actually done anything illegal: the Suez Canal Company was an Egyptian enterprise, which the government in Cairo could nationalize if it wanted, having promised full compensation to its shareholders, who were—apart from the British government—overwhelmingly French. It wasn't doing anything novel here. Britain had spent the years after the Second World War nationalizing everything from the Bank of England to the coal mines. Similarly, all the most important French companies were taken into state ownership in the same period. By taking a crucial strategic asset into public ownership, Nasser was swimming in the very middle of the economic mainstream. But the British and French governments were appalled and tried to create a pretext to intervene. They removed their pilots from the canal, hoping to sabotage its operations. They sent dozens of ships to the canal at once, trying to create lengthy queues. But the Egyptians out-thought them, and kept the canal open. Prime Minister Eden was in a tight spot.

Eden became, or so it looks with hindsight, increasingly unhinged about the threat posed to Britain by Nasser. "It's either him or us, don't forget that," he said. Macmillan agreed. "It's absolutely vital to humiliate Nasser," he said. "We must do it quickly, or we shall ourselves be ruined." Nasser was strong and popular admittedly, but he led a poor country, which could not conceivably threaten Britain militarily. But for the British government, the threat was not one of military defeat but of strategic irrelevance. Nasser represented a new and vital form of Arab leader, one who was catching the imagination of the populations of countries that Britain still dominated, like Jordan, Kuwait and Iraq. If he could turn the Arabs against their colonial masters, the British would have to retreat even faster. The dignified decline of the empire would become a scuttle. The French, who were beset by similar troubles in Algeria, hated Nasser too, so the two fading powers cooked up a secret plan to get rid of him, bringing in the Israelis to help.

The plan was complex, but boiled down to Israel invading

across the Sinai peninsula—the stretch of desert between Israel and the canal. Anglo-French forces would then move in to separate the two sides, as if they hadn't known about the invasion in advance, and in the process accidentally occupy Cairo and impose a friendlier government. It was a ludicrous scheme (kept secret from the Americans), made all the more remarkable by the fact that Britain was simultaneously plotting another coup (kept secret from the French) in Syria, although that one collapsed before it even began. A naval task force brought British troops to Egypt's northern coastline, and so it began.

"We landed in Port Said. It was chaos. Our regiment had the job of mopping up part of the town. Unfortunately our rifles were without firing pins. We had left Cyprus in a hurry. The rifles had been stored in the armory with the firing pins removed for safety," wrote one correspondent to the SVA of the amphibious operation that began in November 1956. "I never had to fire a shot and I'm glad I didn't."

Nevertheless, militarily, despite many more cock-ups, it was a walkover. The Egyptian forces were routed, hundreds of civilians were killed, and the Israeli, French and British invaders took mere handfuls of casualties. Politically, however, it was a disaster. "Anthony, are you out of your mind?" President Eisenhower asked Eden when he heard of the invasion. It was an assessment shared by most of Britain's allies, who could not believe what they were seeing. How could Britain claim to be on the side of the good guys when it was prepared to invade a sovereign nation that just wanted to run its own affairs?

The financial markets sensed weakness in London's isolation, and speculators pounced, selling pounds and putting huge pressure on its exchange rate. Britain no longer had the cushion of overseas wealth to protect its currency, and the Americans refused to help or allow the International Monetary Fund to do so. Sterling was on the brink of collapse, and Britain backed down.

It was as if Bertie Wooster had tried to act independently of his aunt, but then was forced to surrender when she threatened to cut off his allowance. Britain withdrew from Egypt, humbled and humiliated, its position in the world embarrassingly clear—no longer an empire but a regional power dependent on its American paymasters. Historians debate now whether the Suez Crisis was itself a catalyst for British decline, or just an example of it, but that didn't much matter to the servicemen who were there. The campaign has become a byword for a fiasco, still invoked today as the lowest point in Britain's international prestige. The members of the SVA understand very well why no one wants to remember them: they were defeated, and every defeat is an orphan.

Jeff Malone, regular correspondent in the SVA's newsletter, and its long-serving editor, had been due to give a speech at the laying up of the standard in Sunderland. ("It was the only place interested in having our flag," he said when I asked why they'd chosen the northeast for the occasion. "We did try some of the fancier places, like Canterbury, but nothing came of it.") All those plans were postponed by the pandemic, however. Instead, I visited him at his neat bungalow in a suburb of the Shropshire town of Bridgnorth. There I leafed through his collection of newsletters and drank the cups of coffee he brought me. We ended up chatting for hours. He is eighty-five years old, thoughtful and funny. His bookshelves are full of grammars of the languages he has learned, and his walls are full of pictures of his children. Like him, they're engineers, and he totally failed to hide how proud he is.

When he talked of his time in Egypt, however, he was still, even after all these years, bitter about the political failure that had put him in harm's way. The veterans had established the SVA as a forum for those who had survived the ordeal, a way to get together and support each other, and it had served its purpose well, helping them to talk through some of the more distressing memories, to share pleasant ones, and to have a laugh while doing it. It was Malone who organized the tours back to the canal zone, despite having promised himself back in 1956—when his troopship, the *Empire Orwell*, carried him away—never to go near Egypt again. He laughed when he described how one of the hotels had been on exactly the same site as the soldiers' social club, and how the same man still owned the drink store. But then he became serious.

"I remember once, a couple of old ladies rang me up and asked if they could come on the next trip to Egypt. I asked why they wanted to come, and they said their brother was killed out there," he said. "The brother, he was at a crossroads, with a Bren gun set-up, sandbags, all that. An Egyptian came up with a wheelbarrow, but its wheel fell off. It was full of oranges, you know, and he said, 'Just keep an eye on this while I go and find a wheel. Help yourself to an orange.' So the brother got out and helped himself to a couple of oranges, and it was booby-trapped. I showed them where he was buried. I'll say one thing: the place where they're buried, it was beautifully kept."

He paused for a long time, and blinked rapidly before continuing. "The guys who died in World War Two, they died for some reason, you know, but our guys, they died for nothing."

British prestige burned in the fires of Port Said and Ismailya, leaving behind decades of grief for those bereaved by the fighting, lasting ignominy for the prime minister who took an extreme gamble, and a radically changed world. Barely remarked, something new was born from the ashes, however, before the troops even made it home. Britain wasn't the biggest bully in class anymore, but it still knew an awful lot about the bullying business, and that knowledge turned out to be very valuable indeed. To see how that worked, we need to leave Egypt behind and travel to the heart of the dying empire—to the City of London.

3

PRACTICAL PEOPLE

Looking back at the years around the Suez Crisis from the perspective of 1970, the *Guardian*'s financial editor Richard Fry could hardly believe how much had changed. And Fry knew an upheaval when he saw one. He was born in Austria, started out working on a German newspaper but—as a Jew—lost his job when the Nazis took power in Berlin in 1933. He moved to the UK and found a place at the *Manchester Guardian*, where he chronicled the Second World War and the turbulent decades that followed it.

"At the end of the 50s, London seemed to have been left behind in the progress of world trade and finance," he wrote, "such was the prevailing pessimism that the sons of some bankers were training to be farmers."

I grew up on a farm myself, so I'm not entirely sure that was a bad thing, but it is still extraordinary to think back to a time when farming could even come close to competing with finance as a profession, when the brightest minds of a generation might consider raising cattle rather than pouring into offices by the Thames to move money around. In the years after the Second World War aging men ran the City, and once-coveted seats in the Stock Exchange had lost their value. Ambitious young graduates went instead into manufacturing, the law, academia or the civil service. By the end of the 1960s, however, according to Fry, that had all changed.

"To work in the City now seems to hold the promise of moving up fast, not merely to good pay and good social standing but to an early share of responsibility. The merchant banks, the overseas banks, the specialized finance houses and the larger stockbrokers are so swamped with business that a bright newcomer may well get his hand onto real decision-making at a very early age," Fry wrote. "Enterprise and inventiveness flourish." What happened between the Suez Crisis and the end of the 1960s was a rebirth: the City of London was back in the game.

If Westminster was the head of the British empire, and the Royal Navy its muscles, the City was its heart, pumping money out into financial arteries that stretched to every continent and every city on earth. This blood supply—the sterling system—was, more than anything, what held the empire together. Pounds carried the oxygen of capital to any business that needed it. But when the empire declined, the heart became sluggish, beating ever more falteringly. Without the dividends and interest earned from Britain's global possessions, which had been sold off to pay for the world wars, and with British industry outcompeted by its rivals, there was simply too little money flowing into and out of the City to keep the sterling system vital. Sterling remained a global currency, the only rival to the dollar, but Britain's huge debts made sure it was under constant threat of speculative attack, and the restrictions put in the way of capital flows by the postwar financial system prevented City institutions from inventing new ways to respond.

I described this postwar financial system, created at a conference in Bretton Woods in 1944, in *Moneyland* and won't re-describe it here, except to say that it was very different to the one we have now. At the heart of the difference between then and now is an irreconcilable trilemma (like a dilemma, but with three possibilities instead of two). In inter-state financial relations, countries have three options to choose between: fixed exchange rates, which exporters and importers love because they make trade predictable; free capital flows, which banks love because they make investment overseas easy and profitable; and domestic autonomy, which governments love because it allows them to respond to the wishes of their electorates. The trilemma arises from the fact that only two of these are possible at any one time. Whichever two you choose, you have to sacrifice the third. Someone—banks, exporters or governments—is going to be disappointed, whatever you do.

If you have free capital flows and fixed exchange rates, you can't have domestic autonomy, because the markets will severely punish what they deem to be excessive expenditure by making borrowing prohibitively expensive. This is why Greece had such a tough time after the financial crisis of 2007–8; its exchange rate is fixed because it's a member of the euro, and it can't restrict capital flows because of the rules of the European Union, so it had to sacrifice autonomy—its government lost the ability to do what it wanted.

That wasn't acceptable, however, to governments after the Second World War; with the horrors of the Depression of the 1930s still fresh in their minds, they wanted the power to create full employment. This was all part of a settlement that included the New Deal regulations in the United States, the welfare state in the UK and similar structures in other Western countries, all of which required governments to control investment levels in order to improve living standards.

But if governments insisted on the autonomy to do what they wanted, they had to choose between the remaining two options. Would they allow free capital flows, which would please the banks but displease exporters? Or would they fix exchange rates, which would please exporters but prevent the banks from making easy profits? Much of the blame for the Great Depression had been laid on the banks—and on the "hot money" that was deemed to have inflated asset bubbles then caused stock markets to crash—so the decision was an easy one. Governments chose exporters over finance houses. In the language of the time, productive capital would take priority over speculative capital. Capital flows were severely restricted, and the value of one pound sterling was fixed at $2.80, so companies could easily move their goods around the world.

This was bad news for the City of London, the heart of the empire. Without the unimpeded ability to pump pounds out into the sterling system, and to receive back the revenue they generated, its arteries clogged up. It was the financial equivalent of atherosclerosis. Unable to attract young talent, it was stuck in time, dominated by people often hilariously out of step with the supposedly thrusting dynamic of postwar Britain.

George Rowland Stanley Baring, third Earl of Cromer, was one of the most important of these people, as governor of the Bank of England in the first half of the 1960s. He described his time as governor and his career in his family's merchant bank in a lengthy interview a year before he died, in 1991, and it is hard to imagine a man with better Establishment credentials. His paternal grandfather, the first earl, ran Egypt back in the 1880s and headed the Men's League for Opposing Women's Suffrage. Cromer's maternal grandfather—also an earl—was governor general of Canada and then ran India as viceroy. His father, the second earl, was lord chamberlain to the royal household, as well as the British government's representative in the Suez Canal Company. Cromer married the daughter of Viscount

Rothermere, the media baron who owned the *Daily Mail*, and he himself was a royal page at two coronations.

And yet when Cromer described his time at Eton, it is as if he imagined himself to have been a street urchin locked out of a world of privilege and putting a brave face on it. "They were always very nice," he said of his schoolmates. "But I mean, life is, I mean, I think it was out very early in life, one of the things one's nanny taught one is that life isn't, isn't fair. I mean, there are going to be inequalities of one sort of another. As soon as you recognize that, stop beefing about it . . . I didn't feel any resentment about it. I mean, I didn't want to live at Chatsworth."

His interview is part of an oral history project called *City Lives*, which features interviews with almost all the most significant men present at the rebirth of the City of London's financial industry. What is extraordinary is their cultural uniformity. They were wealthy, they were male, they were southerners, they were privately educated; if they hadn't studied at Eton, they went to Harrow. To have been educated at Winchester marked someone out as daringly nonconformist. Within this small world, tiny gradations of status assumed outsize significance. Cameron Cobbold, who headed the Bank of England before Cromer, is described by one historian as a "distinctly Etonian Etonian," and once you've spent time listening to the interviews they gave and reading the transcripts of their speeches, you can see exactly what that means. Cromer, an heir to an earldom whose father organized the king's engagements, could only have counted himself among the world's unfortunates because he had never met anyone who was actually unfortunate. And this is the man who ran Britain's central bank.

It wasn't just that this tribe knew nothing about the lives of their fellow citizens; they had also all known each other since childhood. That meant they shared mannerisms and quirks that helped to exclude anyone from outside. Theirs was the studied indifference of the English gentleman: to call something "embarrassing" was the supreme insult. One key designator—visible in letters and documents throughout City archives—is the way insiders called each other by their first names, but outsiders by their surnames. "Those who were regarded as being below the salt remained called by their surnames for their whole lives, and they worked their way up. They were the quartermaster commissions of the business world, as opposed to the officer-cadet commissions," recalled privately educated John Barkshire, a City grandee who went on to help launch futures trading long after this period, and who we'll hear from again.

This translated into the fact that those on the inside—the people addressed as "Charles" or "Louis" rather than "Smith" or "Perkins"—could be forgiven almost anything. One evening early in his career, when heading home after a day's work, Barkshire reached into his pocket and found a check for £5 million ("a great deal of money in 1956") that he'd neglected to deliver. "It was a very nasty moment, and I assumed that I would be sacked in the morning, but in fact I wasn't."

Sadly, we don't have comparable interviews from the kind of people that got called by their surnames, so we have no idea what they thought about the social division at the heart of their world, but these accounts chime closely with what Jeff Malone said about his officers during his time in Suez. When I asked him if he recognized the traditional description of British soldiers as lions led by donkeys, he laughed and shook his head. "We might have been lions, but we were led by ex-public schoolboys," he said before launching into an account of one base he worked at. "There must have been about fifty or sixty of us repairing all sorts of vehicles. The officer in charge, he had this office that was hanging from the roof, and all the time I was there he never came out of the office down onto the shop floor, he never spoke to any of the guys, which I thought was a bit peculiar. Granted, he didn't know anything about engineering, but still."

Malone might have found plenty to talk to an ex-public schoolboy about; he was bright and well educated, with an expansive and curious view of the world, which has persisted to the present day. But he never got to find out, because his officers never engaged with him, and he was always called—like a servant, or indeed like a younger child at school, which presumably came to the same thing for an Etonian at the time—by his surname. The levers of financial power in postwar Britain were controlled by the same people as before the war: the privately educated children of privately educated fathers, which gave them an extremely limited ability to understand the world.

There is much debate in the academic literature about philosophical splits during this period. Obviously, this being the time of the Cold War, there was the enduring division between communism and capitalism. Within communism there were the disagreements that led to the Sino-Soviet split. And within capitalism there were divisions between those who favored the insurgent Chicago school of neoliberalism, and those who clung to the older Keynesian principles that had informed the recovery from the Great Depression. The more I spend time in the company of the small clique that dominated the City, however, the more I realize that to look at them through a philosophical prism is to totally misunderstand them. They existed on a different axis, and would have rejected the work of Friedrich Hayek as thoroughly as they did that of John Maynard Keynes, or—God forbid—Karl Marx.

They loathed economists and the way they analyzed the world, prizing instead nothing more than "common sense," unless perhaps it was to be "hard-headed" or "practical." They had not themselves graduated from universities and distrusted anyone who had. Within the Bank of England the circle was smaller still. It wasn't just that its governors always came from the banking industry, rather than from other parts of finance—insurance, stockbroking or commodity trading, for example—they also always came from the same part of banking. The most important banks in ordinary people's lives were the clearing banks, which had branches all over the country where people and businesses kept their money. The City's aristocrats were not prepared to soil their hands with such a sordid business, however, and it wasn't until the 1980s that someone was chosen to head the Bank of England who came from anything other than a merchant bank.

Merchant bankers appear to have lacked the curiosity to wonder whether their limited social circles, privileged upbringings and careers within a small part of the finance industry, one that exclusively looked for business from corporations, rather than people, might have colored their outlook. They genuinely believed that there was no politics in their opinions, which were based solely on "common sense." Theirs—they thought—was the natural viewpoint of anyone who knew how the world actually worked, the implication being that someone who thought otherwise was either a fool or a crook, and could thus be disregarded.

"I went down on the Monday to pay my respects to the new chancellor," said Cromer of his first meeting as governor of the Bank of England with James Callaghan, after the Labor Party had won the 1964 general election. "And I told him, which was perfectly true, that I wasn't going to play politics, nor did I.

And that I considered my job was to serve the country and the government of the day, but in that order, which is rather an important difference."

The Bank of England, the institution he headed, would be central to the changes that overtook the City. It had been nationalized by the reforming postwar Labor government as part of, as Cromer put it, "the socialist nonsense after the War" which also created the National Health Service and took Britain into NATO. The governor of the Bank nominally reported to the government, but in reality nothing changed after nationalization: the governor still answered to his peers rather than to any broader constituency. As a result, the Bank was an island of Victorian plenty in the sea of postwar austerity.

Andrew Shonfield, an influential left-leaning economist, wrote in a book published in 1958,

There are none of the civil servant limitations on the size of its staff or on the amounts it pays them. No account is rendered to the public of the Bank's expenditure, since it all comes out of business earnings. One becomes aware of this atmosphere of freedom and ease as soon as one enters the Bank's premises. The contrast with the Treasury building in Great George Street, where people are still living very much in the Gladstonian tradition of saving candle ends—and, one sometimes suspects, working by candlelight in order to give themselves the opportunity to do so—is overwhelming. As one enters the unnaturally tall door of the Bank, let into the fortress wall facing onto Threadneedle Street, and comes into the large vestibule, one is struck at once by the considerable crowd of pink-coated messengers in top hats standing about in attitudes of respectful waiting.

. . . The Bank has more clerks at its disposal for the amount of work to be done and a more elaborate filing system than the Treasury; its offices are much better, and so are many of its other amenities. Its solitary apparent handicap is its inability to build up a staff of bright young men from the universities. But this is perhaps because it does not try very hard . . . the hard core of the executive hierarchy is still public school, rather than university. They are in fact very different people from the prize-winning university graduates who are recruited into the Treasury.

According to Shonfield, the directors of the Bank fundamentally disagreed with the entire world's economic direction, in particular the focus on prioritizing productive capital over speculation. They believed in a different solution to the trilemma that confronts all governments interested in engaging with the global economy. They would strip away the limits on moving money around and bring back the kind of free trade that had benefited Britain in the nineteenth century. The pound would remain fixed against the dollar, so inevitably—as with Greece today—the government would lose the autonomy it enjoyed to create full employment, to build social housing and to expand the health service. This was, Shonfield wrote, "the vicarious reassertion of the political power of the owners of wealth—not businessmen or people active in any way, but just owners—which the postwar revolution in Britain had set out to prevent."

Shonfield knew what he was writing about, and knew the class he was describing. While researching the book, he was working as foreign editor at the *Financial Times*, the house journal of the City of London. He had served in the Royal Artillery and as an intelligence officer during the Second World War, after being educated at St. Paul's, a prestigious London private school, and the equally elite Magdalen College, Oxford. His accent was as plummy as anyone's. But his kind of intellectually rigorous insistence that the Bank of England should represent the nation that owned it, not just the City it was embedded in, was not something the Bank's directors had any sympathy with. In a caustic internal note Deputy Governor Humphrey Mynors referred to him as "Andrew Shonfëld," which was apparently enough to disqualify him from having an opinion worth hearing. What, after all, would a Jew know about how to run England?

The strange aspect of all this is that the Bank belonged to the nation. Surely, therefore, the government could just tell it what to do, replace any directors who opposed its policies and force it to recruit economists to broaden its horizons? There had been some attempts in this direction, with a handful of trade unionists appointed as directors, but no government seemed willing or confident enough to risk a showdown with the City as a whole. Leadership of the Bank remained in the hands of the merchant banking elite, and with it oversight of the country's financial system.

Cromer told a story from the 1960s when, during a brewing financial crisis, a Treasury official tried to tell him what to do. "So I remember saying to him, 'Well, William, look, if you really want to create a crisis, I invite you to issue your direction. Because if you issue the direction, it'll be known that you've issued it. I will resign, so will every member of the Court of the Bank of England resign, and you will have an absolutely first-class financial crisis. Do you think that's a clever thing to do?' And he said, 'Well, I'll have to think about it.'" The direction never came, and the Bank kept doing what it had done ever since it was founded in the seventeenth century as a private bank handling the government debt. It had power without responsibility.

It was the Bank of England that regulated the City, although there was precious little regulation involved. Beyond exchange controls, which restricted how much money anyone could move out of the country, and which had been introduced on the outbreak of war in 1939, financial institutions were largely guided by gentle pressure toward doing the "right thing." If the Bank's governor thought there was too much money out there, and the economy was in danger of overheating, he wrote to the banks, suggesting it would be "an act of cooperation" if they limited lending. The heads of the major banks would occasionally come in and drink tea, and the governor would make suggestions which, as a rule, they went along with. A chap's word was his bond. The directors didn't like to give actual instructions, as Barkshire remembered when he described a bit of financial trickery he invented that allowed him to circumvent the Bank's controls.

"If they had said, 'Look, John, just please don't do that,' we wouldn't have done it. If they'd said to us at the time of doing the swaps, 'Look, just please don't do it,' we wouldn't have done it," he remembered. "What they said was 'We don't like this; you're wrecking the system,' and we might then have said, 'Are you telling us not to?' And they'd have said, 'S'pose not.'"

In short, chaps don't tell other chaps how to behave, and as a rule most chaps don't need telling. Sadly, however, some chaps are cads, which created a gigantic loophole to ride through for anyone who prioritized making money over doing what he was supposed to do. And this brings us at last to the moment when the City of London reinvented itself, which began in a small way, but became the point from which this tiny group of privileged Englishmen changed first Britain and then the world.

It started with two banks in 1955. The first was the Midland, a small bank stuck in a vicious circle. It couldn't attract deposits in the face of competition from the clearing banks that dominated the High Street. Without deposits, it didn't have the resources it needed to make loans. Without loans, it couldn't make profits. Without profits, it couldn't expand so as to get big enough to attract deposits. The second bank was the Moscow Narodny, a Soviet-owned London-based institution that looked after the USSR's dollar deposits, which it kept outside the United States out of concerns they might be frozen in a moment of international tension. If the Midland could only have bought those dollars, it could have used them to fund its activities, but it wasn't allowed to buy them because of the limits on capital movements.

And now came the clever part: someone at the Midland realized it didn't need to buy the dollars; it could just borrow them. The end result was the same—it would have dollars, which it could use to buy pounds, with which it could fund its activities—but the details were different. It was like renting a car rather than buying one: you can still drive wherever you like, but since the car belongs to someone else, you dodge any limitations on car ownership.

And what was in it for the Moscow Narodny? If the Russians lent those dollars to an American bank, a US rule called Regulation Q limited how much interest they could earn to just 1 percent. But in London the Midland would pay anything that could turn a profit, which in practice almost doubled MNB's earnings. It doesn't sound like much, but this odd little idea simultaneously allowed the Midland to dodge the limits placed on its activities in Britain, and let MNB avoid US restrictions. Financial surgeons in the City of London had operated on the heart of the sterling system, and installed a bypass around an obstruction that was stopping capital from flowing freely into the British economy and stopping the Midland from making profits.

The Bank of England thought this was getting dangerously close to caddish behavior, so an official at the Bank invited in a senior manager at Midland for a cup of tea, raised an eyebrow and showed what was called a "warning light." But, this being the City, he didn't actually tell Midland to remove the bypass it had installed, and since the bypass let it attract substantially cheaper funds than its rivals the Midland saw no reason to stop. The trouble was that the Midland wasn't doing anything illegal. It may have been violating the spirit of the law, but not its letter, as a Bank of England official recognized: "it is impossible to say to a London bank that it may accept dollar deposits but not seek them." The Bank of England could not force bankers to abide by voluntary restrictions. That would be that most of ghastly of things, "embarrassing."

And then came the Suez Crisis of 1956, the prolonged stand-off over the nationalization of the canal, the airborne and amphibious landings in Egypt, the speculative attacks on sterling and the UK government's realization that without American support it could not maintain the value of the pound at its fixed peg of $2.80. As the weeks passed in that long autumn, the country spent its dollars on pounds in an attempt to support the currency, but the attacks kept coming, and the store of dollars dwindled away. If the pound couldn't be supported, the whole sterling system, which—sclerotic though it might be—provided the arteries that linked together the remaining members of the British empire and many ex-colonies, allowing them to trade with each other and fund their activities, would go with it. There had never been a global economy without the sterling system, and officials were genuinely terrified that the loss of these arteries might cut off the financial oxygen economies needed to stay alive, that the world might collapse into disconnected organs struggling to survive.

"If sterling were to go the way, for example, of the French franc, the consequences would not be, as is so frequently suggested, that the world fall either into the Dollar Area or the hands of the Bolsheviks," George Bolton, an executive director of the Bank of England, had said in a speech in 1956. "The immediate results would be chaos, anarchy and, unless the gods were very kind, a collapse of civilization as we know it over a very large area of the world."

That may sound absurd with hindsight, now that we know sterling did indeed go the way of the French franc and civilization barely noticed, but Bolton was speaking with the weight of experience. He had helped guide the Bank of England through the horrors of the 1930s and the war; he had been a director at the International Monetary Fund. And even a small chance of the complete collapse of civilization is the kind of thing that will focus any politician's mind. The government had two choices: continue with its invasion of Egypt, maintain Britain's strategic position militarily and risk the end of everything, or abandon the Suez adventure, rescue what was left of sterling's reputation (and save civilization).

Officials tried to find a third option, begging the Americans for help, but the United Nations General Assembly had demanded that the Anglo-French forces leave Egypt and, Washington said, Britain could not expect assistance until it complied. In a desperate attempt to stave off disaster, Britain imposed petrol rationing and promised the Americans it would pull its troops out. "An Englishman's word is his bond," insisted the ambassador when the Americans demanded a deadline for the withdrawal. But the Americans wanted better security than that, and eventually London promised a complete evacuation within a fortnight. The Americans in return promised to lend as much money as was needed. Sterling was saved, but at a huge cost in British prestige, to the British economy and—it turned out, a decade or two down the line—to the United States and the world.

In a desperate attempt to support the pound, the Bank of England had increased its base rate from 5 to 7 percent, and the Treasury imposed yet more restrictions on the use of sterling to finance international trade. The limits helped the pound limp on, but did no more than postpone the inevitable when it came to the geopolitical situation. For the merchant banks of the City, however, the restrictions were existential. The arteries leading from the heart weren't just a bit clogged now, they were clamped shut. The merchant banks had relied on pounds to fund trade and suddenly needed a new source of funds if they were to stay in business. And that's when the Midland Bank's odd little idea went mainstream, but with a twist. The Midland had borrowed dollars in order to buy pounds so as to fund domestic lending. The merchant banks didn't bother with the second half—the pound was dead to them—they just started borrowing dollars in order to do business. And this was the moment when everything changed.

The Bank of England had been obsessed with defending the sterling system and convinced that the only way to do that was to support sterling as a global currency. It had spent its precious store of dollars buying pounds in order to do just that, but its officials were about to discover that they had been prioritizing the wrong half of the sterling system. What mattered was not sterling, but the system. It wasn't the blood that mattered, but the tubes it passed along. If they transfused dollars into those old sclerotic arteries, the blockages fell away, and life-giving capital poured through once more into the global economy; it made London feel young again, and the City had—quite accidentally—invented one of the most consequential financial tools of the twentieth century: the Eurodollar.

You may feel like I've already told you this story before in *Moneyland*, my previous book on financial skulduggery, and indeed there are similarities with the tale of the Eurobond, which is itself central to the rise of kleptocracy. A small, excluded British bank found a source of capital—for Eurodollars, it was the Midland and the Soviet Union; for Eurobonds, it was Warburgs and Switzerland—and created a new business that changed the world. But that's where the similarities stop. Eurobonds were a retail market, allowing tax dodgers, kleptocrats and the occasional refugee to hide illicit funds from governments. Eurodollars were far more important. This was a wholesale market that allowed banks to raise funds without limits or restrictions. Eurobonds are easy to understand—they're secret wealth guaranteed by pieces of papers—Eurodollars are far more complicated. They've had economists puzzled almost ever since they appeared.

One of the first economists to try to understand them was Geoffrey Bell, who I met in his rather grand fourth-floor flat in Holland Park, west London. He has a slight American accent now, thanks to decades living in the United States, but he comes from Grimsby, a fishing town on the Humber estuary in north-eastern Lincolnshire. He was educated at the local technical college and then at the London School of Economics, before joining the Treasury, where he made it his mission to understand what was going on with this new market, which was difficult, because Bank of England officials made it their mission to stop him. He was everything they hated: clever, bookish, working class, provincial, an outsider prying into their affairs.

"I remember the snobbery at the Bank of England and in the City, generally in the City . . . It certainly wasn't in those days a bastion of democracy, to say the least," he told me. "The senior people were very senior, and the junior people knew their place. I remember being excluded from the City workshops. I was excluded from the City. I kept myself to myself."

Bell did much of his research while on secondment to the US central bank—the Federal Reserve—and the Bank of England archives contain the letters that he wrote to Threadneedle Street seeking information about the Eurodollar market, which encapsulate the difficulties he faced in researching it. "Dear John, may I wish you a very happy New Year and I am looking forward to seeing you later this summer," he wrote in the cover note for an article he'd written for an academic publication, which he signed "Geoffrey." A Bank official has annotated it, referring to him—inevitably—as "Bell." In the next letter he tried again ("Dear John" signed "Geoffrey"), asking for permission to publish a paper, provoking an exchange of internal memos. There is something heroic about his insistence on signing himself "Geoffrey," but he was always "Bell" to them, and, an internal note stated, his request was "embarrassing." "It seems to me quite out of order that anyone on the Treasury staff should be allowed to write articles for magazines," one official sniffed in a handwritten annotation to one of his documents. "He might be presumed to have specialized knowledge." When he got his reply ("Dear Bell") it contained no information of use to anyone.

It is little wonder he remained in America, where he worked with economists of the caliber of Paul Volcker and Alan Greenspan, both of whom went on to chair the Federal Reserve. "I got to know them all, because they weren't snobby," he remembered. "Before, I hadn't realized what could be done with research."

He shouldn't have taken the Bank of England's refusal to share information with him personally; it was like that with almost everyone. Its hundreds of officials hoarded their secrets and left the government largely in the dark about this booming new business stream. The Bank's archives show, again and again, instructions not to share information with Whitehall officials, but information did leak out eventually, leading economists to try to analyze this new market and to understand what was going on. That was not an easy task.

The essential problem they faced—and, fair warning, this is where things get confusing—was that Eurodollars simultaneously were and weren't dollars. They were dollars in the sense that you could use them to buy things, just like you could with ordinary dollars; they weren't dollars in the sense that they weren't subject to any of the restrictions faced by ordinary dollars when you used them. There were no limits on the interest rate you could charge, there was no limit on how they could move between countries. Like some kind of peculiar particle in quantum physics, they both were and weren't US currency, although in their case the waveform collapsed not when you observed them, but when you decided what you wanted to do with them.

I read a few years ago about a farmer in Ireland in the 1960s whose land holdings straddled the border between the Republic and the North. He had a petrol tank built with two access points, one on each side of the frontier. He would pour petrol in on the side where it was cheaper, then take it out and resell it on the side where it was more expensive. His petrol was British and Irish at the same time, and only became one or the other when it was advantageous for him to make a choice. Eurodollars were a bit like that, though with less work and much bigger profits.

If you wanted to take advantage of the vitality and strength of the US economy, they were dollars; if you wanted to avoid restrictions imposed by the US government, they weren't. They could only have been invented by the practical men of the City of London, rather than the theorists of academia, since they didn't make sense. For hundreds of years money had meant something, a specific amount of precious metal guaranteed by a specific central bank, and governments did everything they could to keep it that way. In 1956 one dollar bought you 0.03 ounces of gold, by law, guaranteed by the Federal Reserve. With the Eurodollar, however, that was no longer the case: money was worth what someone would pay for it, and there was no backstop at all. If a London bank would pay more than the US government permitted, bring it on; if not, buyer beware.

This was an early example of what has come to be called "financial innovation," a term for the bewildering techniques developed in the City and on Wall Street to move money in more profitable ways. We tend to reflexively approve of innovation, since it brings us new medicines, machines and ideas. It is worth pausing, however, to ask what exactly financial innovation actually is. Unlike the kinds of innovation that have brought us the iPhone or antibiotics, a new financial technique doesn't carve a new niche out of the natural world or find a cleverer way to exploit existing materials. Boiled down to its essentials, finance always does the same thing: it takes money from people who have it but don't need it, and gives it to people who need it and don't have it, and earns a fee for its trouble. Governments try to regulate this process, to direct the funding toward the causes they care about, and financial institutions try to avoid those rules so they can direct the funding toward the causes that will pay the largest fees. That is financial innovation, which is simply an artificial way of exploiting artificial rules governing the artificial thing we call money, and normally involves finding mismatches between regulations in different countries. It's clever, but it adds nothing to the sum of human achievement.

And that's how it worked with Eurodollars. The bankers identified a mismatch between the United States and the United Kingdom and acted accordingly. By basing themselves in London, they avoided US restrictions on how much interest they could pay; by using dollars, they avoided British restrictions on how much money they could move. There was nothing inevitable about the market appearing in London, since this same dynamic could have played out almost anywhere. Indeed, smaller versions emerged in other European countries like France, Germany and Switzerland. The Swiss, French and Germans strangled their markets at birth, however, recognizing early on the risk they posed to financial stability. London's crucial advantage was that the Bank of England's officials saw no need to do the same. If they couldn't rule the world anymore, they wanted to be butler to whoever did.

In 1963 the merchant banker Charles Hambro wrote to the Bank to ask whether he should be getting involved in this new market, about which he clearly had concerns. A Bank official assured him (Hambro was educated at Eton, so the letter began "Dear Charles") that there was nothing to worry about. "It is par excellence an example of the kind of business which London ought to do both well and profitably," the letter said, before going on to give the first example I know of the creed that the City has lived by pretty much ever since. "If we were to stop the business here, it would move to other centers with a consequent loss of earnings for London." It's the greatest excuse for bad behavior there is. As the old song goes: If I don't do it, somebody else will.

In public, however, bankers liked to come up with nobler explanations for why they thought it a good idea to erode the controls on money moving between countries, and unpick the solution to the trilemma imposed at the end of the Second World War. Bolton, who we last saw warning apocalyptically about what would happen if the sterling system collapsed, changed his mind immediately upon leaving the Bank of England. At the merchant bank BOLSA (Bank of London and South America) he had his employees enthusiastically bid for dollar deposits they could use to fund trade and took any opportunity to insist that Eurodollars were not just profitable for him, but beneficial to the world.

In one speech in early 1961 he claimed that expanding financial flows would help ease tensions in the Cold War. "Apart from the commercial benefits there would surely follow a lessening of tension and mistrust," he claimed. "I feel strongly, therefore, that all of us, especially the United States, should concentrate on expanding trade with these countries, including the provision of medium- or even long-term credit on reasonable terms." Just a few days previously he had criticized governments' attempts to keep capital penned inside borders, even if it was helping deliver domestic prosperity. "It fails to take into account Europe's responsibilities toward the under-developed countries," he said. The City of London's new idea was apparently a force for both alleviating poverty and spreading peace, and should therefore be encouraged. If it allowed London banks to profit at the expense of their American counterparts, who were still forced to abide by US regulations, that was all the better.

"The Bank of England people, there weren't many of them who were intellectually curious. They were older, and were executive types rather than strategic thinkers. Their attitude to the burgeoning dollar market was one of benignity," remembered David Walker, who headed the Treasury's exchange control department at the time, when we chatted in his flat in Kensington. "If you said, 'Isn't this a very good thing for the UK and aren't we stealing the Americans' lunch?' no one quite thought of it like that. I think I did a bit, and I'm sure Geoffrey Bell did, but most of the time we took it for granted. It was a very very good thing for the City of London."

The issue was that, from the purely day-to-day perspective of officials like Walker, who were trying to enforce the regulations around money flows, the solution created after the Second World War to the trilemma was kind of annoying. Yes, if you stepped back it was theoretically good, and the democratic argument for it was solid, but what if one of your companies wanted to operate in more than one country? All those regulations stopped a multinational corporation moving money around, and that was expensive, which limited its profits. British officials approved of the democratic case for capital controls, but they wanted Shell Oil to do well too, and juggling those two priorities was hard.

The same went for American officials. They might have wanted all dollar transactions to stay in New York, but it was also quite useful for US corporations to have a place to raise funds when operating overseas that was not as restrictive as the domestic market. This appears to be why US officials didn't put pressure on their British counterparts to stop the trade in Eurodollars. "Although the continental dollar market has somewhat reduced the importance of New York as an international lending center, it has added to the importance of the dollar as an international currency," wrote two Federal Reserve analysts in 1960 in what seems to have been US officials' first attempt to understand what was going on. They did not take it very seriously, however, and no one informed the White House for another three years.

With other banks piling in, the Midland was rapidly eclipsed as a major player in Eurodollars. It held half the market on the eve of the Suez Crisis, but that share had fallen to just 3 percent by 1962, as American, Japanese and other British banks realized the appeal of cheap string-free money. What you could do with it was limited only by your imagination, because it expanded unimpeded trade to the whole world. "The Euro-dollar market knows no politics," said Oscar Altman, deputy director of the International Monetary Fund, in 1964. It was little more than a year after the Cuban Missile Crisis, but capitalist and communist banks alike plugged happily into the City of London's new blood supply, safe from the privations of the Cold War.

It was around the time of the Cuba crisis that American journalists first noticed what was going on. According to the *New York Times*, in July 1962 the market was worth between $2 billion and $5 billion, all of it circulating outside the US financial system. "The frustration of American officials in such a situation is understandable. The entire operation stands beyond the reach of United States law and regulation," the paper noted. American banks joined in for one simple reason: it was profitable. As one senior banker told the paper in 1965 in a quote for the ages, "you can't expect people to remain virtuous when the temptation becomes too great."

By 1967 the market was worth $13 billion, and the US government was increasingly concerned about what this restless pool of dollars meant for domestic stability. The trouble was that bankers moved Eurodollars wherever they could gain the most profit. So, if one country tried to give its economy a boost by lowering interest rates, bankers would sell its currency to seek better returns elsewhere. This weakened the currency, forcing the government either to intervene in the markets to protect it, or to put interest rates back up again. The same dynamic worked in the opposite direction. If a country put up interest rates to calm its economy or restrict inflation, Eurodollars would pour in, strengthening the currency and forcing the government to put interest rates down again. Eurodollars linked all the national money markets together into one huge market, through which money sloshed in waves powerful enough to capsize governments. That restricted governments' freedom of action and thus undermined the autonomy that they had so jealously guarded.

When the US government was concerned about how quickly prices were rising and so sought to limit the supply of money, large banks simply borrowed Eurodollars in London, then sent them to their head offices in New York, allowing them to circumvent the restrictions. By 1969, the Federal Reserve was openly speculating about imposing the same limits on Euro-dollars that it imposed on all dollars. If the dollar was going to be the international currency, then the Fed would have to be the international central bank. "A genie has popped out of a bottle and grown in just a few years to an enormous size. He has no nationality, owes allegiance to no one and roams the world looking for the biggest financial rewards. He is extremely useful. But his uncontrolled antics can frustrate the good intentions of lesser creatures, such as central bankers," wrote the *New York Times* in April 1969 with heavy irony. "The genie is the Eurodollar, a strapping giant, well over $20-billion strong, baffling to the layman and puzzling even to the experts."

Normally, when central bank officials openly muse about

new regulations, that is equivalent to creating them, but this time it didn't work. Bankers knew very well that the Federal Reserve couldn't impose its will in London, even if it wanted to. By December, the *New York Times* said, the volume of funds in the market had hit $40 billion. Like the sorcerer's apprentice bewitching his broom to fetch him water, the central bankers who had conjured up this market couldn't stop it; the more they tried to do so, the higher the water levels rose.

In 1971 the US Congress held hearings on the problem, in which Eugene Birnbaum, vice president of Chase Manhattan, neatly encapsulated it. "Foreign dollar-denominated loans, which had previously fallen under the regulatory guidelines or examination of the Securities and Exchange Commission, the Federal Reserve, or the Comptroller of the Currency, have simply moved out of the jurisdictional reach of these institutions," he said. "British supervisory authorities are aware of the fact that any attempt by them to impose regulations or reserve requirements on such foreign currency-denominated credit activities would tend to drive this thriving international business away to some other locations." If either of the two countries tightened its regulations to rein in this feral market, that simply increased the profits available to the other. If Ireland tried to impose tighter controls on petrol, the more profit could be made by the farmer siphoning petrol in from the UK, and vice versa.

Leslie O'Brien was Cromer's successor as governor of the Bank of England and came to the United States in 1971 to reassure Americans about London's capacity to look after their money. As part of his tour, he gave a speech to the Bankers' Club of Chicago in which he recounted the history of the Eurodollar market, though largely in the passive voice. He gives no sense that the Bank approved the momentous changes that had crippled the US ability to regulate dollar transactions; in his telling they just happened, like the weather. And, as with the weather, there's nothing that can be done about it, except invest in better clothing or perhaps an umbrella.

"If we attempted to solve the problems of international adjustment by legislating the Eurodollar market out of existence, we should discover one of two things. Either the attempt would be largely ineffective, because the Eurodollar market would simply shift its location to an unregulated center; or its effect would be quickly undone, as other mechanisms came into being to take its place," he said.

And here is the second argument the City of London uses to explain its failure to impose regulations. The first is that if it doesn't do something, someone else will. And the second, which interlocks elegantly with the first, is that there is no point refraining from bad behavior until everyone else agrees to do so, because that would achieve nothing. If I don't steal your money, somebody else will; and there's no point in me stopping until everyone else does too. Together these two arguments spelled doom for the Bretton Woods system of capital controls.

Five months later, President Richard Nixon, infuriated by his inability to control inflation by limiting the amount of currency in circulation, abandoned the US dollar's peg to gold. From then on, the dollar would be worth whatever someone would pay for it. All dollars became Eurodollars, and the bankers got their solution to the trilemma. With free capital flows, they could make money wherever they spotted an investment opportunity, and using their bases in London, US banks could escape any attempt to rein them in.

By the end of the 1960s there were more than a hundred foreign banks with branches in London, to the horror of the old City elite. This was not what they'd thought they'd signed up for at all. They had invented this accounting trick to make themselves some extra cash, but it had been seized upon by pushy outsiders who were now elbowing the old Etonians aside. "I'm not saying that their system's not good for the Americans, in America, but I don't think it's very good here," said Cromer in that interview toward the end of his life. "One was much better informed of what was going on in days gone by because it was a smaller circle, I think, and people weren't quite so much after what the Americans call 'the quick buck.'"

Of course, the Americans noticed that their banks were crossing the Atlantic and an ever-larger share of business was moving to London. In 1980, therefore, they copied Britain's lax regulatory regime in an attempt to lure the business back and abolished Regulation Q—the limits on interest rates that had helped inspire the Eurodollar market in the first place—and created "International Banking Facilities," which copied the regulation-free approach of the UK. Stung, in 1987 the British loosened their regulations still further in an epic act of deregulation that stripped away centuries of procedure and was termed the Big Bang. In 1999 the Americans removed more regulations of their own, allowing financial institutions specializing in different activities to combine into huge corporations. It was a deregulatory two-step, the Brits and Americans taking turns to loosen their rules in attempts to attract business to their own financial center.

Most historians credit the decisions of Margaret Thatcher and Ronald Reagan—and their successors—to dismantle the architecture of the welfare state and the New Deal to their shared conservative philosophy, and of course that's important. Just as important, however, was the fact they were trapped in a spiral whereby they had to keep removing regulations to prevent their financial sectors vanishing over the Atlantic. It was as if Ireland and Britain each kept trying to appease that farmer by lowering petrol taxes and loosening the restrictions on his trade, and yet finding that no matter what they did the other side could go further. The important point is that it makes no difference to the farmer which side treats him and his petrol better; he makes a profit either way. And it was the same with the financial institutions. New York and London became one market—perhaps we could call it NY-LON—in which American money filled a British system, meaning neither government could supervise it, and there was no democratic control over wealth. Banks simply moved their activities to whichever side of the Atlantic was more profitable at the time.

"The Euromarkets set in motion a 'transatlantic regulatory feedback loop' that destabilized transatlantic regulatory regimes," writes Jeremy Green, a historian of the Eurodollar. "Many of the deregulatory moves in Britain and America during the ideological transformation of the 'neoliberal era' were incubated during the 1960s."

It is often lamented in Britain that Americans have taken over the City of London, and the UK has lost its autonomy as a result. And it's true that the old merchant banks have all been taken over, and the City institutions that created the Eurodollar market—BOLSA, Hambros, Barings, even the Midland—no longer have any independent existence. For the first time since the Italians were dominant in the Middle Ages, Britain's financial elite is essentially international, with no automatic allegiance to the country that hosts its offices. But what is less remarked upon is that there has been a concurrent decline in autonomy in the opposite direction. The US Treasury lost oversight of its own banks when they moved to the City of London. Both governments lost out, as financial institutions slipped out of their control.

Freed from regulations and oversight, the financial industry was able to attract more and more of the kind of "bright new-comers" graduating from universities that Fry was so pleased to see back in the City in the late 1960s. More than a fifth of recent British graduates now work in banking and finance, three times as many as have gone into manufacturing, and the industry employs more than two million people. Anyone who has studied at a UK university in the last thirty years will remember the City recruiters who came round to careers fairs, promising higher pay than any other sector. The world needs a lot of butlers to move all that money around.

During a speech in 1962 in which he looked back on the Suez humiliation and British decline, former US Secretary of State Dean Acheson let slip a pithy epigram: "Britain has lost an empire and has not yet found a role." The phrase set off a storm of fury in Britain, and has resounded ever since, but he was wrong. Britain had lost an empire, but it had already found a role: as an amoral servant of wealth wherever it could be found, using the skills it had built up over centuries of empire-building to help the owners of wealth avoid having to account to anyone but themselves. And the effects are all around us. I am writing this sentence nine months into the COVID-19 crisis, and have just read a report published by the accounting giant PwC and the banking giant UBS which revealed that between April and July 2020, the world's 2,189 billionaires increased their collective wealth by $2.2 trillion.

How, the report asked, should the world respond to this, particularly with governments facing such huge deficits as the pandemic dented their economies, and their spending surged in response? The report stated that it would not be effective to tax the billionaires, who could just move their money out of the reach of national tax authorities. Instead, governments should allow inflation to increase, to erode what savings the rest of us have left, because that is the money that can be reached. Handing the bill for society to those too poor to avoid paying it has become the default solution to all the challenges we face, and that is the logic that the Eurodollar has bequeathed us. When money can flow wherever it likes, governments need to treat its owners well. This is the consequence of the decision that the Bank of England made in the aftermath of the Suez Crisis, a decision that allowed Britain's merchant banks to free wealth from democratic controls, and we're all living with it.

This shouldn't be a surprise. Shonfield, the economist whose views Bank of England officials dismissed back in the 1950s because he was Jewish, predicted the consequences of an unrestrained flow of money between countries before it even happened. Countries would have to compete with each other to attract this footloose capital, which meant its owners would be able to pick and choose which jurisdiction to favor with their custom. "This at once sets pretty narrow limits to what the government can do about taxation, about social expenditure, about nationalisation, and a number of other major political issues," he wrote. That neuters democracy, and not just in the United Kingdom. If governments can't control their financial systems, they are no longer sovereign.

The British butler had set the banks free to earn profits previously denied them. But, just as when Jeeves has successfully solved one of his gentlemen's latest entanglements, the story does not stop there. There are always new problems to solve, and new fees to earn by doing so. A butler's work is never done.

4

SHELL SHOCK

When Michael Riegels passed his bar exams, he could have walked into most London barristers' chambers. Clever, well spoken, with a degree from Oxford (and an athletics blue to go with it), he was the kind of man who could have slotted right into the British Establishment. He had other plans, however. He was going home to east Africa. Riegels is in his eighties now: straight-backed, white-haired, pink-cheeked, slim-waisted, aquiline-nosed. His accent and his manner are unmistakably English, yet he has—apart from the years of study at Oxford and Gray's Inn—spent barely two years in England in his life. He is a man of empire. He was born in Tanganyika, he went to school in Kenya, and he had no intention of living anywhere else. "I was never tempted to stay in the UK," he told me.

He first looked for a job in Nairobi, but eventually took up an offer in Dar es Salaam, which wasn't too much of a step down. "Tanganyika was the sort of poor relative," he remembered. "We were always a bit smaller than Kenya, but we had a sizable notch. We managed to have all the societies, the sports clubs and motor clubs, amateur dramatic clubs. They were well supported."

That was in 1961, and he came back just in time for independence, when Prince Philip flew in to watch the Union flag come down for the last time, and the green, black and gold banner of the newly independent nation rise in its place. It was an extraordinary period for Africa, as British rule evaporated in a dozen separate states within a decade, but change on the ground was far more gradual than the political upheaval might suggest, particularly for a lawyer. Divorces, business disputes and motor accidents happened regardless of who ran the country, so Riegels had plenty of work, and his life was little different to what he'd known growing up.

As the years passed, however, the impact of independence became clearer. The new leader of Tanganyika, Julius Nyerere, was determined to fix the country's many inequalities, among which were the stark racial divides in its economy. While white people still dominated the professions, people of Asian origin tended to control trade. That left black Africans—the overwhelming majority of the population—as laborers and farmers, and scraping by with very little. Nyerere was committed to treating all races equally, but he was also determined to give the country's majority prosperity, as well as control of their own destiny.

"He was an ex-teacher, and he was always called the teacher, *mwalimu*. No one ever questioned his integrity; he lived in a modest sort of way, that was him," said Riegels. "But he was a dreamer, he was a great believer in the communist principle that everyone should muck in together. They had this policy, *ujamaa*, togetherness, and they set up all these co-ops. The local farmers had always sold all their crops to Indian middlemen, but Nyerere said, 'We don't want that. You will all give your crops to the co-op, and they will sell them.' [But] there was total incompetence, the crops were left outside, and got rotten, or there was a lot of corruption."

This was the time of the Cold War, when the world was

divided between communists and capitalists. At first, it looked like Nyerere would stay friendly with the West. On a state visit to Washington, DC, in 1963, President John F. Kennedy compared him to George Washington as the founding father of his own nation. But the teacher's rigid principles repeatedly clashed with the West's reflexive patronizing of ex-colonies: he fell out with West Germany over his friendship with East Germany; he fell out with Britain over its failure to discipline the rebellious racists in Rhodesia; he fell out with the United States after what seems to have been a slightly farcical misunderstanding over a figurative use of the word "ammunition," which led to a tit-for-tat expulsion of diplomats. He provided shelter for militants fighting colonialism in Congo and Mozambique, which did not endear him to Belgium or Portugal.

His principles were unbending in domestic policy too. He disbanded the army after a mutiny, and rebuilt it from nothing. When students in Dar es Salaam protested over the government's insistence that they do national service and pay a special tax of 40 percent on their post-university income, he had half of them expelled. He nationalized the banks, which cut the country off from the London money markets, depriving companies of the cash they needed to keep open and exacerbating an economic crisis caused by low prices for the country's primary export crops, including coffee. He made strikes illegal, but workers continued to withhold their labor as the economy shrank, and tens of thousands of people were laid off.

Although Nyerere was no friend of the Soviet Union, he became—as the 1960s went on—increasingly close to the rulers of China, which alarmed Riegels and the remaining British community. They definitely did not want to get stuck in Tanganyika—renamed Tanzania after its union with the island nation of Zanzibar in 1964—if the country was planning to transform itself along Maoist lines. So they started looking to hedge their bets.

This occurred across the decolonizing world, not just among the British, but with colonists from France, Belgium, Portugal, the Netherlands and elsewhere. There is a saying that if you're accustomed to privilege, equality feels like oppression, and that is how many Europeans responded to the changes sweeping across Africa and Asia. Accustomed to society being run in their interests, they found the prospect of being ruled by their former subjects and having to pay tax to the new nations' governments hard to accept. So they started to shift their assets out, money that contemporary observers termed "funk money" ("funk" as in "fear," rather than "funk" as in "music").

This was not an entirely spontaneous process. Just as the settlers were looking for a way out for their money, Butler Britain's bankers were anticipating their concerns, gliding into the room soundlessly, giving a discreet cough and waiting to be noticed. "There seems to be an obvious need for residents of such areas to take some sort of evasive action against future legislation in their countries," said a banker from Kleinwort Benson, a London-based investment bank, in the early 1960s. Translation: as a butler, I must find a way to help my clients to pre-emptively break the law, because that's how to keep them happy.

"Why, dash it, if I could think of some way of doing down the income tax people, I should be a rich man. You don't know of a way of doing down the income tax people do you, Bertie?" asks Bertie Wooster's friend Claude "Catsmeat" Potter-Pirbright.

"Sorry, no. I doubt if even Jeeves does," Wooster replies.

The historian Vanessa Ogle has identified what she calls "low white tax morale" as a key driver of the flow of money out of ex-colonies, a way of saying that colonists did not like paying taxes. In most colonies the costs of the administration had long been born by the subject population and by duties at the ports, which meant European settlers could live well and cheaply. White residents were not accustomed to having to pay to support their government, and didn't want to have to start. However, they also didn't want to have to pay the high taxes on income then prevalent across Europe and North America.

London bankers, easing into their role as butler, were happy to service funk money, creating clever financial instruments that allowed its owners to park it in Jersey or the Bahamas or Switzerland while still enjoying its use. "We have for some time felt that an investment medium should be set up for the many people resident in the West Indies, Mediterranean, Africa, Far East, etc. who are either of British origin or who look to London for their financial arrangements, but do not wish to become involved in British income-tax or estate-duty liabilities," noted a banker from Hambros in 1963. Translation: they need help dodging taxes.

Funk money helped to create its own reality. As money left the ex-colonies, the local banks became weaker, which led to financial instability, so customers worried about the banks' solvency, so more money left, and so on. The governments of ex-colonies imposed ever-stricter controls on the movement of money as they tried to support their economies, which just created greater nervousness and ensured even higher fees for anyone who could help the money's owners circumvent the controls. The more serious a problem, the more a butler can earn if he solves it.

"Because the economy went to hell in a hand basket, they introduced stricter and stricter exchange controls. Eventually, by the time we left, you were only allowed to remit foreign currency of £150 every three years," remembered Riegels, who was married by now and had a first child. "We wanted to educate our children overseas, but we couldn't do it because you couldn't get the foreign currency. You had to report all of your foreign assets to the Bank of Tanzania, and they would buy them off you for useless shillings. No one did this of course, so you ended up hiding your assets overseas and hoping nobody ever found out, because they would give you a strict sentence if they did."

Tanzanian shillings had little value overseas, so imports dried up, which severely impacted the Riegels family's lifestyle, from breakfast onward (Kenyan traders had stopped selling bacon and milk to Tanzanians, because they had no hard currency to pay for them). Western products like Raleigh bicycles or Gillette razor blades vanished from the Asian-owned stores for the same reason; then the Asian shops began to vanish too, as their owners had nothing to sell. Passing through Beirut on a business trip, Riegels saw a currency exchange booth that boasted that it would trade anything and thought he might get a price for his otherwise worthless banknotes. "I hopefully trotted round with my Tanzanian shillings, but he said, 'No, no, no, we don't want those.' Those were very hard times. That was just after nationalization, when everything fell apart," he said.

It wasn't just the financial conditions that were pushing Michael Riegels to leave, however. The youth wing of the ruling party had begun to campaign against Western influence in Tanzanian society. Hair straighteners and miniskirts were targeted, and newspapers regularly ran editorials accusing businessmen and lawyers of being accomplices of the colonialists.

Considering what Nyerere's Chinese patrons were doing at the time, it did not take much to imagine Tanzania boiling over into a full-blown cultural revolution like the one Mao Zedong

had unleashed in China, with its millions of arrests and rit-
ualized public shamings of the educated and the bourgeois.
Riegels was both educated and bourgeois, and as a lawyer he
had an insight into the way the Tanzanian legal system was
becoming politicized, so he had no hope that he would find
justice if he were ever arrested. "In one case we were acting
for a client who was accused of corruptly attempting to bribe
a government official. At the client's insistence we engaged a
prominent London QC to handle the case, but he was served
with a deportation order very soon after his arrival in Tanzania. He sought to challenge the deportation order in court, but
after lengthy argument the chief justice excused himself saying
he needed to discuss the matter with the minister of the interior," Riegels said. "Our learned QC went slightly purple in
the face and spluttered, 'But, but you should not be doing that.
This is a matter of law. You are the chief justice. You should
make your decision based on the law.' It did not help him. After
discussing the matter with the minister of the interior the chief
justice returned to court to say, 'Your application is dismissed.'
He was out on the next plane."

Riegels became increasingly worried, whenever he left home
in the morning, that it would be the last time he saw his wife
Norma and their boy. "Michael would say, 'If I'm not home by
seven o'clock, pick up the baby and get the hell out of here. I'll
see you at your parents' house.' My parents were back in the
UK by then," Norma Riegels told me.

And so after almost exactly a decade of independence
they decided to leave. They sold their house in Dar es Salaam,
handed the proceeds to someone prepared to exchange shillings
for pounds at the black market rate and headed back to the UK.
It was 1971. Norma had left Britain aged six, so she knew little
more about the country they were moving to than Michael did.

But if they had hoped for a land of plentiful stability, they were disappointed.

In fact, in the whole second half of the twentieth century, they could hardly have picked a worse time to come home. Inflation was high, eroding what little savings they had after the money changer's cut. Labor unrest was rife, as workers attempted to preserve their wages in the face of the collapsing value of the pound. Electricity and fuel were rationed, as the government sought to keep the lights on. "We hated it, and had another baby," said Norma, laughing. At the time, however, it wasn't funny. They had to ask their relatives for help, and were worried about what would become of them.

One evening they met up with a friend from Tanzania for drinks. He had left Dar es Salaam when his company had been nationalized, and he was in the UK on holiday. After hearing them complain for a while, he asked if Michael would consider coming to work for the law firm that serviced his company, which needed a new partner. But it would mean leaving Britain. Was that OK?

It certainly was. Michael Riegels jumped on a plane and went to have a look. "Michael came out for a look-see, fell in love instantly and said, 'We're going,'" said Norma Riegels. So, after twenty-one long months in the UK, they packed every-thing up once more and moved to a place in the Caribbean that neither they nor almost anyone else they knew had ever heard of, the British Virgin Islands. "When we came here from Tanzania, we thought we'd died and gone to heaven," Michael Riegels remembered. "It was so nice. And it was a change not having everyone saying you're a filthy imperialist swine, which does get wearing after a while."

It was to be a fateful decision, not just for them, and not

just for the BVI, but for the whole world. Britain's butlering sideline was about to take another step into the mainstream.

The British Virgin Islands are a picturesque scattering of fifty or so coral-fringed, white-beached humps projecting from the Caribbean Sea. The largest island is Tortola, which is steep like a dragon's back and spined with spiky vegetation. It hosts most of the population as well as the capital Road Town, which when the Riegels family arrived was just a village, but is now a sprawling low-rise conurbation running from the port along the narrow strip between the sea and the slope. Christopher Columbus named the islands on his second voyage to the Americas in 1493 in honor of St. Ursula and her 11,000 virgins, a group of (hopefully mythical) martyrs beheaded en masse by Huns in Cologne in the fourth century. Unlike the other islands that Columbus sailed to in those early voyages, the Virgin Islands lacked the kind of resources that attracted much European attention, however, and there is a good reason why Riegels had never heard of them: they were extremely poor and spectacularly obscure. Britain took possession in the late seventeenth century, but mainly just to stop someone else—in this case the Dutch—from having them.

"There is no more backward unit in the British Colonial Empire," wrote a former governor of London's Caribbean possessions in the late 1940s. Considering how large and far-flung the empire was at the time, that is quite a claim, and not much had changed some twenty-five years later.

In common with most colonial possessions in the Caribbean, British or otherwise, the BVI had once been sugar islands where African slaves had toiled in the sun to keep a small class of white planters—the plantocracy, as the locals put it—in a life of

shaded ease. Unlike many of Britain's other Caribbean possessions, however, in the Virgin Islands the plantations ceased to
be viable once the slaves won their freedom in 1833. The plantations gradually returned to the bush, the plantocrats moved
away, and the ex-slaves were left to their own devices. In the late
nineteenth century the population was below 5,000, almost all
of them peasant farmers raising scrub cattle and subsistence
crops. "It is possible to get about on horseback, but the roads
have become mere tracks," wrote a colonial official. "Extreme
poverty is only too common, and the government cannot raise
by taxation any revenue sufficient to cope with it."

Part of the problem was that the BVI were so far from any
other British possession. They possessed no strategic or economic value and traded primarily with the other half of the
Virgin Islands archipelago, which was owned by Denmark until
1917, and then by the United States, which bought the islands
to stop the Germans getting them. In comparison with the
British Virgin Islands, the USVI were relatively prosperous and
well populated, importing the BVIslanders' beef and selling
them dry goods, groceries, rope and almost anything else they
needed. Everyone in the BVI had relatives in the USVI, which
are just a short sail away, but they remained separate countries,
which caused serious impediments to trade.

"Each time one of these little boats goes to St. Thomas with
its cargo, its master has to fill out seventeen different forms
required by the United States government, the same number
and identical forms that the captain of the *Queen Mary* or
any other ship has to fill when she enters New York harbor," a
visitor noted. Most of the sloops' skippers were illiterate, and
couldn't be bothered with this kind of bureaucracy, so smuggling was rife, which further undermined what little tax the BVI

administration might have hoped to receive. In the 1950s half of the colony's revenue came from selling stamps to the world's philatelists, which was never going to amount to much of a living. The locals used the US dollar as currency, and largely ignored the government's attempts to control them. "The only elements obviously British at first sight are the Union Jack that flies over the government buildings and the charming British colonel who is the commissioner," wrote an academic from the University of Chicago who visited in the early 1950s.

In return, Britain paid the islands almost as little attention as the locals paid the UK. On the rare occasions when members of Parliament in Westminster did talk about them, a wag would invariably bring up the apocryphal story of a government minister who, when asked where the Virgin Islands were, quipped that they must be "far from the Isle of Man." A plan to turn one of the islands into a holiday resort failed. One MP in 1964 suggested that perhaps Britain should just give the islands to America, but that didn't happen either.

"It was a very sleepy sort of place when we first got here," remembered Michael Riegels, who worked for three months for a Cambridge-educated lawyer called Neville Westwood, before joining his practice as a partner. Westwood had moved to the islands six years previously. "We were chugging along, doing motor claims, things like that. There were a lot of land disputes—that tree belongs to me, not you, that kind of thing."

The moment everything changed came some time in the summer of 1976. No one can remember exactly when it happened, because its significance only became clear in hindsight, but Michael and Norma's son Colin imagined it in an article three decades later; open windows in the office, piles of paper on the desks, overhead fans moving lazily in the thick tropical air, the rotary telephone ringing shrilly. It was Paul Butler, a lawyer with the New York firm of Shearman and Sterling, and he was looking for someone who spoke English.

In their quest for offshore profits, American financiers had not stopped with the Eurodollar market. They had discovered that if US corporations did business via wholly owned subsidiaries on Curaçao—one of the scattering of Dutch islands in the Caribbean—then they could avoid onerous regulations and taxes, thanks to a generous double taxation treaty between the United States and the Netherlands.

Double taxation treaties are foundational to the globalized economy, because they ensure that a company that operates in more than one country isn't taxed twice on the same money. There is a flaw in the system, which is that, if one country undercuts the other on tax rates, companies that base themselves in the first can dramatically reduce the amount they pay into government coffers in the second. As a rule, however, big countries don't play that game, because they lose more in tax than they gain in economic activity. Small jurisdictions, however, see things differently. They never have much tax revenue to lose, and the new business they attract from relocating companies gains them more in fees and economic activity than they lose in taxes. Such countries are now understood and referred to as tax havens, but back in the 1970s they were a new phenomenon, and businesses were exploring them with relish.

Curaçao, which is just off the coast of Venezuela and had long specialized in smuggling and oil refining, was one of the first Caribbean jurisdictions to understand the profits to be made from gaming the system in this way. There was still a problem, however. Curaçao was Dutch, and although Dutch people tend to speak beautiful English, they are still Dutch. That means they write legal documents in Dutch, hold court hearings in

Dutch, and use civil law, which is all quite annoying from the perspective of an American lawyer.

And that is why Paul Butler was trawling the Caribbean for English-speaking common law jurisdictions with a taxation treaty that could provide access to the same kind of loophole without the hassle of having to use translators. History doesn't recount how many places he tried before he discovered the British Virgin Islands, but when he did he lucked out: he had found Riegels and Westwood, who were not only competent, skilled and hard-working lawyers, but also more than happy to incorporate as many companies as he wanted, whenever he wanted. No, thank *you*, Jeeves.

"They had to have someone who could respond to telexes, who could give a legal opinion. Christmas Day, at the drop of a hat," Michael Riegels said, laughing.

"That was Christmas Eve, actually," responded Norma Riegels dryly.

"My wife said she would never talk to me again. Those guys wanted it, and we provided it. We were probably cheaper too. We never charged an arm and a leg."

If a company was deemed to be "managed and controlled" in the BVI, which meant that a majority of its directors had to be resident there, even if it was wholly owned by an American corporation it could take advantage of the United States–BVI double taxation treaty. And that not only avoided US corporate income tax, which at the time was 50 percent, but reduced the tax on exported dividends and income from 30 percent to 15 percent. So if income that originated in the US was paid to a BVI-resident company instead of kept at home, the US tax rate fell from 50 percent to 15 percent, and that was only the start of it. "It wasn't just avoiding taxes, it was also avoiding regulations and making life easy for people," said Michael Riegels.

The dynamic was essentially the same as that which brought the Eurodollar market to London. The US government had imposed onerous restrictions on its finance industry to try to prevent the kind of runaway speculation that had resulted in disaster in the years before the Second World War and levied high taxes to support a generous government. American bankers and lawyers were looking for ways to circumvent those restrictions and dodge those taxes, and were willing to pay good money to anyone who could help them. That was where Michael Riegels came in, which was good news not just for him but also for the British Virgin Islands as a whole.

In the 1970s Britain put its remaining Caribbean colonies on a pathway toward independence, which involved the gradual granting of ever-greater autonomy, so local politicians became increasingly accustomed to running their own affairs. Although the British Virgin Islands have not yet actually become independent, and are still part of the Greater Britain that is such an effective butler, back then they were following the same route as their fellow territories. During the 1970s, therefore, Britain gave gradually greater powers to the islands, and from 1977 the locally elected assembly took charge of the BVI's finances, which had previously been the responsibility of the London-appointed governor. It was an important moment for the islands but also a frustrating one, because their elected representatives had almost no money to spend. They charged few taxes or duties, and had no scope to charge more, which severely limited their revenues and thus their ability to enjoy their new powers.

But this is where Riegels came in. Every time he registered a company, he paid a fee to the administration, and that helped to increase the amount of money the administration had to spend, as if by magic. It was a little like the islands had suddenly struck oil, but without all the messy business of having to dig wells or move viscous liquids around.

As with the Eurodollar market, the US initially had no real objection to this kind of tax dodging. Officials recognized that onerous New Deal–era regulations made it expensive for businesses to raise capital, and were prepared to tolerate a bit of offshore skulduggery if it helped the economy. However, as the trickle of offshore business became a flood, they began to worry about what it might sweep away. Pete Stark, a congressman from California, became particularly outspoken about the way corporations and offshore jurisdictions were colluding to minimize taxes against the interests of the United States as a whole. He called out "tax shelters" and "tax straddles," the artificial tax avoidance schemes created and sold by US law firms, which often made use of companies that began their life on Michael Riegels's desk.

US officials were listening and summoned a BVI delegation to discuss the double taxation treaty. They initially planned to negotiate a new one but in 1982 unceremoniously canceled it altogether. "By the time the US pulled the plug on us," remembered Norma Riegels, "business had picked up. I remember us celebrating because at the end of one month we'd done fifty companies."

"We were a bit cross, but you can't argue with Uncle Sam," said Michael.

It was a worrying time for the lawyers and for the BVI government. The revenue from shell companies had grown to such an extent that it was now equal to the islands' entire education budget, and losing it would set them back years. What were they to do? "The premier of the day, the chief minister, was a chap called Lavity Stoutt, and he said, 'Chaps'—he used to speak very English—'chaps, we've got to do something,'" recalled Michael.

Fortunately, Paul Butler, the appropriately named New York lawyer who had first called up Riegels, had already thought of something. Couldn't the islands pass legislation to create a new kind of company? It might not have access to the double taxation treaty anymore, but, designed right, a shell company could still be a powerful tool for his rich clients in their quest to avoid contributing to society. Butler threw together some ideas, mainly borrowed from legislation in Panama and Delaware, and faxed them down to Road Town. There Lewis Hunte, the islands' recently appointed attorney general, set to work translating them into British legal terminology and then submitted his document to the lawyers for comments.

We are accustomed to complaints about lobbyists having undue access to the legislative process and governments cozying up to corporate interests. That is not what happened here, however. In designing this new piece of legislation, government and business were so completely intertwined that there is no way of seeing where lobby-er stopped and lobby-ee started. The BVI's new companies bill was co-written by what is now called the gang of five—the government's top legal officer, the three partners at Harneys, Westwood and Riegels, and Butler himself. Each afternoon Hunte would sit down with Riegels or one of his colleagues and thrash out some thoughts, then fax them to New York, where Butler would add his edits, have them typed up and fax them back. The next day the process would begin again. And so it continued, day after day.

Eventually Butler got fed up with acting as the BVI's secretary, and shipped out a word processor made by then-cutting-edge Wang Laboratories. The computer lived in Riegels's offices, which allowed Butler to mark up the fax he received and send it right back, leaving the BVI secretaries to do the typing. It was the first computer on the islands, saved laborious and messy work with the duplicating machine, and significantly sped up the process. Everyone wanted this law passed quickly. The islands wanted to plug back into the shell company gusher, and Butler wanted a new product to sell to his clients.

Even a general election in 1983 and the departure of Stoutt as chief minister did nothing to derail the train; the new government simply introduced the legislation as if it had been its own idea all along. "The legislative council was scheduled to meet on Friday, 29 June 1984, at 10 a.m., although it was almost 11 a.m. when the meeting began," wrote Hunte in his autobiography, *Memoirs of a Caribbean Lawyer*, which he signed for me when I stopped by his office in Road Town. "Meetings of the Council never began punctually; they normally began as much as 45 minutes late and I always felt sorry for the chaplain who had to sit around and wait to read the prayers without any consideration being given to the fact that he might have other business demanding his attention."

Normally a government bill was introduced by the chief minister, then seconded by another government minister. Before the second minister could get to his feet, however, something remarkable happened: a member rose from the opposition benches to pledge support, which was unprecedented. "I remember the chief minister being so astounded that his eyes looked like the double one in dominoes," Hunte wrote. The opposition not only agreed to support the bill but suggested that instead of the customary three parliamentary readings they would be happy to make do with just one. The bill was passed within an hour of its introduction, without so much as an altered comma. Hunte, who is very proud of the work he put in to draft the bill, chose to see this as a tribute to his accuracy and diligence. Michael Riegels, however, was rather more sardonic.

"It passed in a day. Unanimous," he told me then gave a wry smile. "No one had a clue what it meant, probably. Everyone just said, 'This is what you need to get you out of the financial doldrums, you've just got to trust us.'"

So what did the new law do? It created something called an international business company (IBC), which was a stripped-down version of a corporation. Much of the legislation is highly technical, but essentially an IBC was tax-free, completely opaque, only had to keep records "as the directors consider necessary" (so not at all), did not have to tell anyone what it was doing, and could be moved to another jurisdiction at any time, for any reason—for example, if the police were after it. IBCs were easy and cheap to create, and perfectly designed to hide behind. "They were tax free and business friendly, and they caught on because the world was dying for something like this," said Michael Riegels.

The first few years were slow, however, with takers—as before—primarily being American tax dodgers. It took two consecutive geopolitical favors for the BVI to really make its mark in the butlering industry. The first favor came from the increasingly tense relationship between the United States and Manuel Noriega, erratic kingmaker and de facto ruler of Panama since 1983. Panama had been Central America's clearing house for all kinds of dodgy business, but in 1988 Noriega was indicted in Miami on drug smuggling charges. As US intervention in Panama looked increasingly likely, investors started looking for somewhere more stable. "We are bringing our clients here, convincing them that the BVI is a good place," Panamanian lawyer Ramon Fonseca of the law firm Mossack Fonseca (of which more later) told local newspaper the *BVI*

Beacon in 1988. Would you like some help hiding that stolen money, Mr. Wooster? Allow me.

The other boost came from the far side of the world. In the mid-1980s Britain agreed to hand Hong Kong back to China, unleashing a wave of funk money as large as anything the world had yet seen. "All the Chinamen got a terrible fright and said we've got to move our assets out of here, where should we go? And somehow the BVI sprang into someone's head," said Riegels. The decision of Li Ka-Shing, Hong Kong's richest man, to transfer his shipping assets to a BVI-registered shell company boosted the islands' prestige, as did some canny marketing. One lawyer, alerted to the fact that the number 8 is considered lucky in Chinese folklore, arranged for a large number of new companies to be registered on August 8, 1988—8/8/88 and thus supposedly the luckiest day of the Chinese century. The registry should have been closed for the Emancipation Festival, the islands' most important public holiday, but good butlers don't take a day off, so it stayed open.

Precise statistics on the number of companies registered on the islands are hard to obtain, not least because companies could be dissolved, then reopened again, then dissolved once more with alarming ease. But by 1997 the BVI was registering more than 50,000 companies a year. They had eclipsed their old rivals in the Dutch Caribbean, and had almost half of the world's offshore company market.

From the islands' perspective this was like a miracle, a discovery of oil in even greater quantities than before. Shell companies made the place rich. Per head of population the British Virgin Islands are now richer than the average for Western Europe, and a third of the economy is directly made up of financial services, which is the biggest single sector, employing every ninth BVIslander. The companies do not contribute much tax (obviously, as part of the point of them is that they're tax-free) but the fees paid by the lawyers that create and maintain them provide almost two-thirds of the government's revenues.

The money has transformed the islands. A century ago, there were tracks barely passable for horses, but now the precipitous hillsides are criss-crossed with metalled roads, running up onto the spines of the hills, where elegant villas look out to sea. Forty years ago, most of the population worked in subsistence agriculture, but now almost all the islands' food is imported, and sold in convenience stores or in vast supermarkets on the edge of Road Town. The cars are boxy and American, and the road signs are printed in white capitals on a green background, in the US style. I searched for any trace of British influence, and eventually found a traditional cast-iron pillar box bearing the royal crest, leaning at a drunken angle in a patch of scrub. It was clear no one had used it to post a message for decades, unless you counted the local dogs.

The governor is still British of course, and via a friend I arranged a meeting with him. His full name is Augustus James Ulysses Jaspert, better known as Gus (though I didn't get on to those kind of terms). We arranged a meeting for mid-morning. I parked my car in a tiny patch of shade that I hoped would still be there when I got back, rang a bell to get past the green-painted fence, then walked across a pleasant little garden toward the modest two-story mansion that houses his offices. Ringing again to enter a lobby, I was instructed to wait.

I sat for a while and scrutinized a plaque bearing the names of all the governors of the BVI. A steady stream of smokers went past me on their way outside, each one asking as they did so whether I was being taken care of. I changed to a seat further from the door and examined a portrait of the Queen in which she strongly resembled my mother-in-law. Then I leafed through the literature provided in a wall-mounted magazine rack: a dog-eared flyer for an American insurance company, a three-year-old copy of a BVI finance pamphlet and a two-year-old glossy about Britain's best brands. It felt like the staff common room at a failing prep school in Herefordshire; it did not feel like the nerve center of the Caribbean outpost of a modern and outward-facing country.

Eventually I was invited upstairs and ushered into the governor's presence. Jaspert was pink-faced and sandy-haired, not quite forty years old, with an appropriate handshake. I would love to tell you what he said, but he made me promise that our conversation was off the record before we sat down. Don't feel too left out, however. Our meeting began ten minutes late, consisted entirely of platitudes, and ended within minutes when one of his underlings appeared in a prearranged-looking manner to tell him he had "a call." I was back outside so quickly that the last two smokers hadn't even finished their cigarettes by the time I walked past them. The patch of shade was still squarely over my car.

One of the few specific comments he made in the meeting was a suggestion that I should read the constitution, so I did, though I'm not sure what I was supposed to gain from it. The preamble notes that the United Kingdom is "the administering power for the time being," from which I concluded that Britain is no more enthusiastic about ruling the BVI than it used to be, or indeed than Gus Jaspert was about meeting me. The joy of being the unelected representative of an unelected head of state in a remote colony is you can treat journalists as the annoyance that they are, without any kind of downside.

But what have the BVI's shell companies meant for the rest of the world?

The islands say that their role is to facilitate investment. The way they explain this is that they ease transactions between countries that have capital and countries that need it in the same way that clean, well-maintained pipes help water and sewage flow freely between houses and processing plants. The islands' law firms provide a reliable, honest service backed ultimately by the British courts, which helps soothe investors' fears that their money might be at risk from capricious politicians in developing nations. According to a study commissioned by the BVI, investment channeled through the islands supports some 2.2 million jobs worldwide, many of them in the Far East: BVI companies invest four times as much in China as US companies do, apparently.

That means BVI companies are powerful entities able to project British jurisprudence into the heart of another country. A company can do most things that a person can—it can own property, open bank accounts, pay taxes, enter into contracts, etc. Admittedly, it can't vote or get married, so it doesn't have all the rights that an individual has, but from an economic perspective it is very useful for ensuring the security of an investment, thus reducing the risk of losing your money. That function is entirely neutral, however, and therefore its utility is completely dependent on the intentions of the company's owners, which is where the problems start.

We have already seen why American corporations liked the idea of moving money via BVI-registered firms in the first place—they didn't want the federal government limiting their freedom of movement or charging them taxes, and the same principles applied to Hong Kong businessmen in the 1990s with far more urgency, as the deadline for the colony to reunite with China approached. Hong Kong's capitalists had extremely "low tax morale," and did not want to contribute anything to the communist Chinese government, which explains the rush to shift their assets behind the protective screens of BVI shell companies before 1997. As for the kind of clients who came via Panama's dodgier law firms, they were after the same service but for even ignobler reasons: they wanted to make sure their corruption, money laundering, drug smuggling and general criminality was kept secret from law enforcement, above all the agencies of the United States. "In the beginning few questions were asked because we wanted to be successful," admitted Michael Riegels. "So undoubtedly rogues took advantage of what was on offer."

So, when you cut past the legal terminology, what is the BVI selling? It is selling discreet and affordable asset protection services, all guaranteed by the pleasant and reassuringly solid presence of the British flag. Those services have been used by North Korean arms smugglers, crooked Afghan officials, American tax dodgers, South American drug cartels, Kremlin insiders, corrupt football administrators and far too many criminals to name. Many of these companies were set up by Mossack Fonseca, the Panamanian law firm that arrived in the 1980s, and we know about them thanks to a vast leak of millions of the company's documents in 2016 and the resulting journalistic frenzy dubbed the Panama Papers. Mossack Fonseca has now quit the BVI—no one wants an offshore lawyer who can't keep secrets—though when I visited the islands the ghostly silhouette of the company name was still visible on the light blue façade of the office building where those companies were created.

The BVI is very keen to stress that Mossack Fonseca is not typical of the islands' businesses. It insists that because its companies make financial transactions more secure, the world is able to undertake more financial transactions, which makes everyone more prosperous. That may indeed be the case, but the islands are far less keen to admit that because its companies make financial crimes more opaque and thus harder to prosecute, more such crimes are committed. This is an uncomfortable fact that lawyers and officials on the islands struggle to talk their way around, although they still try.

"I do not think it is fair to blame the BVI for the ethically challenged people of the world. Such people will use whatever tool is at hand to serve their purpose, and if all else fails just lie. Many useful items such as knives, lasers or the internet can be used for immoral purposes if in the wrong hands," said Michael Riegels. "Undoubtedly many users of IBCs were motivated to hide illegal assets or evade taxes, but such people would generally be motivated to seek this outcome whether the BVI was there or not."

Translation: if I don't do it, somebody else will.

It would be nice to think that politicians in Britain saw what was happening and stepped in before it got out of hand, but they did not. On the contrary, the shell company boom appears to have meant they could now ignore the BVI with a clear conscience, since BVIslanders' standard of living was improving so rapidly. One Conservative MP, an accountant called David Shaw who represented the port city of Dover, understood the threat that the BVI's innovations posed to the rest of the world and in 1992 proposed regulations to stop them. He recognized, decades earlier than his peers, that secrecy encourages fraud, just like dark alleys encourage street crime, and proposed a bill that would stop British accountants and lawyers from working in tax havens. "The main problem caused by tax havens is that they allow transactions to take place in conditions of extreme secrecy," he said. "Too many tax havens have traditional relationships with the United Kingdom. That is no excuse for allowing their economies to develop around fraud."

Even couched in such terms he failed to attract much support, and his proposed legislation didn't even secure a second reading in the House of Commons. Britain, like a neglectful father who doesn't mind his children picking pockets so long as he gets left in peace, was apparently quite content with the BVI going their own way.

In 1997 Michael Riegels retired from his law firm, now called simply Harneys, which remains a dominant presence in Road Town. He went on to head the BVI bar association and then the Financial Services Commission, which regulates the islands' finance sector. He and Norma now live in comfortable retirement in a villa looking southwest, from which they can see the white sails of yachts beating up against the winds that blow steadily over the deep-blue Caribbean Sea. "I just see myself as being in the right place at the right time," he said, before laughing out loud. "I could still be sitting in Ham or somewhere in England, bitching about the weather and Brexit and everything else, but here I couldn't care less. We had no idea it was coming down the pike, as they say in America, and we were just lucky to be here at the time."

We had eaten a lunch of curry cooked by Norma east-African-style with fresh chutneys, and it was clear that they remembered their time in Tanzania fondly—their villa has a Swahili name, *Nyumba Yetu*, which means "Our House," and is decorated with a tasteful selection of African sculptures. Just before the COVID pandemic froze international travel they took the whole family to see where they'd started out and had a very pleasant holiday, although they couldn't help noticing how ramshackle the supposedly five-star facilities still were.

Tourism has been central to Tanzania's attempt to develop a more dynamic economy and to overcome the sclerotic if honest system that Nyerere—who stood down as president in the mid-1980s—bequeathed the country, and that has required substantial investment in the infrastructure that tourists need. In the early 1990s the government asked international companies to submit bids for a radar system to allow more planes—and, thus, more tourists—to use the airport at Dar es Salaam. Not everyone was convinced that this was the best use of the country's scarce resources, but eventually, in 1999, the government entered into a contract with British defense giant BAE Systems and its local agent Shailesh Vithlani for a dual-use radar installation for both military and civilian aircraft, which would cost $40 million.

It took the British government a year to approve the deal, and when it did so the project sailed into a storm of condemnation. This was a huge amount of money for a country that was so terribly poor: life expectancy at birth was just forty-five years, two million people were living with HIV/AIDS, and it already had a national debt of $5.4 billion. Besides, it wasn't just that Tanzania might not need a radar system at all, but that the one it also had chosen was extremely expensive. Forty million dollars was a third of Tanzania's annual expenditure on basic education, and the World Bank said a perfectly adequate system could be bought at a quarter of the price. Britain's own development secretary, Clare Short, opposed the deal, as did leading aid agencies and charities. Tanzanian officials, however, insisted that this was what they needed, and eventually the British government—with an eye on the 250 jobs the deal created—waved it through.

It was only years later that the real nature of the transaction emerged, and we gained an insight into the damage that

Michael Riegels's innovation did to the country of his birth. In 1998, while negotiations for the radar contract were still going on, BAE quietly established a shell company in the British Virgin Islands called Red Diamond Trading Limited, which it never admitted to owning on the documents it had to issue as a publicly traded entity, but which was central to the way the Tanzanian deal worked.

Every time the Tanzanian government paid one of BAE Systems's bills, the defense giant would pass on to Vithlani's Tanzanian company the commission he had earned as its local agent. The amount varied depending on the size of the original bill, but it might be $5,500, $2,750 or $25,000. Simultaneously, and beyond the view of the Tanzanian authorities, BAE Systems would pay Vithlani's BVI company a far larger amount. Again the figure varied—it might be $344,500, $272,250 or $1,780,000—but it was almost always significantly more, and sometimes as much as 100 times more, than what was being paid into the Tanzanian firm's bank account. Vithlani was, according to BAE Systems' internal records, being paid for "technical services," although he knew nothing at all about the technical side of the radar project, as later court documents made clear.

We know all this thanks to a sprawling and interlocking series of criminal investigations into BAE Systems's conduct. The company fought hard against accusations of corruption, but pleaded guilty to other charges, which resulted in it paying a $400 million fine to the US Department of Justice. "BAES established one entity in the British Virgin Islands to conceal BAES's marketing adviser relationships, including who the agent was and how much it was paid; to create obstacles for investigating authorities to penetrate the arrangements; to circumvent laws in countries that did not allow agency relationships; and to assist advisers in avoiding tax," the US charge stated. Just one BVI company could do all that. A BVI company really is a powerful thing.

On the other side of the Atlantic, the investigation was not so wide-ranging. The UK government stepped in to stop the Serious Fraud Office from investigating BAE Systems's relations with Saudi Arabia on national security grounds and, given that the SFO didn't want to prosecute the same crimes covered by its counterpart in Washington, that left it with just the relatively small Tanzanian deal to investigate. Again, BAE Systems refused to accept it had acted corruptly, but in 2010 it pleaded guilty to the technical offense of "breaching its duty to keep accounting records." That meant it had obscured the total of $12 million it had paid Vithlani via its BVI company—which paid the money to another offshore company called Envers. Once again, the BVI company did its job, creating enough confusion about the money's final destination to ensure prosecutors were stymied in their attempts to prove corruption. "It is not now possible to establish precisely what Vithlani did with the money that was paid to him," the SFO lawyer's opening note said. "To lobby is one thing, to corrupt another."

The judge, the highly experienced David Bean, was not happy at all, and his sentencing remarks are packed with so much frustration that he appears to have been close to fury. He criticized the SFO for its decision to prosecute such a small offense and for accepting BAE Systems's word on the purpose of the payments routed via the BVI. "It seems naive in the extreme to think that Vithlani was simply a well paid lobbyist," he noted. "There is no evidence that BAE was party to an agreement to corrupt. They did not wish to be, and did not need to be. The fact that money was paid by them to Red Diamond, by Red Diamond to Envers and by Envers to Mr. Vithlani placed them at two or three removes from any shady activity." He reserved particular ire for BAE Systems's description of the payments to Vithlani as "technical services." "They were making payments to Mr. Vithlani, 97 percent of them via two offshore companies, with the intention that he should have free rein to make such payments to such people as he thought fit to secure the radar contract," the judge wrote. It was the protective shield that the BVI company put around the money that prevented him from going further.

Vithlani himself denied any wrongdoing, as did all the Tanzanian officials involved, although an investigation by a House of Commons committee said MPs had been told at an "informal meeting" with Tanzanian officials that corrupt payments had been made. In Tanzania officials promised that they would prosecute, but nothing ever came of it. The shield that the BVI threw over these payments stymied investigators here too. The crime BAE Systems was charged with—a technical accounting offense—is not one that has a victim, but BAE Systems agreed to make a £29.5 million payment to Tanzania, which it used to buy equipment for schools, and the whole episode was quietly forgotten. When I asked Michael Riegels what he thought about the scandal, he said he had never heard of it.

In 2019 Benjamin Mkapa, who was president of Tanzania when the radar contract was signed, published his memoirs. These contained a verbal shrug as to whether top officials had taken bribes to approve an overpriced radar system the country didn't need. "Though I cannot swear that the 'big man' in the ministry of communications, ministry of defense or the attorney general did not get something, I don't know; frankly, I just don't want to know," he wrote. In fairness to him, he never could have known, again thanks to the British Virgin Islands. And this is a pattern that has played out across Africa. Whatever happened in this case, we know that officials from Nigeria,

Angola, Guinea, South Africa, Kenya, Rwanda, Equatorial Guinea, the Democratic Republic of Congo and many other countries have used companies registered in the BVI as their primary tool to disguise the theft of vast wealth from populations that desperately need it and to prevent them ever being brought to justice. This butler does not concern himself with the moral character of his clients, only with serving their needs.

When Nyerere was president, one of his biggest fears was that Tanzanians had succeeded in ridding themselves of exploitation by the British only to fall victim to a new class of local exploiters. This was one of the reasons he insisted on exerting so much control over the political and legal systems: he was honest, but he couldn't rely on anyone else to be. In 1970 the *New York Times* quoted a "London-trained lawyer" (it wasn't Riegels, though he told me he fully agreed with the sentiment expressed by the lawyer) who had just been to see President Nyerere to complain about the arrest of thirty men accused of bribing officials. "President Nyerere replied that case after case of corruption had failed in the courts because prosecutors were so inept," the article quoted the lawyer as saying. "He felt corruption was a terrible threat in all of Africa, and he had to stop it in Tanzania."

There is a terrible irony in the fact that it was a son of Tanzania that created the tool that undermined Nyerere's attempts to keep public servants honest and outwitted his successors. But, looked at from a British perspective, wasn't this all for the good? The fees earned by butlering accrue to British people operating out of British territories; why should Britain worry about them? This is certainly a question we could ask about the UK government's decision to squash the SFO's attempt to investigate BAE Systems's ties to Saudi Arabia, which also involved substantial payments via companies in the British Virgin Islands. And this argument has been made by defenders of the BVI in evidence to a UK parliamentary committee investigating the islands. "The maximum amount of tax evasion that the BVI could facilitate globally is £750 million, a small fraction of which would be in the UK," said a report from the International Centers Forum, a lobbyist for the BVI and the other British overseas territories (OTs) that make a living in the same way. "Any tax leakage due to the OTs must also be considered in the context of the contribution they make to the UK economy." Translation: yes, we're butlers; yes, we help our clients get away with some pretty bad stuff, but you and I do pretty well out of it, so let's not worry.

In the next chapter I hope to show that it does affect British people, very seriously, and that they should worry about it.

5

ROCK SOLID

Gibraltar became British in the early eighteenth century, around the same time as the BVI. In all other ways, however, the two colonies could barely be more different. Where the British Virgin Islands were an abandoned backwater for centuries, the subject of international indifference, Gibraltar was fought over repeatedly by world powers. It is proverbially steadfast, a symbol of the stubborn might of the British nation. The iconic silhouette of the Rock, a towering limestone lion at the mouth of the Mediterranean, has graced the cover of innumerable war memoirs and boys' weeklies. Any threat to its status conjures up a storm of outrage in the London tabloids. No other colony anywhere has ever been so close to the hearts of its owners.

This is, in truth, slightly odd; Gibraltar is a tiny little peninsula not much bigger than Wimbledon Common, a skin tag hanging off Iberia's bottom. I ran all the way around it in an hour, and that included dips out of and into Spain at beginning and end. Where colonies like India enriched Britain immeasurably, for most of its history Gibraltar never amounted to all that much, even militarily, and what significance it did have was brief. It came into its own with the opening of the Suez Canal in 1869, since that transformed the Mediterranean Sea from a lake into a highway. Possession of the Rock ensured that Britain controlled both the Mediterranean's entrance and its exit.

For the coal-powered Royal Navy before the First World War, Gibraltar was a useful refuelling station, ensuring ships could patrol far from their home bases. For the oil-powered navy of the Second World War, it helped keep the route to the oilfields of the Middle East open and serviced convoys supplying British and American forces in North Africa, Italy, the Balkans and southern France. It was also—for much of the war—the sole part of mainland Europe west of the Soviet Union in Allied hands, which gave it both symbolic and practical significance, not least because it allowed my great-grandmother's cousin Billie to make it home after escaping from a Nazi prisoner of war camp. The war left as a legacy miles upon miles of tunnels within the Rock, which served as hospital, munition store and accommodation for many of the tens of thousands of men who made Gibraltar their home. They are now a popular tourist attraction, alongside the tunnels left by the Rock's defenders in earlier sieges and some attractive natural caverns.

The Rock's original Spanish inhabitants were driven out when London took control in 1704, and were replaced by immigrants from Malta, Morocco, Genoa, India, Britain and elsewhere, who worked in the shipyards, supplied the garrison and engaged in some light smuggling with the Spaniards across the bay. These Gibraltarians in turn lost their homes during the Second World War, being forcibly evacuated to make room for Allied soldiers, sailors and airmen. This experience of evacuation—the sense of unity, the discrimination they suffered in exile, their struggle to return home after the war was over—welded them together and created for the first time an organized and coherent Gibraltarian nation. On their return, they demanded self-government and received it in 1950.

But democratic advance did not mean life was easy. Those were the years of decolonization, when London surrendered control of India, the Suez Canal and many more strategic assets. And the Spaniards not unreasonably asked why the Brits clung on to this little colony when they were giving up so many others. Technically, the Treaty of Utrecht, which was signed in 1713 to end the War of the Spanish Succession, gave Gibraltar to Britain in perpetuity, but times were changing, and the Spanish government demanded that the peninsula be returned.

It is perfectly possible that, given the opportunity, Britain would have hauled down the Union Jack as readily in Gibraltar as it did in Tanganyika. In the age of the ballistic missile and the nuclear-powered submarine, small and exposed military bases like this one looked vulnerable, anachronistic and expensive. But surrendering control of the place was politically impossible: the Gibraltarians and their numerous friends in the United Kingdom were fiercely opposed to rule from Madrid (Spain did have a fascist government at the time after all). After a referendum confirmed that all but forty-four Gibraltarians wanted their country to remain British, London considered the question closed, which infuriated Madrid. In 1969 Caudillo Francisco Franco severed all land, sea and air ties with Spain, and for the next sixteen years Gibraltar was essentially under siege. Its economy was dependent on London, in particular on the dockyards of the Royal Navy.

Gibraltar has always been surprisingly British, but this is when it turned its back on Spain decisively. The local dialect—Llanito, a mixture of Andalusian Spanish, Genoese Italian, English, Hebrew and various other bits and bobs—began to be replaced by the English that its young people learned at university in the UK. Without the steady stream of Spaniards crossing the frontier to work, the shops and restaurants became more dependent than ever on military custom, and thus ever more

British. If you stroll now between the café tables laid out on Casemates Square or down Main Street, you'd be forgiven for thinking you were in a provincial English town, although you might wonder why the weather was so nice.

Gibraltar did try to get into the tax haven business by copying legislative innovations from the Caribbean, but never made much of a success of it. US clients couldn't be bothered to cross the Atlantic, and Europeans already had good and discreet French-, German- or Italian-speaking bankers in Switzerland, Luxembourg, and various assorted micro-states. Occasionally, a lawyer in the Channel Islands would send down some business that was too crooked for them to countenance, but it never amounted to much.

"The economy was two thirds Ministry of Defense in terms of GDP. In terms of employment, right through the 70s and into the early 80s that accounted for 40 percent of the labor force," said Ernest Montado, who in the early 1970s created the colony's statistics service and who still speaks with a trace of the hard-to-place Llanito accent—which makes the speaker sound a little like a well-traveled Welshman. As soon as the frontier was closed, the government in London sent out a mission to study the economic situation, but failed to come up with many useful suggestions. "They said, 'There's not much you can do on this piece of rock, you know.' They were talking about things like shellfish farming. I said, 'Fine, but that's not going to feed many people,'" Montado remembered.

And then came 1981. It started as a good year, with Gibraltarians winning full British citizenship and Prince Charles and Princess Diana coming to the Rock on honeymoon. But in June the government in London announced it was radically changing the way the navy was maintained. Britain needed fewer ships now it no longer had an empire to defend, and the ones it did have were more sophisticated. That meant that it needed fewer and more specialized shipyards, and Gibraltar was not going to be one of them. This was a disaster for the yards' 1,400 employees, and catastrophic for the colony as a whole. The border was still closed, and now it was losing its sole significant employer. "We were going to lose 25 percent of GDP, just like that," said Montado.

General Franco had died by now in Spain, and the newly democratic government in Madrid was easing the restrictions on the border, which at least raised the prospect that Gibraltarians could start trading with their neighbors. But economic diversification was hard when the Ministry of Defense owned almost everything, including most of the colony's real estate. There was accommodation for servicemen, and separate officers' messes and swimming clubs for the navy, army and air force; there were special areas for their bands to practice and wharves kept in reserve just in case a big submarine came in.

The 20,000 Gibraltarians were squashed into a third of the colony's already tiny extent. "We have an area called the Alameda Estate—you can just about see it from here," said Montado, taking me to a window and pointing south across the town. "That's six or seven blocks, the best public housing Gibraltar ever had, housing 4,500 people. It's comfortable and good. A bit further up the Rock there's an area called the Mount, and in surface area it's the same as the Alameda Estate, and that housed just the admiral and his wife. I said, 'Look, you can't expect us to take this knock, diversify our economy, if we can't even build a bloody office block—we don't have the space for it.'"

The colony's government, led from 1988 by a combative union rep called Joe Bossano who had learned his negotiating tactics in east London industrial disputes, fought hard to gain good redundancy terms from the British government for local workers and worked to turn Gibraltar into a more commercially orientated place. Land was reclaimed from the sea, extending the area of the town, and more houses and offices built. People studying in Britain at the time remember how every time they came home, it was as if the colony had gotten bigger.

Bossano wasn't in Gibraltar when I visited, but having heard I wanted to talk to him, he called me one Sunday evening and we chatted for a couple of hours. He led the opposition party before becoming first minister, and the prospect of a committed socialist taking charge of such a strategically significant outpost had alarmed American officials. They had invited him to visit the United States, all expenses paid, the year before the election, in an attempt to persuade him of the virtues of capitalism. "I was very impressed by their candor, their transparency and their honesty, in telling me what they were up to. They wanted me to come over and brainwash me, so I went over," Bossano said. It was from both sides' point of view an extremely successful trip. The rabble rouser met a series of American capitalists and came away transformed.

"I became very left wing from being in West Ham, and then I learned the peculiar aspects of capitalism from having face-to-face meetings with top guys in the United States," he said. "It was incredible. It was almost an electrical thing, as if there were sparks coming out—you could see the energy of the guys. It was almost visual."

On his return, and after his elevation to the top job, he brought in a US company to create better phone links with the rest of the world and unleashed the power of private capital, mainly by doing nothing to stop it. "We didn't bend the rules; we just made them more flexible, so we could adapt them to the needs of the customer," Bossano said.

Notoriously, he did not stop people who had received generous redundancy payouts from investing the money in speedboats with which they could revive Gibraltar's ancestral trade of smuggling. If a Gibraltarian filled up his boat with cigarettes and zipped over to Spain he could clear £5,000 in a few minutes, more than his parents would have made in a month at the old dockyard. And, soon enough, hundreds of people were doing just that. By the early 1990s Gibraltar was importing enough cigarettes for every inhabitant of the Rock to be smoking seven packets a day, most of which went straight to Spain. That earned some £16 million in annual revenue for Bossano's government, around a fifth of its total earnings, as well as vast profits for the criminal gangs that controlled the trade. The smuggling in return cost the Spanish government hundreds of millions of pesetas in lost duties. For years Bossano resisted demands that he shut it down, only doing so when the government in London threatened to impose direct control on the colony.

"The reality is we live on a lump of limestone at the entrance to the Mediterranean with no food and no water. We have to earn a living in ways that are perhaps not the best things to be doing in life," said Bossano. (This sounded fine when he said it, but looks awful written down; he really is one of the most remarkably charming people I've ever spoken to.) "I am not saying that, if I had lots of different things to choose from, that I would develop an economy that depended on military activities, or an economy that depends on selling cheap cigarettes and cheap alcohol. Regrettably, the reality of it is that, if we weren't doing any of those things, in a world that depended on a normal relationship between human life and nature Gibraltar would survive with only half a dozen people."

Fortunately, with the border open, some of the Brits who

holidayed or lived in southern Spain were crossing over to visit the old colony and to enjoy the familiar pleasures of a pint of bitter or a newspaper-wrapped parcel of fish and chips. That brought a bit more money into the economy, which helped the banks, and it helped the tax havenry, because Brits would use Gibraltarian companies to invest in Spanish real estate, and kept their money in Gibraltarian banks. More importantly, however, it also brought in customers for a local businessman who would turn out to be the one to find Gibraltar's specific niche in the butlering business—a man called Freddie Ballester. His impact on the world has been vast, and is growing vaster all the time, but is almost entirely unrecognized. Before I visited Gibraltar I had never heard of him, but he is the colony's equivalent of Michael Riegels.

Ballester is short and stocky, with white hair and a broad smile. We met in a coffee shop on the ground floor of one of the many office blocks built on the land that Bossano's government reclaimed from the sea, and our conversation was regularly interrupted by greetings; he appeared to know everyone who walked by. Born after the Second World War, he was working in a hotel when he got talking to a British bookmaker who had come to Gibraltar to look into buying a local chain of three betting shops called Rock Turf Accountants. The visitor seems to have been impressed by the young Ballester's energy and suggested that he work for him. Ballester was due to go to London on honeymoon, so he visited the bookie's offices while he was there and liked what he saw.

"They sent a general manager out, and he trained me then left eleven months down the road. I kept on running the business, which I did from 1974," Ballester said. With the frontier closed, his clients were mainly British squaddies posted to the

Rock. They came in to bet on British events, particularly foot-ball, as well as horse and dog racing. "It was what it was. There was nothing better, you know."

Running a bookmaker's at the time wasn't a very demand-ing job, once you understood the mathematics of it, and his career could have continued in this manner indefinitely, had the border not opened in the 1980s and his clients begun to change. British expats who lived on the Costa del Sol, which is just along the Mediterranean coast from Gibraltar, would reg-ularly drive down to the colony to experience a taste of home. While their wives went shopping, the men would come into the betting shop and have a flutter. "I got chatting to them and they said, 'We can't come to Gibraltar every day, but if we deposited money with you, we could have a bet.' They would leave, say, fifty quid and would phone up. Up to that amount, win or lose, they would settle up."

This was all very well, but it could have been better. Stand-ing in the way of expanding his business was the law. At the time there was a tax on all bets made in British betting shops that came to around 7.5 percent, but bets placed at racecourses were treated differently and only had to pay 4 percent. So Brits in Spain were phoning up racecourses in the UK and placing bets with bookies there. This undercut the service Ballester was able to offer because his customers had to pay the higher rate of tax.

Gibraltar is a small place where not only does everyone know everyone, but everyone also tends to bump into everyone just walking down the street. That made it easy for Ballester to speak to the government official in charge of taxes, a Brit called Brian Traynor. "I explained about the on-track tax, the betting shop tax, and I said, 'We don't stand much of a chance, but I've noticed that since the frontier has opened fully, we're getting more trade,'" he explained. "I made him a proposition: 'Why don't you allow us to bet at 1 percent tax, and then we'd get business.'"

And in April 1987 Traynor rose to his feet in the colony's parliament to present the Financial Ordinance, an annual piece of legislation that laid out how Gibraltar's revenue would be raised for the coming year. He ran through the state of the economy (a bit better than forecast), the trade deficit (worrying), tourism (encouraging) and the level of bank deposits (hopeful, though nowhere near those of Jersey or Guernsey), before getting on to tax and duty changes. It's funny reading it now, being aware of how significant Ballester's proposal was to become, to see how many things Traynor clearly considered to be more important than betting duty at the time. First, Traynor talked about cars, which would be taxed slightly differently to how they had been, and then he made alterations to the tax-free income allowance and proposed a review of inheritance tax. Then finally, after announcing a change to the fee that passengers on ships paid on arrival in Gibraltar (it rose from thirty to fifty pence), came the reform Ballester had suggested.

"As a measure to encourage non-residents, mainly British expatriates, to place bets through Gibraltar rather than London, a concessionary rate of gaming tax will be introduced," he said. "This will be applicable to telephone bets on credit only, and there will be no public access to the premises either by Gibraltar residents or anyone else."

Ballester had gotten what he wanted. Expats placing bets with him by telephone would get a much lower rate of tax—just 1 percent—than they could get by calling an on-course bookie in Britain, and that made all the difference. He applied for an offshore license, received it in 1989, opened a second floor at the betting shop on Casemates Square, put in more phone lines and waited for the calls to come in. "I employed additional staff to work in the betting shops, and two of the more experienced girls I brought up to the phones to work with me. We started getting accounts from Spain, Portugal, the UK, honest to God, even Australia," he recalled, laughing. "It worked. On the offshore, we were taking in more money than in the betting shops. When some of the big boys, big punters, found out in the UK, they were phoning us up at the 1 percent, because over there they still had to pay 4 percent at the track."

Not only was Gibraltar British, but Ballester was too. The company he worked for was British, its owners—Mr. and Mrs. Coomes—were British, the odds that he quoted in his shop were set in Britain and quoted on events that took place in Britain. He had to check any particularly large bets with his boss in London before agreeing to them, and the clients making the bets were overwhelmingly British too. Yet, by the magic of Gibraltarian autonomy, he could outcompete UK rivals by offering a lower rate of tax.

For a few short years he made them a fortune, but Mr. and Mrs. Coomes do not appear to have appreciated it. In 1994, on the instructions of his employers, Ballester closed down Rock Turf Accountants' offshore betting service and went back to his traditional focus on face-to-face customers. But, thanks to his suggestion, the law had been changed, a seed had been planted, and it would grow into something genuinely huge. "I feel like it's my own contribution to the success story of Gibraltar, in my own small way, without wanting any medals or MBE or OBE," Ballester said.

Gibraltar enabled the gambling industry to escape the restrictions the state had put on it, rather as Jeeves helped one of Bertie Wooster's friends take bets at the racecourse when he'd fallen on hard times. Jeeves's plan didn't work out very well for

P. G. Wodehouse's fictional ninth Earl of Rowcester, who had to flee for his life, pursued by an outraged customer, but in real life things went swimmingly—for Gibraltar, whose clients did spectacularly well out of the scheme.

To understand how Ballester's idea changed first Britain and then an increasingly large part of the world, we need to understand how gambling worked in Britain at the time. Betting shops were legal, and had been since 1961, following a peculiar and hypocritical period when cash betting was illegal but betting over the phone and at racecourses were both considered fine. Since this was a transparent and unfair attempt to stop working-class people from gambling while exempting anyone who could afford a telephone or to travel, it had been widely ignored. Illegal betting shops were common, and the police largely tolerated them. The 1961 legislation was just an acceptance of reality: betting was too deeply embedded in working-class communities to be eradicated, and the government might as well earn some tax revenue out of it and try to keep the cash out of the hands of organized crime.

The government tolerated betting shops but did not encourage them. Bookies were not allowed to advertise, were not allowed to sell drinks or provide seats, could not show sporting events on television and could only open in a neighborhood if they were able to prove there was already a demand for their services. They were strange soul-less places, dominated by large blackboards displaying the latest odds. A radio feed announced the results of races, and their windows were painted over to stop anyone seeing in from outside.

But betting retained its central place in working-class culture. Unlike in the United States, where gambling on sports was illegal almost everywhere but casinos-dominated places like

Las Vegas or Atlantic City, British gamblers disliked games of chance. They wanted to stake their money on a horse or a dog, where there was at least a theoretical chance that they knew more than the bookie and could execute a coup. The house might usually come out on top, but this was still a contest of wits in which the bookmaker was taking a real risk, unlike in roulette, which by design—the o being neither red nor black, thus giving the casino every thirty-seventh spin—is rigged to favor the house.

If anything was resented, it was the heavy taxes. On top of standard business taxes, every gambler had to contribute a fixed percentage of every bet to the government, plus an additional levy to support the horse-racing industry. By the 1990s the combined duty and levy was subtracting 9 percent of every bet before it was even made.

A second issue was that by the 1990s the industry was dominated by a handful of very large companies. Because the industry as a whole could not expand thanks to the heavy taxes and the restrictions on opening new shops, the only ways for companies to expand their profits were to take over smaller rivals and cut costs. An oligopoly had developed, with a handful of household names—William Hill, Ladbrokes, Coral—overwhelmingly dominant. In the years of illegal gambling a bookmaker was a sole trader or a small businessman, part of the same community as his gamblers. Legalization, however, had separated the gamblers from the industry, which saw its customers solely as a source of profit. A neighborhood bookmaker might once have been careful to ensure his customers gambled only what they could spare, rather than their whole weekly pay, but a multinational corporation wasn't bothered.

It was a comfortable existence for the bookmakers—they made steady profits from their customers, they obeyed the regulations, and everything was predictable—but there was change in the air. The government created the National Lottery in 1994, which could advertise. Its popularity vastly increased the amount of money spent on games of chance, and as communications improved and the world opened up, there was also the possibility of seeing if Freddie Ballester's idea of relocating to Gibraltar might not boost profits a little. Ladbrokes was the first big bookmaker to dip a toe into offshore waters to take advantage of the lower taxes in the colony, although it only solicited bets from non-British clients, so it made no difference to the UK situation. But then came Victor Chandler, who was a very different proposition indeed.

Chandler is a caricature of a successful bookmaker: relaxed and tanned, he speaks with a slightly cockneyfied drawl, has a sideways smile and a glint in his eye. He's a master of the killer anecdote, delivered deadpan. He was gambling aristocracy, going back to his grandfather, who left a dog track to his uncle and a bookmaker's to his father. When his father died young, Chandler built the family business into a boutique operation favored by wealthy high-spenders who liked to bet whatever they liked on whatever they liked at any time.

"I've always thought that the best sort of client is someone who stays with me for a lifetime. That means someone who can treat gambling as any other entertainment, whether it's mistresses, wives," he said, with a flicker of a smile in an interview on his YouTube channel. "As the economy changed in the 80s, the City boomed, and businesses boomed generally, and there was a huge influx of foreigners into the UK. My business changed, and we saw high rollers for the first time of any real size . . . I had one Arab that was having fifty or a hundred thousand on at the races."

Unlike the big corporations, and despite his lineage in the

industry, he was still an outsider, seeking to build up a position in a very established market. That meant he either had to slog away against big companies with deep pockets and more outlets than him or else come up with something new they hadn't thought of. The moment of inspiration came around the start of the 1994 World Cup, which was held in the United States but watched all over the world. He tells the story, sitting back in an armchair, one knee up, wearing an expensive-looking suit and holding a large cigar.

He had a phone call from someone who wanted to deposit a large amount of cash with him on behalf of a group of Far Eastern gamblers. They wanted to place their bets at a racecourse so he could give them the lower tax rate, even though they would be betting on football rather than horse races. "He left £800,000 in cash, and took 200 with him to Newbury," Chandler says. "About an hour after he left, forty minutes, the police raided our office with guns, took everyone outside, questioned everyone and confiscated the money. Apparently the bank he'd drawn the money out of thought he was going into a drug deal or something like that. He was stopped on the motorway by a roadblock. All of this was related to me on the phone, so I headed back to the office to have a look at the 800,000 in cash, which was a very rare sight, especially in those days."

It makes a great anecdote, but it was bad for business, not least because he missed out on a day taking bets while sorting out the mess. Wouldn't it be better for all concerned if low-tax betting could be arranged without having to go to a racecourse at all, and without needing to transfer the quantity of physical cash that makes the Met come after you with guns? He looked into jurisdictions where he could legally take tax-free bets offshore and then heard about Freddie Ballester's innovation. "I was lucky enough to be informed that there was a license for sale in Gibraltar, the casino license. The chap had sold the casino at the time, but he'd retained the license for bookmaking," Chandler explained. "I came over and did a deal in a day with him, and bought the license—0001—which had to be printed out on the minister of finance's daughter's computer. Gibraltar's government office at the time didn't have computers."

He had an office up and running—six landline telephones and a dozen mobiles, plus employees who spoke the languages required to answer them—in time for the 1996 European football championships, and took bets from clients in Hong Kong and Singapore. He was still running his British business through his UK company, however. All British bookmakers had voluntarily agreed not to take bets offshore, which may in fact be why Ballester had to close down his offshore operation. They were prepared to deprive foreign governments of tax revenue by basing themselves in Gibraltar, but not to undermine the British Treasury.

It wasn't until 1999 that the decisive change happened. Chandler was apparently in the bath while his wife Carole read him snippets from the *Daily Mail*. One article said the Irish government had cut its betting duty from 10 to 5 percent, which was now lower than the rate in the UK. This intrigued her. If Irish bookmakers could take British bets, which they could, why couldn't he do the same from Gibraltar? That was the light-bulb moment and the end of the gentlemen's agreement. "I went to see a QC a few days later, and it all went from there," Chandler says. "We decided to move the whole UK business to Gibraltar."

The significance of what he had done was immediately apparent. The *Racing Post*, the horse racing industry's most influential publication, splashed with the headline REVOLUTION, and other journalists flocked to write about his coup. In one interview he predicted he'd gain 10,000 clients by the end of the year, and these would be the most profitable ones, those who placed the biggest bets. In another paper he anticipated clearing a billion pounds within six months. His competitors felt they had no choice but to follow. Within months, Coral, Ladbrokes and William Hill had all moved their telephone and nascent internet operations offshore too.

This all came as quite a shock to the Gibraltarian government, which had not intended to dive so wholeheartedly into the butlering business. But local politicians were delighted. They had tried to keep the shipyards going using a succession of private operators, but they had failed one after another. Doing for British bookmakers what Jeeves did for the ninth Earl of Rowcester and helping them run their operations more profitably helped keep the lights on. Within months Chandler was employing more Gibraltarians than what was left of the shipyards. A rival bookmaker had to buy an old hotel just to find somewhere to put its employees. Gibraltar had finally found its niche.

"What serious punter—the average bet in Gibraltar earlier this year was £2,500 from Far East clients—can fail to be attracted by a 3 percent deduction, or service charge, as opposed to the usual deduction of 9 percent in the United Kingdom?" asked the Earl of Huntingdon, formerly the trainer of the Queen's own racehorses, in a debate in the House of Lords that July.

At the time the UK government was earning some £500 million a year from taxes on the gambling industry and could ill afford to lose the income, so it promised urgent action. Initially, they tried to kill off the fledging offshore industry with a ban on advertising, but unsurprisingly that didn't have much of an effect. If you're the kind of client who can drop a few thousand pounds on a bet, you're also the kind of person who doesn't need an advert to know who to bet with. As ministers watched the revenue drain out of the government's accounts and into those of Victor Chandler and his peers, they seized on an idea long favored by John Brown, chairman of Britain's biggest bookmaking company William Hill, but one which officials had previously refused to engage with. This was to radically reform the way gambling was treated by the government, to stop bracketing it with harmful practices like smoking and drinking and treat it like any other leisure activity.

In the past pressure to do this had seemed like the kind of special pleading that any industry makes when trying to lower its tax burden, but with Butler Gibraltar having found a way to give the bookmakers leverage with the UK government, the demand for reform had more force. If the government didn't do what the bookmakers wanted, they'd leave the UK, and the Treasury would be left with nothing. The government capitulated, and that's how gambling was transformed, first in Britain and then everywhere. As with the Eurodollar market, which changed all dollars into offshore dollars, the industry's aim was to make betting everywhere offshore betting and, as with the dollar market, for Britain to dominate. In fact, commentators at the time made a direct comparison between the two.

"Zero tax, claim the bookies, would double betting turnover. With no need to set up offshore, jobs would relocate to Britain, perhaps allowing London to capture the world's betting market, just as it has for foreign exchange. The Chancellor would gain more in income and corporation tax than he lost in betting tax," said an article in the *Daily Telegraph*, a paper which was notably sympathetic to the bookmakers' arguments.

The actual change sounds minor—the government stopped taxing every bet that was made as an individual transaction and instead taxed bookmakers' profits as an aggregate total—but the effects were profound. Instead of taxing turnover, the government taxed profit. Previously, a bet was taxed as if it was equivalent to an alcoholic drink or a packet of cigarettes. These goods are considered harmful, so special duties are levied on them at the point of sale to limit consumption. If the taxes were levied on the profits of brewers, or tobacco companies, the cost of their products would fall, and they could sell far more booze and cigarettes.

The reform essentially meant that the British government—concerned by the potential loss of revenue and perhaps seeking to make its concern look more principled—stopped looking at gambling as a public health issue and instead treated it like a leisure activity. If you've ever wondered why it suddenly became so much easier to gamble in the UK in the early 2000s and marveled at the incredible profusion of adverts for gambling companies on British television, you have Gibraltar to thank.

To be fair to the bookmakers and to Gibraltar, they were pushing at an open door. The "third way" politics of the Tony Blair and Bill Clinton years loved to reject what it saw as the pious moralizing of old-style politics and demonstratively treat citizens as responsible consumers. If multinational betting companies just happened to massively increase their profits in the process—or banks just happened to massively expand risky lending as a result of the parallel move toward the "light touch regulation" of the financial sector—then that was all for the good.

A member of Parliament quoted John Brown, the bookie who came up with the idea, in a debate in the House of Commons without any suggestion that he and his company might have an interest in arguing for a lower tax rate. "This is great news for the British punter, for UK plc and the Treasury," Brown was quoted as saying. "The punter wins because we will make it possible to offer deduction-free betting for the first time since betting shops were introduced. The Treasury wins because we will be able to repatriate our offshore operations, enabling the taxman to share in all the profits we make on our international business. UK plc wins because we have a real opportunity to be the world leaders in online betting." Neither the MP nor indeed John Brown felt the need to mention that it was also great news for the gambling industry.

Further reforms followed, which allowed bookies to advertise and to open shops wherever they wanted without having to prove that demand already existed. Regulation was transferred from the Home Office to the Department for Culture, Media and Sport—from the police to the so-called ministry of fun. "In the future, well-informed adults will have greater freedom and choice to spend their leisure money on gambling if they want to. The law will, for the first time, treat them like grown-ups," said government minister Tessa Jowell in 2003. "Outdated restrictions . . . will be removed and the industry will be able to develop innovative new products."

The big bookmakers moved their operations back to Britain, well satisfied with the new settlement, but it was a strange kind of revolution. There had been no public clamor for gambling to be reformed; quite the reverse. Opinion polls showed ordinary Britons were very happy with the situation as it was. The pressure came from officials worried about losing revenue and gambling companies wanting more freedom and less tax. Without the intervention of Gibraltar, which allowed bookmakers the option of not paying tax, no one would have given the companies' argument five minutes of their time. Thanks to Gibraltar's intervention and the leverage it gave the big companies, the issue became urgent. It was skilled butlering to win concessions by walking out like this. In fact, Jeeves used the same tactic in *Thank You, Jeeves*, leaving Wooster's service and only agreeing to return when his employer stopped playing the banjolele.

Even so, looking back, it is astonishing that government ministers didn't stop and at least try to assess what expanded access to cheaper betting might mean for the more vulnerable members of society. They were not dealing—as Jeeves had been—with an irritating musical instrument after all, but with an extremely addictive product capable of causing huge harm. Instead, these addicts were dubbed "problem gamblers," thus making sure all the blame for their addiction was placed on them, rather than the problem companies selling them the addictive product. Such was the mood of the times. "We do not think the issue of problem gambling should influence the nature of gambling regulation," said the government's Better Regulation Task Force. "Government regulation should not have the effect of preventing mature consumers from exercising their right to spend their money as they see fit. We would urge you to consider self-regulation, such as a code of practice endorsed by the industry."

I am not personally very interested in gambling, and it is possible that my lack of interest has blinded me to something important, but it seems obvious to me that when businesses sell something addictive, whether that's drink, cigarettes, drugs or gambling products, it is not wise to expect them to do the right thing by their clients. That is asking them to turn away free money, and as a rule companies struggle to do that. Even gambling insiders were alarmed by the potential impact of what the reforms to their industry might unleash.

"We were astonished, to be honest, it went far beyond what we had hoped for," said one bookmaker quoted anonymously in the academic Rebecca Cassidy's *Vicious Games*, a study of the gambling industry based on years of research. He had gone to the pub with two friends for a celebration that turned into something more akin to a wake. "We were three old-timers sitting there on what should have been the best or the most profitable or promising change to our industry for a generation and two of us were singing from the old Methodist hymn sheet! We'd pushed at the door and the whole house fell over. That's how it felt."

Bookmakers no longer had to worry about the state taking a stake out of every bet, so they could offer much more attractive odds and encourage higher-frequency betting. They did this by bringing in machines—fixed-odds betting terminals—which gave gamblers instant and repetitive gratification. FOBTs are normally a version of roulette, with the outcome decided by a random-number generator, and bookies reported how clusters of punters would stand behind the gambler, watching him play. There were horse races being shown on televisions all around the shop, but the FOBTs were so addictive that staring at them was preferable to watching live racing. As with casino roulette, the machines are mathematically rigged in favor of the house. With horses, dogs or any other live sport there is at least the possibility of outwitting the bookmaker, thanks to your superior knowledge of form; with FOBTs, if you play for long enough, and the machines are designed to make sure you do, the bookie literally always wins. They are a one-way bet. By 2007 there were 30,000 of them in Britain's betting shops.

"FOBTs? Money hoovers. They literally suck up any cash that is lying about the place. I think of us as like a massive cleaner," said one senior manager at a British bookmaker interviewed anonymously by Rebecca Cassidy. "In we go to a neighborhood. Any spare cash, mate? In this slot here! That's it, just shove it all in there. Oh, and enjoy a free cup of coffee while you're at it, you fucking mug."

Inevitably, the big companies put their betting shops in places where punters could be relied upon to lose as much money as possible. This was predation on the most vulnerable members of society by huge corporations armed with ever more finely honed addictive machines. There was a direct correlation between the concentration of betting shops and the level of deprivation in a district. Within a decade, the machines were earning bookies almost £2 billion a year in profits. On average, that's a loss of almost £100 from each family in Britain, and the money was coming overwhelmingly from those families least able to afford to lose it. "I'm a bookie through and through, cut me and I bleed bookmaking," said Stan, another one of Cassidy's interviewees, who had previously run an independent network of bookmakers in southeast London but become disgusted by the way the industry had changed. "I've retired because of the machines. I've sold up. I'm off to Spain. You've got to earn a living, but you need to look in the mirror when you shave or else you'll cut your throat."

But what did this mean for Gibraltar? If it had become so easy for the big betting companies to make huge profits while operating in the UK, did this mean the little colony had to go back to scratching a living? Not exactly, because the butler had a new idea.

The reforms had been intended to unleash the British gambling industry. The theory was that places like Europe and the United States would eventually catch up with the British advance, but by this point the big UK bookmakers would be so entrenched they would be the Google and Amazon of gambling. At first, this looked like a good bet by the government in

London—the big bookmakers moved their operations back to the UK and paid their taxes into the British Treasury—but the theory had a flaw: if you base your strategy on under-regulating and under-taxing your rivals, there is always the possibility that someone will do the same to you.

A good butler does not stop trying to help his client just because his client has secured better treatment; instead, he looks for further ways to improve the situation.

When Freddie Ballester closed down his offshore operations in 1994, he still thought the idea of offshore gambling was a good one, so he took out his own license and kept renewing it year after year. And that proved to be a wise investment because, even before the British companies went home, other gambling companies had moved in. In 2000 he teamed up with a company called sportsbook.com, which wanted a permit allowing it to offer online betting from the Rock. In 2003 he moved to a new company, Party Gaming, which also wanted to open up in Gibraltar and offer gambling over the internet. Just when the government in London was congratulating itself, Butler Gibraltar was planning a whole new strategy for its client.

"The real explosion came in 2002, 2003, not because we went looking for it, but because the likes of 888 and Party Gaming were looking for a European base from which to effect a listing in London," said Peter Montegriffo, who was a minister in the Gibraltar government from 1996 to 2000, the period when the first online companies opened their offices. "Since 2002–3, it has been absolutely dramatic . . . If you look at the economic pie, it now represents in employment terms one fifth or even one quarter, but not just that, it also brought in a type of skill and a profile of individual, many of them young of course, who really provided a great boost to the human capital of the place."

Butlering has totally transformed Gibraltar, with the business of helping bookmakers avoid other countries' regulations and taxes proving profitable and enduring. By 2003, the UK Ministry of Defense contributed just 4 percent of the colony's economy, which meant Gibraltar no longer worried so much about upsetting people in London. The Rock's online companies were selling betting products into Britain, tax-free, while Britain's world-leading gambling companies, weighed down by the costs incurred by any established business, were not the Amazon or Google of gambling after all. On the contrary, they suddenly faced the prospect of being Blockbuster Video to Gibraltar's Netflix.

They had promised the UK government to come back onshore if it did what they asked, but that promise didn't last out the decade. Jeeves whispered to them that moving to Gibraltar had worked for them in the past, so why not do it again? In August 2009 William Hill moved its online business to Gibraltar, and was followed within a week by Ladbrokes. Betfair, one of the new generation of "betting exchanges," which provides a platform for people to bet with each other, followed in 2011, expecting to save £20 million from the switch, as did pretty much all the others. "We should not criticize them for doing so. They have a duty to their shareholders," said Philip Davies, an MP from the then opposition Conservative Party in 2009, shortly after William Hill and Ladbrokes broke their promises to stay in the UK. "It has become totally unsustainable for them to keep their business here. For every £100 profit they make online, they will pay £1 or £2 in tax offshore, whereas they would pay £36 in the UK . . . Clearly, it is an absolute no-brainer for them."

Davies, a former bookmaker himself who was later forced to apologize for failing to declare gifts he received from Ladbrokes, said the government should repeat the trick it tried after

Chandler moved to Gibraltar and cut taxes again in the hope it would lure the bookmakers back once more. The issue was urgent—according to one estimate, the government was losing £300 million a year in taxes by 2013—but his argument was fallacious. However much the UK cut its taxes and regulations, it would never be able to match Gibraltar. The skilled butler can find advantages anywhere, even in the gaps between different bits of Britain. "Gambling operators have made hay exploiting the laissez-faire regime that has existed hitherto, while successive governments and regulators have failed to keep up with the revolution," concluded a report from a House of Lords committee set up to look at gambling in 2020.

By 2017 gambling companies were investing the money they saved on taxes on expanding their businesses, spending £1.5 billion on advertising. That explains why it's hard to turn on a commercial television channel without being encouraged to place a bet, and the money poured in. In the five years up to 2019 the amount of money gambled online in the UK increased from an annual total of £13.4 billion, which is already more than £200 for every person in the country, to a scarcely imaginable £121.3 billion. That's almost £2,000 for every single person in the UK and, since not a penny of it was staked by me, at least one person is getting a double share. Over the same period, the bookies' online profits rose from £1.5 billion to £5.5 billion, mostly from the casino games that proved so addictive on FOBTs. That means the companies now make a greater profit online than they do from their betting shops, which have been earning less and less money over the last five years. It is so easy to bet from your smartphone, that why would you bother walking down the road to a betting shop? Somewhere between 40 and 60 percent of all those online bets end up in Gibraltar.

"I just think people are weak," an account manager at a

Gibraltar-based gambling company told Cassidy. "If you get addicted it's because you are weak, you have no willpower. Maybe I'm harsh. I see everything in black and white. I am addicted to cars because I want to be."

But that is not what is happening. Bookmakers have learned all the tricks of what Shoshana Zuboff calls surveillance capitalism, the system invented in Silicon Valley that monetizes customers' data to get ever better at predicting what they will want and then selling it to them. The computer learns your habits and how to indulge you to keep you playing: notifications come at the right time to encourage you to have a bet at the weekend. If you lose regularly on elaborate long-odds accumulators—what bookies used to call mug's bets—you are rewarded with "free cash," to keep playing. If you make careful, selective bets that earn you the kind of steady profits made by a clever gambler in the old days, the computer automatically limits your stakes to reduce the company's losses. This is an industry that knows ever more about how to get people hooked on its products, while discarding the kind of punters who eat the worm off the hook without getting snagged. "The people most at risk are the most profitable to the industry; the greater the problem, the bigger the profit," said the House of Lords committee in its 2020 report.

Official studies suggest that somewhere between 250,000 and 460,000 people are—to use the term favored by the UK government—"problem gamblers." That is almost certainly more than are addicted to opiates and crack cocaine put together, but it underestimates the problem, since for every gambling addict a whole circle of relatives and friends are affected too. Some 55,000 children are already addicted to gambling, and away from the old male-dominated world of the betting shop, women gamble online almost as enthusiastically as men. Surveys of the homeless show they are disproportionately likely to be addicted to gambling, as are ethnic minorities and people with the least to lose. "Those in the lowest income quintile were spending an average of 12 to 14 percent of their net income, compared to only 2 percent or less in the highest quintile," the House of Lords study said.

The Gambling Commission, created during those sweeping early 2000s reforms, argued in 2018 that the government needed to stop treating gambling as part of the entertainment business and see it as a health crisis. "These are not small numbers. They suggest a significant public health issue, which has received remarkably little attention relative to other population level concerns," it said. This warning came at least a decade too late for the parents who set up Gambling with Lives, a group that tries to raise awareness of the risk of suicide among people who have lost everything through gambling, and which estimates that 650 suicides a year are linked to gambling addiction. "Our children had all struggled with their gambling addiction for years," says the group's website, which features the portraits and details of twelve heartbreakingly young men and one young woman who all killed themselves after failing to escape their addiction. "Often being clear for many months at a time . . . but always dragged back in by an industry offering 'free bets' and other give-aways. They all felt that they could never break free."

One estimate of the financial cost of gambling addiction to Britain puts it at between £260 million and £1.2 billion, which is a spread so wide that it demonstrates clearly how much additional research is needed before we know what exactly is going on. The government meanwhile earns some £3 billion from the industry, around 0.4 percent of its total tax take. It is remarkable how when Parliament debates gambling, MPs are more concerned about the interests of racehorse owners than of gambling addicts. In 2017 a Scottish member of Parliament suggested in the House of Commons that a special levy should be imposed on the gambling industry to raise money to help addicts, without apparently knowing that such a levy was already made possible by the 2005 Gambling Act. It was just never actually set up.

Gambling companies regularly issue press releases to highlight how much money they donate to charities devoted to reducing the harm they cause, but the total is just £8 million a year, compared to £97 million provided to support racehorses. That means the industry provides owners with £7,000 a year per horse. Meanwhile it spends as little as £19 annually per gambling addict, while making almost ten times that much in profit, every second.

Bookmakers still like to evoke traditions of working-class Englishness ("You may as well have surrendered to the Germans all them years ago as tell a man he can't have a bet," said one bookie at a meeting attended by Cassidy in 2013), but they are now about as rooted in local communities as Amazon. In the last couple of years there have been suggestions that a compulsory levy to support addiction services could be imposed, and the biggest companies have suggested they could raise their voluntary contributions. However, whenever they do so, hidden within their statements is an implicit threat, repeated word for word in statement after statement from the Betting and Gaming Council: "We mustn't drive customers to offshore, black market, illegal operators that don't have any of our safeguards." Translation: if you try to impose rules on us, we'll just leave.

This is not to say that the Gambling Commission has done nothing to rein in Gibraltar-based operators. In 2017 it fined

888 £7.8 million for allowing customers to gamble even though they had asked for their accounts to be blocked, something customers can do to break the cycle of gambling addiction. In June 2019 it fined Gamesys £1.2 million for allowing customers to gamble with stolen money. In October 2019 it fined Petfre £322,000 for money-laundering failures. These may look like significant sums of money, but compared to annual profits measured in the billions, they vanish like single coins fed into a slot machine.

"The online gambling industry is the apotheosis of Big Tech, in terms of its algorithms, its flow of capital, its rootlessness, its addictiveness, its marketing techniques, its ability to permeate into the essential elements of our economic, social and cultural lives," wrote James Noyes, a former adviser to the deputy leader of the Labor Party and author of a study of the gambling industry, in 2020.

> This is the absurdity of talking about the "nanny state," as though we are back in the cozy world of Milton Friedman talking about automobile sales and safety, instead of a world in which the cash reserves of some companies are now equal to the forex reserves of many major developed economies, where capital is left to roam freely around the world, untethered from any semblance of territory, of productivity, of accountability, of reciprocity of value—if online gambling is not at the heart of the daunting world that we all now face, then what is?

And Britain could have approached this very differently. The United States faced the same difficulties as Britain in the late 1990s, with the birth of offshore operations and punters being tempted by gambling sites based in places like Antigua and the

Dominican Republic, plus more casinos opening on sovereign Native American territory and elsewhere. Many of the pioneering operators in Gibraltar predicted that it was just a matter of time before the US government accepted the inevitable and abolished restrictions on gambling; in 1996 the Clinton administration, however, decided to create a special commission to study the issue before deciding what to do about it. "Too often public officials view gambling as a quick and easy way to raise revenues without focusing on gambling's hidden social, economic and political costs," Clinton said when he signed the act establishing the commission.

The commission didn't publish its report for another three years, just in time for British officials to read it before changing their own laws. Although its conclusions are not entirely applicable to the situation in the UK because Americans tended to gamble in casinos rather than on sports, many should have been heeded, not least the direct and obvious comparison between gambling addiction and alcoholism. "Indebtedness tends to increase with legalized gambling, as does youth crime, forgery and credit card theft, domestic violence, child neglect, problem gambling, and alcohol and drug offenses," the report stated.

It was hard, the authors said, to put a cost on the damage that gambling causes, but politicians needed to recognize that there was a trade-off. If you allowed gambling in order to raise revenue, you were causing damage to people's lives by doing so and ultimately undermining society. Unlike insurance or other productive financial services, this is a zero sum industry: bookies' profits are simply gamblers' losses, and there is no broader societal benefit. The United States resolved not to follow the British example and instead to be far more cautious about opening up its market. In 2009 it showed what it thought of companies that tried to escape its restrictions by fining Party

Gaming, the Gibraltar-registered company that employed Ballester for a while, $105 million for taking money from American gamblers in contravention of US law. Party Gaming had been making almost all its revenue from the United States, and its share price fell by two thirds.

By 2019 the gambling industry—or "gaming" as Gibraltarians insist on calling it—employed 3,800 people on the Rock, twice as many as in 2011. It now provides the largest share of corporate and individual taxes, and regulating the industry costs the Gibraltarian government less than a million pounds a year. Gibraltar has outgrown itself: the old sea wall is still in place, built of handsome dressed stone, intended to withstand the ravages of a winter storm. But now the black cannons don't stare out to sea, but over a lane of traffic directly into the plate-glass windows of a rampart of office blocks. The low-rise old town is almost completely ringed by blocky towers built on what used to be the harbor.

According to the Gibraltarian government's own figures, the Rock is now the third richest place per head of population in the world, with a gross domestic produce per capita of $111,505, ahead of Luxembourg but behind Monaco and top-ranked Qatar. The government admits the figure is significantly distorted by having so many people enter the colony from Spain to work every day, but it's still quite an extraordinary development for a place that feared the loss of a Royal Navy shipyard meant bankruptcy. And it goes some way to explaining why Gibraltarians see no need to rein gambling in.

"In Gibraltar today nobody moans about anything—it's incredible. Everybody's well off. There may be the odd pocket, but everything's better than ever, everybody's got a better house than ever, everybody is employed," said Joe Garcia, veteran editor of Gibraltarian news magazine *Panorama*, which he started after training as a draftsman in the dockyard. "We write in the paper about a problem or this and that, and people don't notice—where's the problem? Everything is positive, and people seem to be happy. Gibraltar has never had it so good."

Unlike Nevada, however, where gambling is similarly important to the local economy, in Gibraltar you can't see it. There is a betting shop on Casemates Square, much as there would be in any town square in the UK, and there is a floating casino, but gambling operates as a financial services industry. Just as the BVI feels divorced from the reality of how its shell companies allow kleptocrats to hide their crimes and wealthy companies to reduce their taxes to nothing, Gibraltar is a world away from the reality of young people spending money they don't have on online games rigged to ensure they can't win. And this shouldn't be surprising. A butler is indistinguishable from any other prosperous-looking man on the street. It is his actions that define him. And so it is with Gibraltar. Its gleaming but anonymous office blocks couldn't look less relevant to the reality of gambling addiction in Britain's most deprived neighborhoods.

Joe Bossano, the man who as Gibraltarian premier ordered the reclamation of the land on which the office blocks now stand, is incredibly proud of what he achieved. Gibraltarians have access to subsidized flats, which ensures everyone can afford to get on the housing ladder; young people receive subsidized education at British universities if they want it; there is a hospital, and public amenities, and more. It seems a little strange for an avowed socialist to have made an alliance with online gambling, which is one of the most cutthroat sectors of an already viciously capitalist internet, but he doesn't see it like that at all.

"If you think of China and President Xi's concept of socialism with Chinese characteristics, without knowing it, what I was doing in 1988 was socialism with Gibraltarian character-istics," he said.

And that, to me, is just a witty way of saying that Gibraltar has become wealthy from being a butler to the giant gambling companies. This is just the start too. It wasn't too long ago that the border between Spain and Gibraltar was closed altogether, but Gibraltarian gambling companies now advertise on the shirts of Spanish football teams and in their stadiums, just like they advertise in the English leagues. These voracious online predators are expanding everywhere the internet reaches and taking advantage—as BVI shell companies did before them—of the inability of developing nations to regulate them. In 2019 the leading medical journal the *Lancet* referred to this as "the utter evil of an industry that does indeed prey on those facing social peril and financial precarity." Evil is not a word that medical journals throw around lightly.

And this raises questions about Butler Britain, because if even British people fall victims to this evil, then how does Britain benefit from it? The answer to that is that it doesn't, or not necessarily anyway.

"In real life," said Bossano, "you haven't got the choice of doing everything that is right, and everything that is good, and everything that is best. You have the choice of doing, quite fre-quently, the least worst that you can get."

The butler's client is whoever will pay it the most, and if the client wishes to pay the butler to help inflict evil on his fellow citizens, then he will do that with as much diligence and skill as he will do anything else. Having accepted that he can't afford morals, because morals are bad for business, he can find clients in the most unlikely places, and help them move truly vast sums of money, as we're going to find out.

6

THE SCOTTISH LAUNDROMAT

In the spring of 2015 David Leask drove out to Gartcosh, the newly opened nerve center of Police Scotland, which had been purpose built on the site of an old steelworks by the M73, for a press briefing. Leask was a journalist at the *Herald*, a Glasgow-based newspaper that has always served as a sort of scrappier counterpart to its Edinburgh—and more Establishment—rival the *Scotsman*, and is the kind of reporter that other journalists really appreciate. He's thorough, he's resourceful and, once he's on the track of a story, he does not stop following it until he's run it into the ground. The meeting at Gartcosh was about to set him chasing a new scent.

To outsiders (me at any rate), Gartcosh doesn't have a great reputation, which is entirely due to the cynicism of the hard-drinking superannuated coppers in Ian Rankin's crime thrillers. For Rankin's old-timers, Gartcosh is everything that's bad about modern policing. A policeman's place was on the street; his information came from his sources; he might break the rules or the odd suspect's nose, but he got the job done. Gartcosh is the antithesis of that, a "closed compound that was trying its damnedest to resemble a new-build university, one aimed at the elite," inhabited by police officers with high opinions of themselves. For the campus's designers, however, this was an experiment in a new kind of law enforcement, in which different disciplines worked alongside each other, dismantling the barriers that had all too often stopped tax authorities, criminologists, forensic specialists and others from working together to catch the baddies.

"I was there getting a briefing on something entirely different one day, and on my way out a guy I knew basically handed me the report and said, 'This is something else, man, this is really worrying us what's going on here,'" Leask remembered. The report his source handed him was labeled "Project Tenor— Scoping Phase." It had been written by the US-based corporate investigations company Kroll, and was strewn with warnings declaring it to be private and confidential. "In that police-y hint-y way, they had said, 'You ought to read this.' There were Scottish things in there if I kept looking, so I brought it back to the office," Leask said.

The report is dense, complicated and highly detailed, but once you get past the complexity, it is an account of what is— relative to the size of the country where it happened—probably the biggest bank robbery of all time. Somehow, a group of criminals stole a billion dollars from banks in Moldova, vanishing with their loot without leaving a trace to show where the money had gone.

Moldova, an ex-Soviet sliver sandwiched between Ukraine and Romania, is Europe's poorest country. In 2015 the average family was getting by on around $300 a month, and many young Moldovans had emigrated in search of a living on the building sites of Moscow or in the strip clubs of the Gulf. A billion dollars therefore was an incredible amount of money, an eighth of the country's annual gross domestic product. A bank job of equivalent scale in the UK would net its perpetrators around $360 billion, in the US more like $2.5 trillion, which is why the National Bank of Moldova had brought in Kroll to help it find out what had happened to all the cash.

Three banks, it seemed, had lent money to each other in a circle, using the proceeds of each loan to back the next, each one larger than the one before. The banks were all supposedly separate but were in reality secretly controlled by a 28-year-old businessman called Ilan Shor, whose extravagant lifestyle suggested he had plenty of uses for extra cash. In November 2014, however, someone yanked up the handbrake on this financial merry-go-round, the music stopped, and the money vanished, all but bankrupting the entire Moldovan financial system. "I do not have an answer for you on how it is possible to steal so much money from a small country," said the EU ambassador to Moldova at the time.

The precise details of the scam remain contested, with Shor insisting he's the blameless victim of corrupt insiders, and politicians blaming him, or each other, or Russia, for perpetrating the heist. The Kroll report was an initial probe into the evidence rather than a definitive account, which is why the agency intended it to be a confidential document with very limited circulation. But the speaker of Moldova's parliament leaked it, posting it on his personal blog in what he said was an exercise in transparency but his enemies maintained was a bid to make sure Shor got the blame. We know he leaked it because his name, his job title and "copy 33 of 33" are on the bottom of every one of the report's eighty-three pages.

I'm not going to examine the claims and counterclaims of the Moldovan elite, try to work out who was to blame for this crime or attempt to trace the money, which has comprehensively vanished. Moldova is sadly no nearer a reckoning than it was in 2014. I am more interested in what the fallout from this saga says about Britain—about how it goes about its work as a butler and how, at an institutional level, it resists efforts to stop it from doing so. This chapter is about indifference toward the suffering of the weak, and craven accommodation of the whims of the powerful, about a system that has—seemingly without anyone noticing—been designed to stop anyone interfering in the profits that flow into the butler's pockets. Fair warning: this chapter is going to be pretty depressing.

Leask took the Kroll report back to his office and sat down to read it. It did not take him long to spot what his police contact had been hinting at. There, on page 12, Kroll had specified the last known destination of the money, a UK-registered shell company. And there, on page 65, was the Scottish connection: the shell company was registered on Royston Mains Street in Edinburgh. The final owner of the billion dollars stolen from Moldova turned out to be based in an ordinary residential house in Pilton, a gritty Edinburgh suburb best known as the setting of *Trainspotting*, the 1990s book and film of heroin addiction and petty crime. So on June 20, 2015 Leask published his scoop: an account of the crime and its Scottish underpinning, full of details of Shor's pop-star wife and glamorous lifestyle, containing promises from politicians in Edinburgh that this would never happen again.

Four days later, Leask's colleague Ian Fraser—together with a freelance investigator called Richard Smith—followed up in the *Herald*'s Sunday equivalent. Their article contained details of the Lithuanian couple that had created the billion-dollar shell company, which was called Fortuna United LP (the letters stand for "limited partnership"), as well as 437 other limited partnerships registered at their house. And it explained why these structures were perfect for criminals looking to hide their ownership of stolen money. Fortuna United LP might be registered in Scotland and therefore look respectable to the casual observer, but it was actually controlled by two companies in the Seychelles, a notorious tax haven where ownership of companies is a closely guarded secret. A Scottish limited partnership (SLP) could import the dodgiest excesses of tax havens into the UK and turn them into a respectable-looking investment vehicle. A Seychelles-registered company was an automatic red flag for any half-competent bank compliance officer, but a partnership based in Scotland looked legitimate. In reality, an SLP was even worse than a shell company in a tax haven. We have no way of knowing who owns a company in the Seychelles, but at least someone in the Seychelles does. British regulators had no idea who the true owners of an SLP were because those owners didn't have to register their actual identity anywhere. And that is why SLPs were the perfect tool for anonymously moving money around.

The follow-up article by Fraser and Smith made clear that the use of Scottish limited partnerships was not a one-off: they had found SLPs linked to the Moldovan bank job at an address in Inverness and at a house in Edinburgh's East End. It turned out that, via accounts at banks in the Baltic states, a whole network of opaque Scotland-registered structures had helped the Moldovan criminals bankrupt the three banks and hide the proceeds. For the Scottish journalists it was the financial equivalent of discovering that robbers had bought the guns used to hold up a bank in your hometown, legally and in broad daylight, and that no one had noticed or cared.

In October 2015 a BBC radio reporter took the story to an even larger audience, entering the house in Pilton where Fortuna United LP was based and describing how internally it looked even less like the home of a billion dollars than it did from the outside: "It's a very bare, rather dirty entrance. There's a bike parked here, some old crates and boxes at the back." The BBC journalist spoke to Viktoriya Zirneleyte, the 36-year-old Lithuanian who created the shell companies involved. "We don't ask details about the business," she told him. "Obviously, one of the companies which we registered was used in the structure for money laundering, but really we don't know anything about it. . . . Find the people who made this fraud and convict them— we're nothing to do with this."

She and her partner also signed official documents on behalf of both the Seychelles-based shell companies that owned Fortuna United, meaning they were technically responsible for their conduct, and thus for the whole limited partnership. But Zirneleyte said neither she nor he knew anything about the firms' financial affairs: they just signed the bits of paper required, and took payment for it. These two people were the human cutouts between the criminals and the crime. They might have sold the gun, but they didn't stick up the bank.

Once upon a time, back in the 1970s, thieves and crooks deposited their loot—in cash, in a big sack—in a numbered Swiss or Austrian bank account, where the details of their identity would be a secret between themselves and their banker. International money-laundering rules are more thorough these days, so that kind of setup is impossible, but SLPs provided a perfect substitute. If you owned an account in a bank somewhere in the Baltic states, in Cyprus or in pretty much any country where bankers put profits before probity—via one of the structures that Zirneleyte created—your identity was as comprehensively hidden as it was in Zurich in its prime. And it was cheaper too: a Swiss bank account costs thousands, but a ready-made plug-and-play SLP with bank account costs just a couple of hundred quid.

If you have read *Moneyland*, you may be thinking that I'm covering old ground here. British shell companies are notorious for their role in financial crime, and British politicians are notorious for failing to do anything about them. In 2016 I published a long article revealing how fraudsters had been using companies registered at London's 29 Harley Street for years to defraud their victims. At the time I naively assumed that someone in power would read the article and close the loophole I'd revealed, but that didn't happen; instead it was totally ignored. In fact it was worse than ignored. Three years later journalists from *The Times* published their own investigation into 29 Harley Street, repeating the same allegations and exposing exactly the same crimes as I had, and still no one in power did anything. Seeing a robbery being committed and not stopping to help can perhaps be excused once, but when the same crime is exposed a second time yet still you pass by on the other side of the road, that begins to look like a pattern. Butler Britain exists to help its clients. It has no interest in stopping them from misbehaving when there's profit in it.

Once Leask had broken the first SLP story, he continued with revelation after revelation: how SLPs had been used in the arms trade between Ukraine and the Gulf, in sending mercenaries to eastern Ukraine, in the counterfeit vodka trade, in industrial-scale copyright infringement, in selling illegal "male virility enhancement" pills, in enabling unregulated gambling (all those stories in the space of just eighteen months). The Moldovan heist was clearly just one Scotland-enabled fraud among many, costing victims around the world perhaps hundreds of billions of dollars. In this respect Leask's reporting was like mine on 29 Harley Street, since that also involved many frauds all based out of one address. In one important respect, however, his work was different: politicians ignored my articles, but they didn't ignore his.

Some six weeks before Leask's first scoop was published, a

general election had brought a historic breakthrough for the Scottish National Party, which went from having just six MPs to becoming the third-biggest party at Westminster. Its haul of fifty-six seats was only three away from a clean sweep north of the border. From its many new MPs, the SNP appointed as its Treasury spokesman a parliamentary novice called Roger Mullin. He had caused the biggest shock of the already seismic election by winning the seat previously held by ex-prime minister Gordon Brown. Mullin read about the Moldovan fraud and how it was enabled out of Scotland, and was appalled. The Scottish limited partnership was a product of Scots law, but the legal architecture is set in London. If Scotland was going to get out of the money-laundering business, he would have to persuade his new colleagues in the Westminster Parliament to change the law. That did not look like an easy task: limited partnerships were an obscure twig on an already pretty unfashionable branch of the law, and this was a scandal involving Moldova, a country almost no one knew or cared anything about. But with a neophyte's enthusiasm, he set to work anyway, determined to get results.

Partnerships are a very ancient instrument and for centuries existed only in the common law established by judicial decisions, but the Victorians codified them in an 1890 act which contained seventeen words that would a century or so later cause all the trouble: "in Scotland a firm is a legal person distinct from the partners of whom it is composed." The law does not say why a Scottish partnership (and from 1907, when they were introduced, a limited partnership) was different from a partnership in England, Ireland or Wales, or give any details about what that meant, but those seventeen words established a distinction that would prove extremely costly for Moldova's national bank and extremely profitable for the bank robbers and their butler.

There were only a few hundred Scottish limited partnerships in existence for most of the twentieth century, and they were largely used to hold agricultural tenancies because they allowed Scottish landlords to deprive tenants of rights. Like all partnerships, SLPs had no obligation to publish the kind of financial accounts that companies have to, and were not themselves taxed; any money flowed through to the partners, who paid tax as individuals. Unlike partnerships elsewhere in the United Kingdom, however—thanks to those seventeen words—SLPs could own property, enter into contracts, sue or be sued and generally behave like a company. And because the liability of partners in SLPs could be limited, as with a company but unlike in a traditional partnership, they only risked the money they had specifically invested, rather than everything they owned. If the venture went bankrupt, the rest of their assets were not at risk. No disclosure, no taxes, no drawbacks, no risks: this gave SLPs the "Heads I win, tails you lose" quality so appreciated by very wealthy people looking to structure their business affairs in the most profitable way. And the qualities that appealed to Scotland's largest landowners also, as it turned out, appealed to Eastern Europe's most sophisticated money launderers.

Leask was not the only investigator exploring the strange world of SLPs, or the only one finding it hard to do so. SLPs were difficult to probe because, unlike the corporate registrations I found at 29 Harley Street, the documents relating to limited partnership were filed on the Companies House website as images, rather than entered as data. That meant if you wanted to analyze the documents, you had to read each entry individually; data mining software was useless. That was not only time consuming and frustrating but, at the time, expensive.

Obtaining the documents related to every SLP would have cost more than £6,000. Richard Smith, however, ran through what he could and revealed a situation even more worrying than anyone had thought.

He calculated that if you picked a random SLP from the register you would be more likely than not to find one owned by anonymous offshore companies, registered at a nondescript house somewhere in Scotland, perfectly designed for financial crime. Some 80 percent of all SLPs created in the previous eight years were on exactly this pattern. "Whoops," wrote Smith, who has a very dry sense of humor, on his blog. "How did that happen without anyone noticing?"

The boom in the popularity of SLPs had been sudden and remarkable. More were registered in 2016 than in the entire century that followed their creation in 1907, and more than two thirds of them at just ten addresses. Criminals from Eastern Europe and elsewhere were using SLPs on an industrial scale to hide stolen money intended to build schools or hospitals, or to pay wages, benefits and pensions. SLPs became so notorious in Scotland that Ian Rankin built an entire novel around them, complete with organized criminals, crooked lawyers and his trademark noir-ish Edinburgh backdrop. All the parties represented in the Scottish Parliament committed to reforming the system, and Roger Mullin took the cause to Westminster.

"I was armed with lots of information, not just from David Leask's articles but also from the likes of Richard Smith, who gave me information as well," Mullin told me. "When I spoke in the Commons, hopefully I seemed to be well informed about examples of criminality. My strategy, such as it was—it feels a little grand calling it a strategy—was that I had to use every device that was open to me to be heard in the formal channels."

Mullin rose to address the Commons on the subject of SLPs

for the first time on 5 September 2016, then did so again a day later. He was back in October and December that same year, then in February and March 2017. He persuaded his party's leader in the Commons to ask a question of the prime minister and invited Leask to Westminster to give evidence to a committee looking into criminal finance, to help the journalist's revelations about the SLPs to reach a wider audience of MPs. "It is essentially a do-it-yourself kit for tax avoidance at best and money laundering at worst," Leask told the committee. "They will pick on the weakest regulatory regime they can for any part of their kit to launder money. In the case of companies, I am sorry to say that I think that is Britain."

Rarely can a single subject have had such a committed parliamentary advocate, and Mullin was almost immediately successful. In January 2017, eighteen months after Leask's first article, the government's business department said that it would review the laws around limited partnerships and asked for concerned parties to send in any thoughts they had. This was the first step toward shutting the loophole that had allowed a billion dollars of Moldova's money to slip through the front door of a house in Pilton and never come out again.

"There do not appear to be any legitimate benefits of limited partnerships over a limited company other than the benefit of the lack of transparency. Furthermore, there appears to be little economic benefit to Scotland from the increase in SLP registrations," said the Association of Accounting Technicians in its submission to the government's consultation. This seemed a statement of the obvious, and one that surely presaged these weird anachronisms being swept away.

At this stage you may be feeling a bit let down. This doesn't look depressing at all, but instead like a happy story of politicians acting quickly and decisively to right a wrong as soon as it was brought to their attention by the press. I promised a depressing chapter, however, and I won't let you down now, because the situation was less clear cut than it looked. Mullin, for example, had already had intimations that the fight to deprive Butler Britain of this useful tool for its clients was going to be hard. In 2016 he asked for a meeting at the Treasury specifically to discuss SLPs and found a junior minister and two officials with a very different agenda to the one he had brought with him.

"I remember being really surprised by one thing, which was how little the officials seemed to know about this," he said. "You would have thought they would have prepared for the meeting, but there was little sense of that, other than—the one thing I do remember—they kept on saying, 'We have got to be concerned about the competitiveness of the City.' I remember being told that a major competitor was Luxembourg, and we didn't want to disadvantage ourselves in relation to that."

It was most confusing. He was talking about organized criminals in the former Soviet Union, not financiers in Luxembourg, but he wasn't the only person receiving suggestions that the financial services industry would rather SLPs be left alone. One journalist looking into SLPs told me that he had been invited to a meeting at a prominent law firm and told that if he went ahead with his article the firm would never advertise in his newspaper again. In its submission to the government's consultation the Scottish Property Federation saw nothing to worry about in the growth in SLP numbers, which it thought reflected an increasingly sophisticated investment scene. It seemed primarily concerned that Leask's and other journalists' revelations about money laundering might lose the sector business. "There is a concern because investors will be sensitive to adverse publicity," it wrote.

The Law Society of Scotland took the same tack. It professed itself concerned by suggestions that SLPs might be used for criminal purposes but—in a classic example of the adage that you can always ignore anything that appears in a sentence before the word "but"—it had other concerns too. "In considering any proposed measures, care should be taken not to introduce measures which may impose a burden on legitimate businesses," its submission to the consultation stated. "Except for recent media reported use of SLPs for criminal purposes, we are not aware of transparency problems." If you don't look for problems, it's surprising how few you find, particularly if your income depends on you not finding any. The submission did contain one interesting snippet, however, which was that—thanks to a new law regulating tenancies in Scotland—landlords no longer found SLPs a useful way to manage their tenants. It had been widely assumed that the primary legitimate use of SLPs was in agricultural tenancies, but if this was no longer the case, why did they still exist? And why was anyone defending them at all? The answer lay in the financial services industry, which it turns out had discovered the magical qualities of SLPs long before the criminals had.

A butler does not only work for criminals, remember, but for anyone rich enough to be able to employ his services. Wealthy people, whether their wealth is dirty or clean, almost invariably all like the same things: low taxes, minimal scrutiny, no transparency. The first butlers to use SLPs to shield their clients' wealth from view had not been working for Moldovan money launderers at all, but for money men in the City of London, and it was these money men who emerged now to demand that their butlers' tricks be protected.

Back in the 1980s private equity funds had realized that if their investments were made through a stack of limited partnerships, with a Scottish limited partnership ending up as the final destination for any profits that were paid out, they could legally pay the barest minimum in tax and disclose the barest minimum to regulators. Unlike companies, SLPs were not themselves taxed, so profits flowed through tax-free to their partners. Less tax means more profit. Syndicates at Lloyd's insurance market started to use SLPs, as did hedge funds. Whether legitimate or otherwise, everyone with money likes a best-of-both-worlds setup, and SLPs were very definitely that.

Elspeth Berry, an academic at Nottingham Law School, is Britain's foremost expert on partnership law. She told me that, quite gradually and behind the scenes, the private equity industry took over the whole debate about how these structures should be regulated. "UK limited partnerships are now the most commonly used structure for European (including UK) private equity, hedge funds and venture capital funds," she wrote in an academic article published in 2018.

> Private equity includes both a wealthy elite of investors, and a well-financed interest group in the form of investment fund managers and their professional advisers, who can more easily monitor, promote or challenge decisions that will affect them. It is easier for government to work with them than against them, particularly where, as in the case with limited partnerships, there is not organized countervailing influence and government activities are unlikely to be the subject of sustained (or indeed any) public attention.

If Mullin thought he had his enemies on the run, therefore, he was wrong. It turned out that not only were they not going to submit to additional regulation without a battle, but they had also, unnoticed by anyone, been quietly fighting this war long before anyone else realized it was even happening. Intensive lobbying from the private equity industry had already managed to doom proposals made in 2003 for a total overhaul of partnership law, which would have among other things removed the irrational distinction between Scottish and English limited partnerships. Then they had gone on the offensive. Literally within a week of the announcement of the consultation into Scottish limited partnerships came a second announcement, which he remains amazed by.

"So, at the same time that I was pursuing SLPs, along came this move from the Regulatory Reform Committee to create a limited partnership for fund managers in London," he said.

Mullin, supported by anti-corruption groups in Britain and across Europe, was seeking to tighten regulations on SLPs, so they could no longer be used to launder billions of stolen dollars. The idea was to prevent crooks from looting desperately poor countries, and instead give those countries a chance of building sustainable economies.

Unbeknownst to Mullin and indeed to pretty much everyone else, the Treasury and the private equity industry were actually seeking to loosen those same regulations, so limited partnerships would have to report even less information to the authorities than they already did. They had no interest in whether Eastern European money launderers could or could not do business, but they did want investments to be even more profitable than they already were. Remember how the Bank of England doomed controls on international money flows in the 1950s? The Treasury was doing exactly the same thing now.

And the Treasury had a great advantage in this battle, thanks to a little-known provision in parliamentary rules called a legislative reform order. To get tighter restrictions on SLPs,

Mullin needed to pass an actual law, have it read three times in both houses of Parliament with scrutiny and debate, and gain royal assent, as well as the rest of the parliamentary rigmarole. But an LRO is a formality passed by a simple vote in committee. Even better, an LRO can only be used to deregulate, to remove obstacles to business, not to regulate. Even had he wanted to, Mullin could not have used this tool to secure his goals. An LRO is like a built-in ratchet, deliberately designed to make it easy to remove regulations, while forcing the advocates of greater restrictions to win their battles the hard way. It's the butler's creed: free to those that can afford it, very expensive to those that can't.

Perhaps if Mullin had been in Parliament for longer he wouldn't have been shocked by this, but he was still new to the job, and it felt like his opponents had cheated. The mechanism they had used was intended only for "non-controversial matters," according to the rules, so how could they use it for this? "I can hardly think of anything more controversial than a mechanism that has been used for international criminal assets and money laundering," he told the House of Commons in February 2017. "Not only are we creating a new form of limited partnership, but we are doing so with considerably less regulation than is in place for existing limited partnerships that have been a front for international criminality."

But he was outgunned and outmaneuvered. No one was listening, and if anyone cared they gave no sign of it. The LRO needed to be approved by the Legislative Reform Committee, whose chair was an MP called Andrew Bridgen, a man of the Conservative Party's right wing, a headbanger who campaigned hard for Brexit and then voted on all three occasions against Theresa May's Brexit deal. He tended to plot against almost everyone, and according to an article in *The Times* even his fellow Conservatives disliked him—calling him, in a nod to his past as a potato retailer—"spud-u-hate." If Mullin was looking for an ally in his attempt to prevent even looser regulation of limited partnerships, Bridgen would not have been his first choice.

"I was questioning a couple of officials, and Andrew Bridgen came in and said, 'Oh yes, we've got to protect the competitiveness of the City of London.' That was the big pitch there: here was the chair of the Committee on Regulatory Reform, giving exactly the same message as you were getting from the Treasury," Mullin said.

The committee did convene a hearing on the proposals, and the Treasury sent in Gwyneth Nurse, its director of financial services, to explain why regulations needed to be even looser than they already were. It all came down to money, she said, and to the same kind of international competition that sent the gambling industry to Gibraltar and the shell company industry to the BVI. In regulatory terms Britain had been undercut by Luxembourg, Jersey and Delaware and needed to match them if it wanted to retain the financial services industry. The changes would, Nurse estimated, over the lifetime of the average investment fund save it between £14,800 and £27,600. That added up to a total saving of £3.26 million for all the funds added together over the course of a decade. "It sends a message that we are interested in this area, that the UK is open for business; that we are interested in modernizing our regulatory regime," said Nurse. If Butler Britain's clients were not allowed to behave as they wished, they would take their free-spending ways to another country, and where would the rest of us be without their custom?

Mullin attempted to raise his concerns, pointing out that Britain already had major problems with criminals using its under-regulated limited partnerships to launder money. The proposals would regulate them even less. Shouldn't the changes at least do something to clamp down? "They are definitely not going to clamp down," Nurse said.

And so in April 2017 the LRO became law, and fund managers got their deregulated structure: the private fund limited partnership, which (unfortunately for anyone trying to search for it online) shares its PFLP acronym with the Popular Front for the Liberation of Palestine. Two months later came another general election, and Mullin lost his seat. The advocates of tightening up had lost their champion and their focus. The government's consultation developed in a fractal manner, with each consultation spawning proposals for more consultations, and then more consultations from them. "It would be our intention to legislate as soon as parliamentary time allows," it promised not very reassuringly.

The financial services industry smelled victory. The British Private Equity and Venture Capital Association said further changes would be a "needless act of self-harm." The Scottish Property Federation cautioned that the government risked driving business offshore if it was overscrupulous in checking the origin of money. A government minister told the House of Lords that Britain's departure from the European Union made the need for deregulation timely and urgent (in a way that, apparently, the looting of Moldova did not).

Britain's fund industry at the time looked after £142 billion in assets and generated more than £5 billion a year in fees. If these super-deregulated structures do indeed save the industry the kind of sums that the Treasury predicted, then that is I'm sure very welcome. But it is incredible to me that, in both her written and spoken evidence to the Regulatory Reform Committee, Nurse didn't acknowledge that there is a cost as well as a benefit to loosened regulations. The easier you make it for fund managers to set up limited partnerships, the easier you make it for organized criminals to do the same. Moldova lost a billion dollars it couldn't afford thanks to Britain's skilled butlering services and the determination of the UK government not to put any obstacles in their way. If all the cumulative savings generated by the new reform (as estimated by Nurse) were added together, it would take more than 230 years to earn back enough to make up for the loss that Moldova suffered. Or to put that another way, those savings are equal to approximately 0.006 percent of the fund management industry's annual profits.

Faced with the choice between protecting Europe's poorest country or saving the City an amount so small it wouldn't even be a rounding error on a fund's balance sheet, Butler Britain backed the wealthy and powerful over the poor and weak, again.

Of course the Treasury had its reasons for the change; everyone can find reasons for something they already want to do. Its international competitors were undercutting the UK; the City could ill afford to lose the business; the financial sector wanted it, so it must be a good idea; Britain must declare itself open for business; and so on. What's remarkable is that precisely those arguments were used when limited partnerships were first introduced all the way back in 1907. Even a century ago some prescient MPs worried that this was a deregulatory step too far, that LPs would spread criminality. And back came the reply that if LPs were not introduced Britain would lose out to its competitors, and the financial industry would go elsewhere. "It was a measure which received in this house the support of the hon. Baronet the Member for the City of London and, therefore, they might be sure that it could not have anything very objectionable or contentious in it," a government minister said—supposedly reassuringly—back in the days of the Queen's great-grandfather.

This argument seemed so reminiscent of those that Mullin heard from ministers when he spoke out against limited partnerships that when I found it in the parliamentary record I rang him up to tell him about it. He laughed out loud. "What a wonderful link that is. That's the first I've heard about that. That's absolutely fascinating—more than a century later and they're wheeling out the same arguments," he said. His laugh had an edge to it though.

Among the various legal and property companies that responded to the government's ever-expanding hubbub of consultations, a consensus emerged: the publicity around SLPs has driven criminals away from them, as have some technical changes to European law and Companies House regulations. It would be best now if everyone stopped talking about the issue because that same negative publicity might drive away the legitimate investors that Britain needs if it is to make a success of Brexit. The disease has been cured, so it's time to move on in case further operations do more harm than good to the patient. It is true that far fewer SLPs are being set up these days, but their misdeeds do not appear to have stopped. Police Scotland received sixty-six international requests for assistance in finding out the owner of an SLP in the two years after 2016, and Leask kept publishing his stories, including about criminals' use of SLPs in a huge Brazilian bribery scandal.

And in 2018 came the biggest scandal of all with the publication of a report into Danske Bank's Estonian branch and its laundering of €200 billion out of the former Soviet Union, much of it hidden behind limited partnerships that the bankers were themselves creating to help their clients keep their names off the bank accounts. "You're looking for customers.

That's how it should work, otherwise it's not profitable," one of those bankers said.

The Danske Bank scandal only came to light because of a British whistleblower called Howard Wilkinson who noticed discrepancies between the public documents of limited partnerships and the private accounts they held at Danske Bank. In 2020 Wilkinson won the Allard Prize, a prestigious international award given to anyone who has shown "exceptional courage and leadership in combating corruption or protecting human rights." He has given evidence to the Danish and European parliaments about the scandal he uncovered and the central role played by limited partnerships in hiding the identities of criminals. He and I talk regularly on the phone, but I have never met him in person and have no idea where he lives. He has to be very careful about revealing his whereabouts, in case of retribution from the many powerful criminals whose money-laundering scheme he exposed. I asked him if anyone in the British government had ever contacted him about the scam he uncovered, perhaps so as to help with its supposedly still ongoing consultations into the use of shell companies to hide financial crime.

"As regards the response of the UK authorities, I must have blinked and missed it," he said. "Even the Marshall Islands authorities were more active. Certainly no one has reached out to me from a policy perspective."

Nothing has been done to solve the problems that allowed Scottish limited partnerships to be used to fleece Moldova and to launder many billions through Danske Bank. It is still possible to own SLPs anonymously with offshore companies, to avoid filing accounts and to keep your identity secret. Now, however, you have an even less regulated vehicle—the private fund limited partnership—to do that with too, should you want to. No one checks the information you provide when you set one up, so you too can pretend to be a fund manager, just like a money launderer can. You don't even have to reveal what jurisdiction your offshore companies are registered in anymore, thanks to the new rules, or what sphere of business you intend to operate in. The best irony of all is that—all still thanks to those seventeen words passed into law in 1890—there is now such a thing as a Scottish private fund limited partnership, which is even more perfectly designed for anonymously moving money around, whether it's legal or illegal or something in between.

Alarmingly, there has recently been a small but noticeable rise in the registration of Northern Irish limited partnerships, and no one is entirely sure why, or if they do know they aren't telling. It is perhaps naive to expect the government to do anything other than encourage the business. When you are a butler, you don't turn your client in to the police, not if you want to keep being employed.

Police officers are reluctant to talk on the record about a subject as sensitive as this, but one investigator who has tried to bring money-laundering cases against those abusing British corporate structures was pretty clear about the root of the problem. Limited partnerships make it easy, quick and cheap to move money. They help the money's owners to hide what they're doing from competitors and regulators and they keep taxes and compliance to an absolute minimum. Everyone with money likes that, whatever the source of the money. If the tools fund managers use are also used by criminals to immiserate an already miserable country on the other side of Europe, that's not their problem. If you are a responsible gun owner, why should your right to bear arms be restricted just because criminals behave differently?

Elspeth Berry, the academic expert in Nottingham, said

that she had taught partnership law for decades with barely a mention of limited partnerships. For almost that whole period LPs were a technicality used for a handful of obscure purposes, and she still hadn't gotten accustomed to being called up about them by people like me. "I think, and this is my personal view, not a legal view, that the government is in hock to a lot of big financial institutions," she told me. "Every time the financial services industry says, 'Oh, but we bring so much money into the economy, and we could go offshore if you don't behave your-selves,' the British government panics. There are victims here, but they're not the people the government is worried about."

I spoke to Leask during lockdown, while he was taking a walk in the hills of Fife. He no longer works for the *Herald*, which like many newspapers has had to make deep cuts to its staff numbers thanks to the collapse in the advertising market and a decline in circulation. He still publishes articles, but he doesn't have the kind of back-up that a staffer has to break stories on the controversial topics that he once specialized in.

Sorry, Moldovans, but you're on your own. Britain could help, but that would cost the fund management industry a few thousand pounds, which is obviously not a sacrifice that any self-respecting butler would encourage his client to make. This is not to say, however, that British politicians are not interested in *some* Eastern Europeans. They very much are. And in the next chapter I'm going to look at the interest they showed in one man in particular, the kind of man who could afford a lot of butler's fees.

7

DOWN THE TUBES

When Boris Johnson—the journalist-turned-politician who is, at the time of writing, still prime minister—was Mayor of London, he used to hold regular public events where ordinary Londoners could ask him questions. They were billed as exercises in transparency, which no doubt they were, but they also gave a man who liked performing an opportunity to perform. The mayor made people laugh with his tousled-hair posh-boy shtick, which he probably hoped was enough for many of his constituents.

In July 2009, however, his bluff was called. At an auditorium in Croydon a man called Ajit Chambers, a smooth-cheeked former banker with close-cropped hair turning silvery at the temples, rose to ask a question. He had, he said, identified forty disused London Underground stations, and he wanted to transform them into tourist attractions. "San Francisco has Alcatraz; Paris has its catacombs," he said. "I have a proposal. I have been trying to get it to TfL."

Johnson jumped in. TfL—Transport for London, which oversees the capital's trains, buses, taxis, trams and other modes of public transport—is one of the few bodies that the mayor runs, so this was something he could theoretically do something about. And it was the kind of unusual idea that would catch the eye of any journalist, not least one as successful as him. "It is brilliant. I love it. London Underground. OK, we are going underground," he said.

The mayor asked Chambers a few follow-up questions about these "ghost stations," which Johnson appears not to have heard of, although they're pretty well known among people who travel on the Tube. If you know when to stare out into the darkness, you can even see the old platforms as they flash by. Johnson promised that his staff would evaluate the proposal and follow up. This was great news for Chambers, who had been trying to interest the mayor's office in the plan via more official channels but had struggled to get it past City Hall officials. His peculiar business idea finally had the chance to break through.

There is undeniably something romantic about the ghost stations, about the idea of space which once thronged with people and bustle but is now abandoned to mice and dust. I have a recurrent dream about opening a door in my house and wandering through room after room that I have for some reason never been into, and the old stations have that same appeal: free space thick with history and ripe with potential. And there is undeniably a business case for opening up old transport infrastructure; the High Line in Manhattan is just a long walkway to nowhere in particular, but people love the chance to stroll where the trains once rattled along, and do so in their thousands.

That does not of course mean Chambers's business idea was necessarily a viable proposition. For one thing, although dozens of stations have been closed over the years, there aren't forty actual ghost stations in the sense of places you could walk into and convert into something new. Most have been demolished. For another thing, the ghost stations that do exist are still stations, packed with power lines and machinery and—at platform level—speeding trains. For a final thing, space in London is expensive: almost any surplus building in the capital that can be reused has long ago been reused.

However, if anyone was going to make a go of breathing life back into the ghosts it was Ajit Chambers, who was almost comically persistent. He took to haunting Johnson's public events, and his appearances became so predictable that a columnist at *The Times* called him "London's foremost Boris-botherer." Chambers would rise to his feet and appeal to the mayor to cut through whatever objections had been raised in private by officials. Johnson had built his career on being a plain-speaking critic of the nannying tendencies of the state, and it was hard for him to publicly block free enterprise. In official emails City Hall officials would try to kill off Chambers's idea on the grounds of health, safety, cost or something else, only for Johnson to bring it back to life at public events. "All I want to know from you is that we can do this at no cost to the taxpayer," said Johnson at a public meeting a year after that first encounter. Chambers insisted that he could, and the adventure was back on track. Chambers identified the most promising place to start: Brompton Road, a ghost station in west London about halfway between Harrods and the Victoria and Albert Museum, which was closed in the 1930s for lack of passengers.

His vision for the site—of holographic passengers in period dress at platform level, a rooftop bar and an event space for album launches or other corporate events in the old ticket hall—was sufficiently exciting to catch not just the attention of newspaper columnists but even a publication as sober as *The Economist*. And it does sound pretty cool: "a veritable Tutankhamen's tomb of discarded treasures—huge industrial fans, gas-sealed doors, even a cinema for the troops stationed there for the war." A handful of events actually took place in the station, and people who attended them still excitedly describe the thrill of descending the old stairs to platform level, of seeing a huge map dating from when this was an anti-aircraft command post in the Second World War, of the sign saying DANGER AMMUNITION. Chambers's persistence had won through. All he needed was for public officials to sign over the lease, and those years of Boris-bothering would have paid off.

And that is where the plan fell apart. Butler Britain had different ideas.

The fact that events were held at the Brompton Road site, and held successfully, shows that it would have been possible to use it as a tourist attraction and to sensitively showcase this bit of London's history, even if the idea of holographic soldiers descending from a holographic train sounds far-fetched. It might even have been possible to make a decent profit from it. There will always be demand for another bar or restaurant in Knightsbridge, and the station would undeniably have been a unique event space. The true obstacle to Chambers's plan, however, was not health-and-safety legislation or even doubts over profitability, but something that Britain's work as a butler has embedded so deeply in government that I suspect most politicians don't even know it's there. To hand over the old Brompton Road station to Ajit Chambers, the government department that owned it—which, since the Second World War had been the Ministry of Defense—would have to overcome the reflex to sell things to the highest bidder, whoever they are and whatever their intentions. Chambers claimed to have raised £25 million to back his project, but as it turned out that wouldn't even have bought half of the ghost on Brompton Road when it finally changed hands in early 2014.

That sale was the final act in a remarkable tale that demonstrates how Britain is prepared to be butler to anybody, no questions asked, if the price is right. When the government was asked to choose between helping an entrepreneur to realize an eccentric dream that would enrich its capital city in a truly unique way or selling an asset to the highest bidder, there was only going to be one winner, and it wasn't going to be Ajit Chambers.

It's a well hidden story that requires some excavating. So, as Boris Johnson put it in that first encounter with Chambers, we're going underground.

First of all, we need to dig into where the money that bought the ghost station came from. To understand that, we need to go back in time to the days of the Cold War, when the Communist Party still wielded unchecked power over Russia and the other Soviet republics. The Soviet Union, which had been seen as a great economic rival of the West in the years after the Second World War, was falling rapidly behind. By the 1970s, it was clear that Moscow's plans to provide prosperity for all had been indefinitely postponed. Indeed, it was all the country could do to cling on to the gains it had made. While prosperity, mass fashion, pop culture, and labor-saving devices spread through North America and Western Europe, Soviet citizens queued for hours for basic essentials.

The USSR did, however, have one thing that the West lacked: vast quantities of natural gas, which it used to power its factories, to heat its homes and to earn valuable dollars as exports to the West. This abundance of gas—controlled by the country's first state-run corporation, Gazprom—helped stitch the Soviet economy together, and nowhere more so than in Ukraine, which was a center of heavy industry second only to Russia. Ukraine's factories and chemical works were dependent on pipelines bringing fuel from the same distant Russian and Central Asian gas fields that exported gas to Europe. Thanks to this subsidized source of energy, the factories could compete with their rivals, and millions of Ukrainians had stable, well-paid jobs.

And then in 1991 everything changed. The Soviet Union collapsed. Ukraine became independent and went overnight from being an energy-rich country to being energy poor. Its factories were only viable because of cheap natural gas, and it had hardly any gas of its own. Without its factories, its people would have no work; if its people had no work, its economy would collapse. Logically, one of two things should then have happened. Ukraine should either have rapidly become far more efficient in its use of gas, closing the hungrier industries, finding new ways to earn a living, so its imports and exports could balance each other, or it should have been essentially reabsorbed into Russia. The first option was economically ruinous; the second option was politically inconceivable.

Fortunately the need to reach an immediate decision was postponed by the fact that Russia also relied on gas. Its economy survived thanks to the hard currency it earned by exporting gas to Europe, and almost all those exports passed through Ukraine. That meant that if Ukraine couldn't pay its gas bills, it could just steal it from the pipelines that transited its territory, and Russia couldn't turn off the taps without also cutting off its high-paying customers farther west. As a result, the politicians in Kyiv never had to make the hard decision about the future of their industries that rational economics demanded that they should, and instead persisted in a strange limbo between the future and the past. Thus was born a uniquely Ukrainian phenomenon, which economists call "rents of energy dependency."

It is well established that large reserves of oil or gas almost invariably corrupt countries—think of Angola, Nigeria, Venezuela or indeed Russia—since those in power battle to control the money flows rather than serve the public. Ukraine became very corrupt as well, but in a different way: the corruption derived not from controlling the gas, but from the pipelines that moved it, and thus the ability to reward supporters with valuable shipments, or export licenses. This wasn't so much rent-seeking behavior as toll-seeking. Insiders in Russia and Ukraine teamed up to create shady intermediary companies that took gas from Gazprom at the Russian border, sold it to high-paying Europeans and split the proceeds. Often they paid for the gas not with money but with goods, and barter transactions added a layer of opacity to the deals, which made them even harder for ordinary citizens to understand. Nothing did more to corrupt Ukraine or to maintain its dependence on Moscow than its politicians' addiction to this money. Russia added the cost of the stolen gas to Ukraine's bill, but the insiders didn't care, since they were allowed to keep the profits.

When Vladimir Putin became Russian president in 2000, however, he decided that—at least at the Russian end—this wealth machine needed to be brought in house. If anyone was going to get rich from exporting gas, it was going to be him and his friends, not Gazprom managers and their shady enablers. It took him a little while to wrestle the old guard out of the door, but eventually he had a loyalist in charge of the giant gas concern. There would still be an intermediary company between Russia and Ukraine, so the money flows would remain hidden, but that company would be half-owned by Gazprom to ensure Putin got his share. Its name was RosUkrEnergo (RUE), and it took over gas supplies between the two countries in July 2004.

That was a big year in Ukraine. In the autumn the prime minister, a thug called Viktor Yanukovich who was heavily backed by Putin, tried to win the presidency by rigging an election. Hundreds of thousands of Ukrainians took to the streets of Kyiv, waving the orange flags of Yanukovich's rival Viktor Yushchenko, whose surname became the demonstrators' three-syllable battle cry. After weeks of continuous protests, the election was re-held, Yanukovich lost, and Kyiv held a giant party called the Orange Revolution. For young Ukrainians it was a glorious expression of how ordinary people can triumph over the corrupting influence of oligarchs and their money.

For Putin, however, who had spent time and money backing Yanukovich, Ukraine's revolution was a personal humiliation. Fortunately, he had a useful way to remind Ukrainians—and any other countries tempted to follow Ukraine's lead—why humiliating the Kremlin was a bad idea. Gazprom told the post-revolutionary government it would be renegotiating its gas supply contract, and when Ukraine refused to agree to its terms, cut it off. In the depths of winter the whole country suddenly realized quite how dependent it was on Russian goodwill.

There's a plaintive account in the State Department archive released by Wikileaks of a meeting between the US ambassador and Yushchenko's prime minister. It describes the sudden urgency of the choice that had previously been postponed since 1991. "He was on the horns of a dilemma. If he went ahead with the deal with RUE, he and the Our Ukraine Party would be accused of corruption. If he rejected the deal, he would be accused of plunging Ukraine into the deep freeze as Russia cut off gas." In some parts of Ukraine it was minus thirty degrees Celsius. Those kinds of temperatures kill, so it was really no choice at all. Kyiv capitulated.

Yushchenko signed the new deal with RUE, a humiliation that irretrievably split the coalition that had powered the revolution and from which his reputation never recovered. RUE was already doing well under the old contract. It made $500

million in 2005, which was before the contract was renegoti-
ated, and the money really started to flow. Ukraine's state gas
company, unable to put up its prices to consumers without
risking even further political fallout, lost $500 million in the
first three months of 2006—all profits for RUE's owners.

"Only one source of power proved to be stronger than the
Orange Revolution," wrote a historian. "Not (former) PM
Viktor Yanukovich, not Russia, but the power of energy-related
interests." But who were those interests? Who actually were the
owners of RUE? Everyone knew that Gazprom owned half of
the company, but who owned the other half? Which individual
was making the kind of money that only comes when you face
down a government and win?

Global Witness, a London-based campaign group that
works to expose corruption around natural resources, dug as
deep into the contract as it could. It identified the shell companies and the bank accounts, and it picked out a few individuals
who seemed to be involved: an Israeli lawyer, a former Hungarian minister, a British businessman, politicians in Turkmenistan
and various Ukrainians and Russians, including a notorious
mobster called Semyon Mogilevich. But it failed to answer the
question of who actually controlled the company. "How is it
in the interests of Ukraine, or indeed of Europe, to have such
a vital country's gas supply controlled by complex and opaque
business structures?" their report asked.

A couple of days after the report was published, as if to taunt
its authors, the owner of the other half of RUE revealed himself.
His name was Dmitry Firtash. Global Witness had mentioned
him in its report but struggled to find out much about him. His
biography was sketchy, and in place of a photograph they had
put a question mark. Firtash was only thirty-nine years old, but

his company had defeated a government still riding high on the emotions of a popular revolution, and no one even knew what he looked like. That's power.

In a public relations blitz, Firtash sat down for interviews with the *Financial Times*, the *Wall Street Journal*, and others, telling them details of his life and his plans for the future. Photographs showed him to be a suave businessman in a gray suit with a permanent five-day beard and a slight double chin. According to the accounts he gave, he started out in business selling food to Central Asia, but when his customers failed to pay their bills, he accepted payment in gas, which he sold at a profit in Europe. It was in this complex barter trade that he learned the skills required to run RUE. It never became entirely clear why Putin's Kremlin should have selected Firtash in particular to be its chosen partner in Kyiv rather than one of the country's better-known oligarchs. The articles did include allegations that he was linked to the notorious Russian mobster Mogilevich, which might perhaps explain it, but he denied there were direct business ties between them.

Implicit in all the interviews was Firtash's political heft. Thanks to his alliance with Gazprom and by extension with Putin, he had become not just vastly rich but also hugely influential: the Kremlin's man in Ukraine, a gas-fueled kingmaker. This was controversial in his home country, where revolutionaries accused him of restoring Russia's influence over their homeland. It is perhaps unsurprising therefore that Firtash started looking around for a foreign country where he might buy a second home, somewhere that would be more appreciative of his business prowess.

I did ask why Firtash specifically chose the UK to be the beneficiary of his largesse, but received no answer to this, or indeed to any of the other questions I sent over, but it may have something to do with a Ukrainian spin doctor called Vladimir Granovski, who had worked for Yanukovich in the Orange Revolution—and who also failed to reply to my attempts to contact him. He relocated to London on one of the visa programs reserved for "highly skilled migrants," bought a house for £5.4 million and went into business with Raymond Asquith, an aristocrat and former spy who once smuggled a defector out of the Soviet Union in the boot of his car, as bespoke consultants for wealthy ex-Soviet citizens looking to engage with the UK. Asquith & Granovski Associates devised a plan to integrate Firtash into the UK, and it was extremely successful.

In February 2007 the British Ukrainian Society (BUS) was incorporated, headquartered in Knightsbridge. Granovski and Asquith became directors, along with Firtash's right-hand man Robert Shetler-Jones; plus a reliable Conservative MP called Richard Spring who provided Asquith & Granovski with advice on "political, economic and current affairs matters" in exchange for £35,000–40,000 a year. "Are we trying to improve our reputation? Of course," Firtash later told the *Wall Street Journal*. "I can't just be the place where people throw darts."

Another MP, a Labor backbencher called John Grogan, worked closely with the BUS. He'd become interested in Ukraine after being inspired by the Orange Revolution, and he chaired an all-party parliamentary group on the country. "I was slightly naive perhaps. At that stage I wasn't aware of the funding arrangements," he told me. I asked him what he thought Firtash was trying to do by supporting the BUS. Grogan said the model was the British Syrian Society, which had been established by Bashar al-Assad's father-in-law to help build links between London and Damascus and which also had Spring on the board. The BUS's founding documents laid out objectives that were almost word for word the same as those of its Syrian counterpart. In 2008, in his capacity as chairman of the BUS, Spring secured a parliamentary debate on Ukraine, which is the kind of thing that makes any organization look influential. In the debate he talked at length about how Britain's interests lay in a democratic, Western-orientated Ukraine free of the taint of corruption.

"For a relatively small amount of money, it's trying to get influence and good contacts right in the highest reaches of government," said Grogan. "I suppose reputationally the kind of things the BUS did were in themselves pretty harmless—cultural events or lectures or whatever. No doubt, Firtash was trying to gain friends and influence. I have no idea if he personally met the people involved."

It doesn't cost much money to fund a lobbying group, and Firtash's associates looked around for other projects, which is what took them to a dinner in memory of the composer Pyotr Tchaikovsky at Cambridge University. Ukrainians studying for postgraduate qualifications had organized the event, which was pretty sumptuous by student standards. Held in King's College's great hall, with a formal dress code, tickets cost sixty-five pounds a head, and musicians performed some of the composer's works. According to a source in Cambridge, one of the speakers at the event mentioned that the Ukrainian language was not taught at the university, which seems to have inspired a new project for the oligarch. "Some of these British representatives associated with Firtash approached the organizers of the dinner and asked how much they would need to have Ukrainian taught in one way or another," the source said.

A mutually acceptable total was agreed, and the university's Slavic Department organized language classes open to anyone who wanted to learn Ukrainian. "That was where the first few thousand quid came from. Though whether that was actually

Dmitry Firtash's money, I don't know. I think it was. At that point the foundation didn't exist as an establishment or institution legally," the source told me.

The DF Foundation, dedicated to funding education about Ukraine and giving scholarships to students, was created early in 2008. With that, Dmitry Firtash's British structures were in place. In 2010 Cambridge University created a formal Ukrainian Studies course thanks to a donation of £4 million. "This gift ensures that Cambridge will be a vibrant home for the study of Ukraine for many generations to come," said Professor Simon Franklin, head of the School of Arts and Humanities, in a press release at the time. "Mr. Firtash has opened up new possibilities for teaching and research at the University of Cambridge." In March 2011 he was welcomed into Cambridge's prestigious Guild of Benefactors by none other than the Duke of Edinburgh, the Queen's husband.

Firtash was busy elsewhere too: he grouped all his businesses into one BVI-based holding company called Group DF. According to later analysis by Reuters, he was able to earn $3 billion just by reselling the gas that Gazprom sold him, thanks to receiving it at an artificially low price, so he was extremely cash-rich. With billions of dollars more in loans from Gazprombank—which made him the Russian bank's largest single borrower—he expanded fast into fertilizer, titanium, banking and the media. He became president of the Federation of Employers of Ukraine, a lobbyist for companies. He had funded Yanukovich's successful political comeback—the former prime minister won the 2010 presidential election—so had an ally running his homeland, and thanks to his philanthropy he had met the husband of the queen of his adopted second home too. Everything he touched was turning to gold.

This was a truly astonishing ascent. In little more than the time it took a postgraduate student at Cambridge to earn a doctorate Firtash had gone from being so anonymous that no one knew what he looked like to meeting Prince Philip. He seems to have realized the value of having a public profile in the UK when he took to the British courts to sue a Ukrainian newspaper for reporting on allegations of corruption in the gas trade. The case failed, but Ukrainian journalists told me that just the fact that he had brought it made them think twice before writing about Firtash. British libel cases are easy to lose, and very expensive to fight.

Firtash took to visiting Cambridge quite often, meeting the students whose scholarships he was paying for and bringing along a television crew to see him doing so. Flattery came from the students ("You are offering such a great deal of liberty involved in the program—how come you require nothing in exchange?" asked one student, according to an account on Firtash's website) and from the university, which gave him a special medal for his outstanding philanthropy.

And he bought himself a London residence, a mansion just down the road from Harrods built by the luxury developer Mike Spink, which according to a property publication cost something in the region of £60 million. Built in an understated fashion in pale brick, it looks relatively modest until you realize there is as much of it underground as there is above. It has a swimming pool in the second basement, and it punches all the way through the block; an anonymous-looking basement flat on a parallel street gives it a discreet back exit.

The location is lovely, with its balconies looking down onto a stretch of pedestrianized garden beside two adjacent churches, the London Oratory and Holy Trinity Brompton. During the London Kleptocracy Tours (they're based on the Hollywood Tours, but my friends and I highlight properties belonging to people accused of corruption rather than those belonging to people involved in films) this open space provides a convenient spot for the group to stand while we tell them about Firtash. There was a satisfying period when every time we turned up someone in the house would call the police. On one occasion the two officers who drove up within minutes of our arrival had apparently been informed we were extreme Russian nationalists, which was fun for us if a bit confusing for them. After the misunderstanding was ironed out, they stayed to listen to my presentation, however, and I was pleased to see them nodding along by the end.

With this London base, Firtash's infiltration of the British Establishment became even more ambitious. Toward the end of 2013 he agreed to another donation to Cambridge University and, in a series of events called the Days of Ukraine, opened trading on the London Stock Exchange and visited Parliament with his wife. "We are grateful to Firtash Foundation and all individuals who helped this to happen. We are also grateful to the Chairperson of the Foundation, Lada Firtash, who put all her energy and dedication in the implementation of this project," said John Bercow, Speaker of the House of Commons, according to a curiously ungrammatical Group DF statement.

"The fact that we are hosted at the British Parliament, and that its Speaker came in person to greet us, demonstrates how important our country is to the UK," said Firtash in the same statement. In a photograph of the occasion Bercow and Firtash are shaking hands, while Lord Risby—as Richard Spring has been known since he was elevated to the House of Lords—leans slightly forward in the background, hands clasped around a highball glass, with the kind of rapt smile you'd see on the face of a proud father watching his son pick his way through a piano recital.

Back at home, however, Ukraine was entering a turbulent time. Firtash had helped Viktor Yanukovich become president in 2010—indeed, in one of its classified cables the US embassy referred to Firtash as his "patron"—but ordinary Ukrainians were unhappy. Yanukovich's corruption became ever more blatant, and his profligacy ever more obscene with the building of a huge palace on the outskirts of Kyiv. When Yanukovich announced he would end integration with the European Union and instead align Ukraine with Russia, it proved the final indignity. Protests swelled over the next months into another revolution, and in February 2014 Yanukovich fled to Russia, while Moscow sent troops to seize the Ukrainian peninsula of Crimea. If Firtash was concerned by this turn of events, however, he did not show it. As the British government scrambled to make sense of what was happening in Kyiv, the oligarch was invited into the Foreign Office. According to a later statement in Parliament, they did not discuss matters of national security, although some important issues must have been aired, considering that Putin was about to plunge Europe into a crisis that persists to this day. "I tried to persuade them that imposing sanctions against Russia was a bad idea," Firtash said, according to a report by a Russian news agency. "That will only make things worse. America provoked Putin into this situation."

In less than a decade Firtash had gone from an unknown and shadowy businessman who had helped Putin dominate Ukraine to a widely praised philanthropist advising a NATO power on how to approach the Russian president, but even this wasn't quite the high-water mark of Firtash's influence in Britain. That came three days later, when his purchase of the Brompton Road Tube station for £53 million from the Ministry of Defense was finalized, and Ajit Chambers's business dream was destroyed. The ghost station directly adjoined Firtash's

London property, and it's not hard to imagine that he would have loathed Chambers's plan to create a rooftop bar and restaurant. Late-night revellers would have had a view straight down into his back garden.

He seems to have lacked any equivalent vision of his own for the site, however. The government's press release announcing the sale made much of the station's history and the unique features that had so appealed to Chambers, but Firtash showed no sign of being interested in either aspect. "The whole underground station thing isn't really that interesting," Mike Spink, who advised Firtash on the sale, wrote to me by email. "In reality, it's just another prime central London site."

How's that for butlering? Britain provided Firtash with a luxury home, welcomed him into the deepest recesses of the Establishment's bosom, awarded him a medal—containing nearly 500 grams of sterling silver, designed by Jane McAdam Freud and individually numbered—showered him with attention from members of both houses of Parliament, including the Speaker, sold him a central London landmark and asked him to come in and share some thoughts with the Foreign Office. In return it got money for a major university, extra cash for members of Parliament, support for its property developers and millions of pounds straight into the state budget in exchange for an old Tube station that the Ministry of Defense wasn't even using much.

Criticizing Britain for this may seem a little unfair. Isn't it just an example of how one butler outcompetes his rivals and serves his clients? Any country would have welcomed Firtash's money and expertise, so it would have been self-defeating to turn it away, right? Britain should be congratulated, not condemned. As the old song goes, if I don't do it, somebody else will.

This is a troubling argument. Firtash was Putin's man in Ukraine, and yet Britain integrated him so enthusiastically into the Establishment that he advised the government on Putin's invasion. Should it really be talking to a man like this? Or accepting his money? Or selling him a property with access to the London Underground system? Or, indeed anything at all?

"This has clear implications for national security," noted Parliament's Foreign Affairs Committee a few years later about the tendency to invite Kremlin-aligned oligarchs to buy what they liked in the UK. "Turning a blind eye to London's role in hiding the proceeds of Kremlin-connected corruption risks signaling that the UK is not serious about confronting the full spectrum of President Putin's offensive measures."

There are certainly plenty of other Western countries that have helped Firtash transform himself. Cyprus, Hungary and Switzerland sold him his shell companies; Austria provided him with a bank account; ex-politicians from all over Europe have been happy to hitch their names to his various foundations. But other countries behaving badly is no reason for Britain to do so too, not least because Firtash's integration went so much further in the UK than it did elsewhere. And the response of the United States to his activities provides a fascinating contrast to what happened in the UK and shows that there is an entirely different way to behave. If you look at both sides of the saga of Dmitry Firtash—the American half and the British half—you start to consider the troubling idea that if Britain doesn't do it, perhaps nobody else will. There don't *have* to be butlers.

After the collapse of the Soviet Union in 1991 euphoria in the United States over having "won the Cold War" rapidly changed to concern. There were messy environmental issues to resolve, economic questions to answer, wars to manage, as well as the

USSR's nuclear arsenal to secure. All these matters were intractable in their own right, but they were made even less tractable by a fifth problem, organized crime. Mafia groups took over chunks of the ex-Soviet Union's economy and used parts of its territory—particularly the ports of Odessa and St. Petersburg—to smuggle illegal goods into the West. There was much about these mafia groups that was unclear, not least the extent to which they intertwined with official bodies. Were they just a criminal challenge to the Western order, or were they a security challenge too?

Representatives of law enforcement agencies from the United States, Italy, Russia and Germany met in Moscow in 1994 in an attempt to map the emerging mafia structures, which were becoming influential throughout the former Soviet bloc, and were expanding into Israel, Western Europe and the US. American officials were concerned not just about street thugs in Russian-speaking sections of New York, but also by infiltration of the financial system, which was allowing Russian criminals to exert influence in the United States from safe havens overseas.

Many of the ex-communist countries lacked the capacity to investigate organized crime, but also refused to allow the Americans access to the information they needed to conduct their own investigations. Hungary, however, was an exception. It recognized its weakness and invited the Americans to help investigate a Kyiv-born Budapest-based money launderer called Semyon Mogilevich who was gaining influence in the country's prostitution, smuggling, fraud and corruption rackets. Mogilevich has become infamous in the years since, and is now the most notorious of all the Russian mafiosi, so much so that he is often presented in the media as a Russian boss of bosses. One US source told me, however, that their choice to focus on him in particular had more to do with the available opportunities than with his intrinsic significance. "There were lots of other mob bosses. We went after Mogilevich because he was the only one directing criminal activities in a country that was interested in working with us."

The Budapest Project, as the FBI called it as if it was a Tom Clancy novel, was not a straightforward operation. Senior Hungarian police officers were on the Mogilevich payroll, so it was hard to know who to trust, and the mobster's hoods controlled the streets and the nightclubs. "Black-leather-clad gangsters committed brazen extortions and other acts of violence against local citizens and visitors, including United States military personnel en route to peacekeeping duties in the Balkans," wrote a senior FBI agent in a later article. You can see why Washington was concerned: this was a confident criminal. Most mafia bosses would draw a line at shaking down US servicemen, but not Mogilevich.

In 2000 the FBI opened a permanent base in Budapest, where its officers were embedded with local police and had the same right to carry weapons that they enjoyed at home. The effect was immediate: Mogilevich fled to Moscow, and—in his absence—officials provided thousands of pages of evidence about his money-laundering operations to US investigators. Three years later the FBI indicted him, added him to the list of its Top Ten Most Wanted Criminals, and continued to investigate his associates. One area that investigators became concerned about were gas shipments through Ukraine, and inevitably their attention fell on Dmitry Firtash.

In April 2006, just months after Firtash's big gas deal helped doom the prospect of Ukraine's Orange Revolution, the *Wall Street Journal* announced that US law enforcement was investigating RUE's ties to organized crime. It was this investigation rather than that of Global Witness that seems to have finally forced Firtash to go public about owning half of RUE's shares. The *WSJ* reported that Asquith had gone to Washington on Firtash's behalf to deny any connection to Mogilevich, which is a denial that Firtash has had to make on a regular basis ever since. "There is no business connection between Mr. Mogilevich and me. I have never had any direct business dealings with him, nor does he have any interests in any of my companies," Firtash wrote in a letter to the *WSJ* in 2007. According to an account of a meeting between Firtash and US officials a year later, and released by Wikileaks, "Firtash acknowledged that he needed, and received, permission from Mogilevich when he established various businesses, but he denied any close relationship with him." (After the cable was published, Firtash issued a statement denying he had ever acknowledged this, and suggested the claim was a "mistranslation or misunderstanding.")

None of this lobbying succeeded in persuading US officials to stop investigating him, however. While members of the British Parliament took Firtash's money, the Duke of Edinburgh shook his hand and Cambridge offered him its highest honors, the US embassy in Kyiv kept cabling its suspicions about what he was up to, and FBI agents kept following them up. "Given Firtash's swift ascent from failing canned foods company manager to multi-billionaire dollar gas magnate, he might still be beholden to the forces that helped him rise so quickly," one cable noted laconically, after Firtash bought himself a bank.

Hungary became a less welcoming place for FBI agents with the ascent to power of the illiberal kleptocrat-adjacent Victor Orban, which ultimately doomed the Budapest Project, but there were already enough promising leads to follow. It took them years to finally finish the investigation to their satisfaction ("Welcome to the world of doing international cases," as my US source put it), but eventually they had enough evidence to convince a grand jury to approve an indictment. On March 12, 2014 Austrian police officers arrested Dmitry Firtash in Vienna at the FBI's request. It was exactly a fortnight after the final approval of his purchase of the Brompton Road Tube station from the British government. Rarely if ever have the contrasting approaches of the US and Butler Britain toward fortunes of questionable origin been displayed in starker contrast.

The immediate response to Firtash's arrest was confusion, because US officials provided few details of what they suspected him of, beyond making clear that it was something to do with "international corruption conspiracy" and insisting that it was nothing to do with the revolution that had just decapitated the Ukrainian government. Enlightenment came two weeks later when the indictment was unsealed. Prosecutors accused Firtash of having bribed officials in India with more than $18.5 million in order to gain access to titanium resources which in turn he was planning to sell to Boeing. The aircraft giant's corporate headquarters is in Chicago, and the FBI's Illinois office was investigating. The indictment showed that the alleged scheme dated back to April 2006, shortly after Firtash's big win in the post-Orange Revolution gas deal, and had continued for years.

Firtash fought back hard, posting bail of €125 million and issuing a statement to condemn the indictment as absurd. He was being targeted for political reasons, he said, in order to allow US officials to cement their influence over his home-land's new post-revolutionary government. "I will not allow my reputation to be ruined by those who are driven by political motivations and are not interested in Ukraine and its people," he said in a line that was hammered home in every interview he and his associates gave, a stance in which he was ably assisted by Lord Bell, the veteran British PR magnate, who now lent his expertise to Firtash, while Robert Shetler-Jones told the *Wall*

Street Journal, "It is not a coincidence that the US is trying to extradite our chairman at the moment when Mr. Firtash is needed for the economic and political reconstruction of Ukraine."

Apart from bland denials of such accusations, US officials were unable to respond, since they could not risk undermining their case, which is why my source was only prepared to discuss it anonymously. The source insisted that since the indictment had been sealed back in June, long before Ukrainians rose against their president, any suggestion of political motivation was absurd. The long delay in issuing the arrest warrant had been entirely a result of waiting for Firtash to fly to a country which might be prepared to extradite him. The US has no extradition treaty with Ukraine, so he couldn't be arrested at home, and previous attempts to extradite suspects from the UK had convinced them there was little prospect of bringing him to Chicago from London either. "Look at Julian Assange. Whether you agree or disagree with what his crimes are, it's been, what, ten years? The sheikh who was part of 9/11 planning, he took years to get to the US," the source said. "The only other option was France, and they're even worse than the UK. We only had a few places we could go to, because he only went to a few places, so the choice we had was Austria."

And the suggestion that the case was political? "We don't ever do cases based on political motivation. I can't speak for counter-intelligence, but on the criminal side we have to put all of this into a court, and you can't hide that if it's politically motivated. That's a big frustration."

For a little while Firtash's absorption into British high society continued, despite his arrest. In mid-March Cambridge held a ceremony to welcome Lada Firtash into its Guild of Benefactors, but press coverage was hostile, and protesters greeted her car as it arrived at the venue. The university announced that it would place the most recent donation from the Firtashes in a bank account, and would only spend it if he was acquitted. It also promised to improve checks on the provenance of donations. The Ministry of Defense was also challenged over why it had been prepared to sell him the Brompton Road ghost station, and similarly struggled to answer.

"The site was sold on the open market to achieve best value for money for the taxpayer, and we were not aware of the FBI investigation into Mr. Firtash at the point of sale. The sale followed all guidelines set out by the Treasury, and the MoD is satisfied that all legal checks were carried out," a spokesman said. In Parliament a minister explained what those checks consisted of: "all funds were paid to the MoD through UK regulated solicitors, in accordance with normal practice, to ensure that appropriate financial checks were made on their client."

The fact that US authorities were investigating Firtash's companies had been reported in the press years previously, so this was not a convincing argument. The British government's focus had been on making as much money as possible, and it had actually subcontracted its checks on the origin of that money to Firtash's own lawyers while ignoring anything that stood in the way of closing the sale. It wasn't a good look, and it left the MPs and peers who had so willingly accepted the money with some explaining to do. Many of the details about what Firtash has done in the UK are known thanks to Helen Goodman, a Labor MP who became the party's expert on Ukraine and got to know several of the country's human rights and anti-corruption activists as a result. She said that parliamentarians involved in the BUS had offered to pay for her to go to Kyiv, saying the money came from "somebody in oil and gas," but she turned the offer down and arranged her own transport. "It was just obvious that Firtash was corrupting Ukrainian politics, and equally clear that Firtash has an agenda. Why did he want to buy British politicians as well as Ukrainian politicians? What was his agenda? That's the thing that bothered me. What was he trying to hide?" she told me. "The thing seemed to stink. Every aspect of it seemed really weird."

Asquith did not respond to my many emails or phone calls, and neither did Lord Risby. One parliamentarian involved in the British Ukrainian Society did agree to talk to me, provided I didn't identify them in any way, but seemed ignorant about the fact that Firtash was involved in creating the BUS. "You might say I'm a bit of a useful idiot, but this didn't occur to me," the individual said. I'm still not sure if that is better or worse than getting involved in full knowledge of where the funding came from.

A politician who was prepared to talk to me on the record was John Whittingdale, a Conservative MP to whom I emailed a list of questions and who then rang me up just after I arrived for lunch at my in-laws' golf club. Whittingdale did not end his connection to the BUS until long after Firtash's arrest and accepted more than £3,000 in donations to fund a trip to a 2015 conference held in Vienna and addressed by Firtash. A contemporary statement on Firtash's website made much of the fact that Whittingdale had attended, and I asked Whittingdale—who at the time of our conversation was culture minister in the UK government, but at the time of the conference was just a backbench MP—whether he wasn't concerned that his involvement had given Firtash a degree of credibility that he otherwise would have lacked.

"Do you think so? I'm not sure that it gives him much credibility. Goodness, one meets a lot of people. Just meeting them I don't think enables them to claim any credit. I was briefly director of the BUS, but it is very much an arm's length operation," he said. "I am aware of the support for Oxford University, or Cambridge, whichever it is. That's a matter for them . . . We are a free society, and as long as it's legal it's up to them."

And the Tube station? Wasn't he worried about potentially tainted money being used to buy property from the British government? "That's not a bribe or anything, it's a commercial transaction. I am dimly aware that he did buy a Tube station somewhere in west London to turn it into a property or something, I don't know the detail at all. At the moment he's sitting in Austria somewhere, but there are much more dodgy—" He stopped and appeared to reconsider what he was about to say. "If Ukrainians come and produce evidence for instance that his money had been illegally acquired, or stolen from the people, then obviously that would be something we should look into, and if so then take action over. But as far as I'm aware they haven't, and there are plenty of other oligarchs who have money in London . . . Nobody in Ukraine has ever expressed any concern about this."

He was a government minister with a country to run, and I had lunch waiting, so we ended our conversation there, but that last remark stayed with me because it was so at variance with my own experience. I have spent many months in Ukraine, and almost everyone I talk to expresses concern about Britain giving a safe haven to oligarchs and their money. Whittingdale said Ukrainian prosecutors would have to win a case against Firtash if it wanted Britain to act, but those prosecutors are so demoralized, corrupted and out-resourced that such a victory is an impossible dream (it's hard enough in Britain, as we will see). Even if they do bring a prosecution, cases from other countries show that the oligarch concerned would simply argue that the proceedings were politically motivated and claim asylum in the UK or another Western country. If an oligarch is not prosecuted, Britain doesn't investigate; if the oligarch is prosecuted, Britain doesn't investigate either. The fact that a government minister fails to acknowledge this "Heads they win, tails we lose" injustice helps explain why Britain has consistently failed to interrogate the origin of suspect wealth.

I'm not saying Britain should necessarily have prosecuted Firtash, as the FBI did, but it could easily have been more standoffish. There is plenty of ground between opening criminal proceedings against someone, and welcoming him into your country so enthusiastically that he meets senior royalty and senior parliamentarians and opens trading on the Stock Exchange. It isn't as if no one in the UK had concerns about the origins of Firtash's wealth. In 2010 a Conservative politician failed the vetting process for the job of national security adviser, thanks to having accepted money from Shetler-Jones. But that was a rare exception to the general governmental willingness to accept money from anywhere, which has so distinguished Britain since it got started in the butlering business.

In 2020 Parliament's Intelligence and Security Committee published a report on Russian influence in the UK. The report failed to gain as much attention as it deserved thanks in part to Prime Minister Boris Johnson dismissing it as an attempt to delegitimize the Brexit referendum. This was a shame because it was a thoughtful analysis of the kind of blind spot that has led Britain to accept money directly from Russian oligarchs, as well as from Russia-allied businessmen like Firtash, without looking into where it comes from. "The inherent tension between the government's prosperity agenda and the need to protect national security that has led to the current situation has been played out across Whitehall departments," the report said.

"Prosperity agenda" is another way of saying that the

government prioritizes earning money over all other foreign policy concerns, which is what I call being a butler. My source in the United States said that their team had come across this kind of attitude from British counterparts again and again. "'All of these high-ranking and wealthy people in the UK,' a police officer said to me a couple of years ago, 'they only come on vacation.' And I looked at him and said, 'What do you think they're vacationing on? They're vacationing on stolen money.' He just says, 'Well, we can't make a case on that.' But the US can, and we're going to, we put our money where our mouth is."

As of this being written, which is in the short dark days between Christmas and New Year 2020, Dmitry Firtash is still in Vienna and still battling extradition to the United States. His extradition hearings have bounced between courts, with different Austrian judges ruling different ways, while in Chicago his US-based lawyers have sought to have the whole case thrown out. A number of US citizens have happily taken Firtash's money to lobby on his behalf, but prosecutors are sticking to their task and still hope he'll arrive in Chicago eventually.

Ajit Chambers's business idea has never really recovered from the setback he suffered when he lost the chance to buy the Brompton Road ghost station in 2014, and it's clear money is tighter for him than it was in the days when he was badgering Boris Johnson at public event after public event. He spoke to me at length for this chapter, but then said I couldn't use his words unless I paid him, which is a shame because what he told me was interesting and I would have liked to have quoted him. It is hard not to regret Chambers's failure to take control of the ghost on Brompton Road and turn it into an eccentric cultural venue. The old station has been shuttered since Firtash took possession, a forlorn monument to his ambitions, like a dead dolphin washed up on a beach, a smelly and rotting reminder of how high the tide once was.

Britain's failure to do anything about Firtash's property empire was clearly an issue chewing away at my American source because after our conversation had moved on they told me a story about a case their team had worked on, years before, when a woman from a religious congregation blew the whistle on a fellow believer who was making money from financial crime. The woman had apparently gone to the leader of the congregation and explained the situation, saying that the fraudster should be expelled, but he had taken no action. The victims of the crimes were non-believers, so he didn't care about what was happening to them. "I feel like that's the way Britain treats people like Firtash. He's committing crimes, but he's not committing crimes against UK citizens, so no one cares."

Not only does no one care now, but no one has cared for a long time. Indifference is not simply a passing phenomenon, but something deeply embedded in how British institutions are structured, in how they work and in what capabilities they have. It's not just that Britain didn't investigate Firtash, it's not clear that it would have been able had it wanted to. After all, there is no profit to be had by turning away a client, and a clever butler wants to minimize any chance of that ever happening. And that's the topic I want to turn to next.

8

GIVING EVIDENCE

In March 2018 I filed into an upstairs corridor in the Houses of Parliament, on my way to give evidence about this British tendency to accept money from anyone that has it. The poisoning of the Russian defector Sergei Skripal in Salisbury by Kremlin agents a few weeks before and the almost simultaneous screening of the television show *McMafia*, which vividly depicted the consequences of corruption via the life of a privileged Russian family, had suddenly awakened politicians' concerns that the national butlering business might not be such a good thing, at least with regard to Russians. This was quite a handbrake turn. Ever since the 1990s British politicians had welcomed Russian money. They had celebrated when oligarchs bought football clubs, cheered when they listed their companies on the Stock Exchange and partied on their yachts. They had gladly accepted political donations and patronized oligarchs' charitable foundations without worrying too much about where the money came from. The question the Foreign Affairs Select Committee wanted to ask was: could this money corrupt our politicians, as it had corrupted politicians in Moscow? Were we selling Putin the rope with which he would hang us?

The poisoning was still fresh in everyone's memory, and public interest in the committee hearing ran higher than it might otherwise have done. The room was grand, lined with linenfold paneling and commanding a view over the River Thames, but it was not large. All the seats along the back wall were occupied, while other attendees stood in any space they could find, and it became stuffy quickly. I was seated with three other witnesses along a table facing the parliamentarians who would be asking the questions. I had decided to wear my suit, which is somber (I bought it for my grandmother's funeral), having calculated that—in combination with a sober tie—it would give my words more weight than if I wore jeans. Looking back at the video of the session now, however, I'm not sure that was wise. Thanks to a failure to brush my hair or iron my shirt, the outfit made me look more like a defendant in a trial than the sober businessman effect that I was aiming for. Still, the politicians didn't seem to mind, and the first question was directed at me: "Can you give the committee a sense of the scale of the so-called dirty money being laundered through London?"

The question threw me, but I should not have been surprised. Every time—and it happens surprisingly frequently—MPs convene a committee to examine the wisdom of butlering, one of them is certain to ask how much money Britain's clients bring into the country. Presumably, they're interested either in ascertaining if it's a big enough problem to care about or whether it's so profitable they should leave it undisturbed. Either way, it's a nuisance, partly because the question is impossible to answer but mainly because attempting to answer it is a distraction from more important points. Witnesses with more experience than me have become accustomed to throwing out numbers—£36 billion, £90 billion, £100 billion, hundreds of billions of pounds—just to move the discussion on, but I was unprepared for it. "Blimey, that is a tough one," I spluttered, before waffling about private schools, mansions, luxury goods and the errors and omissions line in the UK's national balance of payments data. It wasn't my most coherent few minutes.

What I should have done, I now realize, was to copy Mark Thompson of the Serious Fraud Office, when a different committee asked him how big the problem was, and whether it could be quantified. "The short answers would be 'Big' and 'No,'" he replied curtly. "My view after twenty-odd years in this field is that I am pretty skeptical of most attempts to quantify economic crime."

This is logical. Britain is a butler, the best one there is, and a good butler disguises his client's misdeeds on the principle that, if you can't see the crime, you won't find the criminal. Britain's commitment to disguising capital flows—to cleansing money of any taint left by how its owner acquired it—has been so complete, and has continued for so long, that even knowing how to begin estimating how much cash its clients have hidden over the years is all but impossible. I wish now that, instead of attempting to answer the question, I had pointed out to Priti Patel, the MP who asked it, that thanks to decades of dedicated butlering Britain has made it unanswerable. She is now home secretary and in charge of the UK's law enforcement apparatus, and thus has the power to change things. Perhaps my words would have lodged in her brain and influenced her to act. Or conversely, perhaps she would have ignored them, thus following the example of her predecessors, who have consistently left Butler Britain's clients in peace. The story of Dmitry Firtash may look extraordinary, but it is only exceptional in that we know it; men in possession of questionable fortunes almost invariably integrate into London society without anyone being any the wiser.

But this raises large questions of its own: how is this not common knowledge? And why is Britain not ostracized from the community of civilized nations as a result? The answer is that there is a large and largely unrecognized gulf between what British politicians say and what British institutions actually do. A few days before I spoke at that committee hearing about Russian oligarchs and their wealth, Prime Minister Theresa May had stood up in Parliament and thundered, "There is no place for these people, or their money, in our country." The MPs behind her rumbled their agreement, but the claim was transparently untrue. There very much is a place for both these people and their money in our country, as I could easily have shown her. The son of one of Putin's oldest friends owns a house within a few minutes' walk of Parliament; his former deputy prime minister owns a duplex apartment a short walk along the Embankment in the other direction. If she'd been prepared to hop into a taxi, I could have shown her a whole fleet of mansions belonging to many of Russia's richest and best-connected men. It takes more than a few words in the House of Commons to wean Britain off its money-laundering habit.

The concept of money laundering—the process by which criminal money is made to look legitimate—dates back to the 1920s, when American law enforcement officers became concerned about the ease with which Mafia gangs were hiding their earnings. But the phenomenon vastly expanded in scope and significance as the financial system globalized in the 1950s and 60s, thanks to the offshore facilities offered first by the City of London, then by its offshoots and finally by its competitors. For decades this money flowed undisturbed, but the increasing prevalence of heroin and crack cocaine and the wealth flowing to the drug cartels finally shocked governments into action. In 1989 the G7 group of wealthy Western countries created the Financial Action Task Force (FATF) to draw up a common approach to tackling drug money and to assess each other's efforts. Over the years the FATF has expanded its focus from drug money to terrorists' money, to kleptocratic money, and now aims to combat money laundering of any kind.

"Why does money laundering matter?" asked Alison Barker of Britain's Financial Conduct Authority in 2019. "It pays for human trafficking. It facilitates drugs. It cheats society of a legitimate economy. Money laundering deprives our schools, hospitals and roads. It causes violence and intimidation—it makes our communities unsafe."

The logic underpinning the FATF's principles is sound, and runs as follows. Criminals commit crimes to earn money, so if we can take away the money, they won't commit the crimes. It's like any job: if you stop paying someone, they won't turn up to work. That sounds simple, but the simplicity is deceptive. Money laundering is not an easy crime to fight, because everyone involved is happy to keep it quiet. The criminal who earns the money and the launderer who passes that money into the financial system are both complicit, while the victim is somewhere else entirely, trying to work out where their money has gone. This means that the normal mechanisms for tackling crime—reports from victims, interviews, looking for clues, etc.—do not work for money laundering. As a result, the countries in the FATF realized quickly that they had to effectively deputize the financial system to help. And this did not just mean bankers, but also lawyers, accountants and any other professional who can move money around. All these gatekeepers have to act as adjuncts to the law enforcement system, not only behaving impeccably themselves but also reporting any suspicions they have about others.

In the three decades since the FATF started out, British politicians have incorporated its principles into law in far-reaching ways—so much so, in fact, that in the last FATF assessment, published in 2018, Britain gained a near-perfect score: "stronger than any country assessed to date," as the government's press release crowed at the time. This was a dispiriting outcome for those of us who were hoping that the FATF would put a bit more pressure on the government to do better, because the system the UK has created is paper-thin. It has all the appearance of tackling financial crime but none of the substance. By the most conservative estimate, hundreds of billions of pounds of criminal money flow through the City of London every year, most of it stolen from vulnerable people in some of the world's poorest countries. The annual cost of organized crime to people in Britain itself is estimated at £37 billion, with fraud costing another £193 billion—that's almost £4,000 for every adult in the country. All this money is laundered, and only a fraction of it is ever recovered. Giving a top score to Britain's efforts is like assessing a hospital solely on how many operations its surgeons perform without asking how many of the patients recover, how many of those patients were ill in the first place, why rates of disease are getting higher and whether doctors are complicit in spreading the diseases they're supposed to be curing. Butler Britain has built an elaborate, expensive and extravagant anti-money-laundering machine, but it is incoherent, ineffective and incompetent. This may look illogical, but actually it makes perfect sense, as doing otherwise would have obliged Britain to turn away clients.

In order to prevent financial professionals laundering money, FATF principles require them to be regulated to ensure they are abiding by the rules that restrict the handling of dirty money. Some countries have a single regulator to do this job, while others separate out the regulation of the legal system, the financial system and accountancy. Britain, however, has chosen a unique path: there are twenty-two different organizations empowered with regulating professionals, plus the Gambling Commission (for casinos), the Financial Conduct Authority (for banks) and Her Majesty's Revenue and Customs (for anyone not otherwise regulated), which makes a total of twenty-five. A couple of years ago the government was concerned about the resulting incoherence and created a super-regulator to regulate most but not all of the other regulators, thus bringing the total to twenty-six. Despite the supposed rationalization brought by the super-regulator, which was successful in the same way that bolting an extra wheel to a car makes it go faster, the system remains baffling. Lawyers have different regulators depending on whether they're barristers, advocates or solicitors, and on whether they're in England and Wales, Scotland or Northern Ireland. Accountants have fourteen different regulators—the Association of Account Technicians, the Association of Chartered Certified Accountants, the Association of International Accountants, the Association of Taxation Technicians, etc., etc., etc., which they can choose between more or less at will, although they don't have to be regulated by any of them if they don't want to be, since anyone can call him- or herself an accountant if they wish.

Britain has essentially outsourced responsibility for stopping money laundering to the money launderers, and is failing to stop dirty money as a result. Much of the time the same bodies tasked with regulating professionals' financial transactions are also charged with lobbying government on their behalf, while also relying on those same professionals' membership fees to keep solvent. "The vast majority of sectors are performing very badly in terms of identifying and reporting money laundering," a Transparency International report from five years ago said. And not much has changed in the years since. According to analysis from the FCA from 2019, almost a quarter of these regulators were doing no supervision at all, almost a fifth had not identified who they needed to supervise and fully 90 percent had not collected the information they needed in order to identify the riskiest companies on their lists. "We were told, particularly in the accountancy sector, that professional bodies believed their members would leave if they took robust enforcement action," the FCA said. Imagine trying to stage a game of football if, when the referee blew his whistle, the players could leave to join a different game, and the referee would lose his job. Expecting sophisticated financial professionals to submit to voluntary law enforcement is clearly a bad way to fight crime.

This is not yet, however, the most surprising aspect of Britain's anti-money-laundering regime. To me, the single weirdest element of this odd state of affairs is the role it provides to the Church of England. Before I start on this, I'd like to make clear I have nothing against the Church of England, and I recognize that Christianity has had sound views on the regulation of the financial sector ever since Jesus drove the money changers out of the Temple. I have two good friends who are vicars, and they do tireless work helping right the wrongs of society, including trying to help disadvantaged parishioners access the banking system. They would, however, be the first to admit that the financial sector has become significantly more complex since the first century AD, and their own expertise does not extend to exposing the misdeeds of sophisticated money launderers.

And yet, buried at tenth place in the long list of money-laundering supervisors empowered with ensuring the cleanliness of Britain's financial system is the Faculty Office of the Archbishop of Canterbury, an anomalous outgrowth of the Anglican Church housed in a honey-gold Gothic Revival building adjacent to Westminster Abbey, which assumed various regulatory roles when Henry VIII broke with the pope in 1533 and which has clung on to them ever since. Specifically, it's in charge of notaries, members of an ancient and rather withered branch of the legal profession who play a role in some property transactions. It is a tiny regulator—there are fewer than a thousand notaries in England and Wales, compared to 150,000 solicitors—but it is nevertheless tasked with helping to defend the twenty-first-century financial system against criminals. Finding out that the Archbishop of Canterbury's Faculty Office oversees part of the financial system thanks to a deal cooked up by Thomas Cromwell five centuries ago to help the king get a divorce is a little like discovering that the Worshipful Society of Apothecaries is in charge of vaccinations, or that the Cinque Ports of Essex, Kent and Sussex are responsible for patrolling coastal waters. It's the kind of anachronism that suggests that the people overseeing the system care more about appearance than results.

"If you were starting from a blank piece of paper, then clearly I suspect you wouldn't end up with what we've got now," said Neil Turpin, chief clerk of the Faculty Office and the man ultimately responsible for ensuring notaries stick to the rules. "But we're not. We are where we are."

His inspectors, who are senior notaries, check up on around twenty notarial practices a year, but there are 700 such practices, so each one will only be inspected every three and a half decades, or just once in the average notary's professional life, which is clearly not much of a deterrent to bad behavior and means the integrity of the profession is dependent not on the inspectors finding bad behavior but on notaries reporting it themselves. Like other financial professionals, if they see something suspicious, they are obliged to file a Suspicious Activity Report (SAR) to alert the authorities. "We do collect data on how many SARs are issued by notaries each year. There's normally about a dozen. There are some who are clearly concerned and make reports," Turpin said.

Turpin is enthusiastic and friendly, and loves his job; he is a lawyer married to a priest, and a former church warden, so the job is a pretty perfect fit. He stumbled into it after seeing an advert in the *Church Times*: "successful candidate will have a knowledge of the workings of the Church of England; a legal background would be helpful but not essential." The problem with this system is implicit in that last comment.

As he explained, if financial professionals are concerned, they make reports, and that is as it should be. But what about financial professionals who are not concerned because they are complicit in laundering money? They keep quiet, which means law enforcement has no idea what they're up to. The system is a little like relying on the church confessional to fight organized crime: you'll hear a lot of people grumbling about their neighbors, but very little about mafia hitmen. And for the same reason, as Mark Hayward, of the estate agents' professional body Propertymark, explained, "Some people are afraid that if they make a SAR, three years later, at nine o'clock on a Saturday night, there will be a knock on the door and someone will be there with a shotgun wanting to know why."

Britain's entire system for regulating money laundering is therefore reliant on money launderers blowing the whistle on criminals, with no prospect of any personal benefit from doing so, and in full knowledge of the fact they'll face retribution if the criminals find out. Unsurprisingly, therefore, not many whistles get blown. In 2019–20 lawyers filed 3,006 Suspicious Activity Reports, which was a slight increase on the previous year's total, but not very many if you consider how many billions of pounds of dirty money is moving through the financial system each year. Accountants filed a few more—just over 5,000—while estate agents and "high value dealers" (auctioneers, for example) filed around 1,000 between them. As one senior law enforcement source, who is long past being shocked by this, put it when we were chatting over a beer, "We rely on people being diligently suspicious, but there's not much money in being diligently suspicious, so . . ." He shrugged.

Actually, it's worse than that, because he was talking about lawyers, and they are only part of the problem. While lawyers and estate agents are under-reporting their suspicions ("They are paid on results, and would it be in their interests to submit a report if there is a particularly large fee at the end of it?" asked one estate agent rhetorically in evidence to a parliamentary committee), bankers are doing the opposite. They are sending in so many SARs that the system is swamped. In 2019–20 financial institutions filed 546,976 reports, which is more than one a minute, for every minute of the year, and the vast majority of these come from banks. The reason for this is simple. Banks operate internationally, which means they use dollars and are desperately worried about getting into trouble with the US Department of Justice, which likes to impose fines with nine zeros at the end.

After the DoJ fined HSBC $1.9 billion for laundering Mexican drug money in 2012, it totally overhauled its compliance apparatus, spending a billion dollars on a system that is able to monitor more than half a billion transactions a month and automatically alerts bank employees to anything that could be considered dodgy. That generates alerts on about 450,000 transactions, which are checked by staff members who then pass on anything that could conceivably be deemed suspicious to the authorities. Every other London-based bank does the same at a total cost to the financial sector of about £5 billion a year, which creates a vast surge of spam, which piles into the UK National

Crime Agency's Financial Intelligence Unit and is increasing by around 20 percent each year. This is an expensive exercise for the banks, but it's like paying an insurance premium to avoid the risk of catastrophe. Banks after all are in the business of offloading risk, and if any of them gets hauled up by the DoJ, they can point out—entirely correctly—how compliant they have been. This doesn't mean they like it. On the contrary, they get extremely frustrated by the waste of time and money.

"The current system diverts too much resource toward low value compliance activity that does little to detect criminals or protect customers," said a report by UK Finance, which lobbies on behalf of the financial sector, in a submission to Parliament. "There are increasing compliance and reporting obligations which are not matched by an uplift in economic crime prevention."

A 2017 report from the European Police Agency—Europol—totted up how many SARs had been sent in for each EU member state between 2006 and 2014. The UK's finance sector is bigger than those in other European countries, but it's still remarkable that Britain was responsible for 2.3 million SARs over that period, which is more than the total for Germany, France, Italy, Spain, Luxembourg, Ireland and twenty other member states all added together. The only country that came close to Britain's total was the Netherlands, and that was solely due to an anomalous Dutch policy that obliged money transfer businesses to report a transaction to the authorities if it was worth more than €2,000.

When the Law Commission looked at the system, it concluded that it was driven by financial professionals covering themselves against prosecution rather than trying to fight financial crime. "We must have a regime in place that allows law enforcement agencies to investigate and disrupt money laundering at an early stage," said David Ormerod, a senior barrister who looked at the SARs regime for the commission. "But the reporting scheme isn't working as well as it should. Enforcement agencies are struggling with a significant number of low-quality reports and criminals could be slipping through the net."

The commission had some recommendations for the government, but the problem is the whole system. Everyone involved wants to minimize the risk of being prosecuted. For big institutions with US operations, that means reporting everything; for professionals without any prospect of being targeted by the Americans, that means keeping quiet. Very occasionally something unexpected comes along to upset this calculation, and exposes how far removed it is from any efforts to actually stop suspicious money, but they are extremely rare.

Such an unexpected event was the media storm in April 2016 that journalists called the Panama Papers. Sourced from a leak of millions of emails to and from the Panamanian law firm Mossack Fonseca (the outfit that did so much to bring business to the BVI back in the 1980s), the documents revealed how wealthy and powerful people had hidden illicit financial activities deep in the system for years. One of the many revelations was how a London law firm had helped the daughters of Azerbaijan's president create offshore structures to invest in UK property. Azerbaijan's current president took over the presidency from his father, and the whole first family has done very well out of its decades at the top of the ex-Soviet oil-rich republic. Like many rich people they have enjoyed spending time in London, where they bought luxury houses. Selling them properties was all in a day's work for Butler Britain, but under money-laundering laws they count as "politically exposed persons," whose wealth should be given extra scrutiny to ensure it does not derive from corruption. And that did not happen, as the *Guardian* revealed.

The solicitor concerned, Khalid Mohammed Sharif of Child & Child, did not even do cursory checks on the two women before agreeing to act on their behalf. It was just one of many scandals exposed by the Panama Papers but it provoked a rare thing: a disciplinary hearing against a British professional in the UK, and not just any British professional, but a member of the elite.

Child & Child is a top-end law firm, with offices a couple of hundred meters from Buckingham Palace. It is very much not the kind of fraud-mill that might be expected to launder cash, but it was remarkably blasé about accepting potentially criminal money. The Solicitors Regulation Authority's ruling in Sharif's case revealed that he only filed a SAR on the transaction a month after the *Guardian* had told the world about it, so the report was clearly a response to the article rather than to any actual suspicions. In his evidence to the tribunal Sharif admitted that not only had he failed to conduct even an internet search on his clients to ascertain whether there were any corruption allegations leveled against them or their family (which there are), but he failed to have any direct communication with them at all.

"Warning signs disclosed an objective risk that money laundering was taking place. In particular, the size of the payments, the source of the funds being Azerbaijan, and the use of offshore companies presented a significant risk," the ruling stated.

Sharif's defense was that he was just doing what everyone else did. "His office was surrounded by multi-million-pound properties and he dealt with some of the most expensive property in London . . . from the respondent's perspective, there was nothing unusual about the transaction. The high value and use of offshore companies were commonplace." In mitigation he claimed there was nothing about the names of his clients to suggest they were politically exposed, an unconvincing excuse given they shared a surname with the president of Azerbaijan.

The SRA fined him £45,000, which is better than nothing, but the ruling revealed that its primary concern was whether Sharif had damaged the reputation of his profession and made no mention at all of the damage that money laundering does to the victims of corruption in Azerbaijan. It took comfort from the fact that "no client had suffered loss as a result" of Sharif's conduct, which is particularly perverse because the whole point of filing a suspicious activity report is to allow the authorities to confiscate criminal wealth. Clients are *supposed* to suffer loss. The SRA did not even block Sharif from working as a solicitor, so he was free to return to his desk and do more deals, and there was no separate criminal prosecution. If the whole episode has a motto, it was "Don't get caught."

It's hard to know if this is typical of the UK's approach to regulation, since there have been so few cases, but what fines there have been show Britain is remarkably lenient in comparison with the US, where HSBC was stung for almost $2 billion. A London money-transfer company was fined £7.9 million in 2019, but that was an outlier, since few other fines have breached six figures. Countrywide estate agency was forced to pay £215,000 for its failings in 2018, which sounds like a lot until you realize it has annual revenues of more than £600 million. A year later, the estate agents Purplebricks was fined £266,793, which again won't have put much of a dent in that year's income of almost £50 million.

"The average annual level of anti-money-laundering monetary penalty in the banking sector—the industry identified by the UK government as having the highest money-laundering risk—has been approximately £8 million. Compared to the overall scale of expected money laundering in the UK and the profits made by the financial services firms from this money, it remains questionable whether the level of fines levied currently has a sufficient deterrent effect," concluded Transparency International with careful understatement.

Ministers responsible for law enforcement find Britain's failure to stop criminal money extremely frustrating, but suffer from the fact that it is very difficult to measure how much wealth is being laundered, since it is so well hidden. As a result, they focus on what they can measure—the number of SARs being generated—and fixate on the need for ever more of them, as if all it will take to stop the torrent is just one more report. "They all need to do much more. It isn't rocket science to make out SAR's!" tweeted Ben Wallace, the minister responsible for economic crime, in 2019 in a classic example of how focusing on process rather than outcomes can have perverse consequences. The authorities are swamped by the volume of submissions they receive, and lawyers and accountants grumble that they get no feedback or gratitude for the unpaid work they do to help law enforcement, which is understandable but also unsurprising. The authorities can hardly be expected to write more than half a million personalized thank-you letters every year.

"The UK Anti-money-laundering regime appears to be suffering from an identity crisis at present," said the Institute of Chartered Accountants in England and Wales (one of the many regulators of accountants) in 2018. "The purpose of the regime is no longer clear. Is it designed to address all instances of financial crime (e.g. omitting £50 from a tax return), or the most serious (billions of drug money entering the London financial system)?"

I don't think it's intended to do either of those things; I

think it's intended to give the impression of extreme activity while doing nothing to stop the butler from helping his clients get away with money laundering. If that wasn't the case, Britain would have upgraded its system for handling SARs years ago. The software system that receives suspicious activity reports, which is rather endearingly called ELMER, was designed for about 20,000 documents a year and yet is now expected to handle twenty-five times that many. That is clearly far too many for actual people to read, so to try to bring order to this flood the Financial Intelligence Unit (FIU) asks that the most important alerts be coded differently—they are called defense against money laundering (DAML) SARs, and filing one protects you from being prosecuted for money laundering—but there are now more than 60,000 even of these in a year. Officers have a week to respond to a DAML SAR, once it's in, and the FIU has fewer than 200 employees. If they were doing nothing but checking these reports, every member of staff would need to be processing one every working day of the year, which is clearly impossible, considering that they deal with complex transactions.

"I am trying to work out what the deterrent factor is for you and your colleagues in the industry," asked an MP of Henry Pryor, an estate agent and regular media commentator on property matters.

"Tiny," Pryor replied.

In the government's defense, it is not just measuring money laundering that is hard; prosecuting it is difficult too. Before you can show that money has been laundered, you need to prove that it derives from criminal activity. To do that, you need evidence that can stand up in a British court, which is difficult to obtain from many foreign jurisdictions where the courts are politically controlled. If foreign jurisdictions do provide evidence then defense lawyers can, quite justifiably, point out that the evidence is proof more of their client being out of political favor than being a criminal—the Kremlin, for example, does not prosecute its friends. On top of that, offshore shell companies such as those registered in the British Virgin Islands or in even more opaque tax havens like Nevis or Nevada disguise the ownership of assets so effectively that it is often all but impossible to see who owns something. Britain may be the best butler in the world, but it is not the only one, and wealthy clients will employ several to make sure they have the best service available when it comes to hiding their wealth.

Thanks to the work of Transparency International and Global Witness, as well as the publicity generated by our London Kleptocracy Tours, which began in 2016, many MPs have become increasingly concerned about Britain's failure to do anything about the dirty money flowing through its system. It was to answer their concerns and to cut through the problems created by criminals hiding their wealth in multiple jurisdictions that the government brought in a new tool, the unexplained wealth order (UWO), which came into effect in early 2018. Since UWOs passed into law just before the screening of the *McMafia* television show, they inevitably came to be dubbed the McMafia law, and were widely hyped in the press. Ministers revelled in the unaccustomed praise and their new image as sheriffs riding into London Town to drive out the bad guys.

"This government is determined not to let organized criminals—like the McMafia mob—act with impunity," wrote Wallace, the minister for economic crime, in the *Sun*. "Theresa May is to launch a major crackdown on the 'dirty money' that Vladimir Putin's McMafia-style cronies have sheltered in London," declared the *Daily Mail*.

UWOs are a good idea, and at the time I found myself in the unexpected position of being non-cynical about a British government initiative. UWOs had the potential to finally turn the country away from butlering. They are designed to work by allowing the authorities to cut through all the offshore defenses and political obfuscation that can be built around criminal wealth to stop the authorities from confiscating it. If served with a UWO, the owner of wealth has to explain where it came from, whereas normally prosecutors have to show that it's criminal. In its assessment at the time the Home Office estimated that, once the law had bedded in, about twenty UWOs would be issued each year, at a relatively low cost to law enforcement of no more than £1.5 million over the next decade, set against the recovery of at least £6 million of criminal wealth. That meant the government would even make a profit from the law.

National Crime Agency officers were excited about these new powers and privately canvassed many of Britain's leading anti-corruption activists about which oligarchs they should be targeting first, since they were determined to win their first cases. Early victories would not only establish relevant precedents but also make clear that London was no longer a safe space for dodgy money. But 2018's first UWO was a bit of a disappointment, being targeted at property owned by the wife of an Azeri banker who had already been jailed in Baku. In Azerbaijan he had been prosecuted for embezzlement, but since it is a place dominated by a small clique of oligarchs, his real crime is more likely to have involved falling out with the ruling family. He wasn't exactly the kind of whale that the government had said it was going after; UWOs were supposed to target bigger cetaceans than that.

Fortunately, however, 2019 brought better news, with the

announcement of an unexplained wealth order against properties linked to the ruling family of Kazakhstan, a post-Soviet kleptocracy that had been dominated by former president Nursultan Nazarbayev since independence in 1991. Back in 2015 Global Witness had published an extensive report into London properties that appeared to be owned either by the president's grandson or by Rakhat Aliyev, who had divorced the president's daughter Dariga Nazarbayeva in 2007 but then, shortly before the report came out, killed himself in an Austrian prison cell while awaiting trial for murder. It was true that Aliyev had fallen out with his ex-father-in-law and been driven out of the first family, which meant that targeting him wasn't quite like going after a top-ranking kleptocrat, but he had been notorious for using his position as head of Kazakhstan's security service to extort wealth and steal businesses, so his was precisely the kind of "McMafia money" London should not be sheltering. At last there was the kind of action that the government had promised when UWOs were introduced. If dirty money, even if it belonged to a sundered offshoot of the ruling family of an oil-rich kleptocratic state, could be driven out of London, it would be an unmistakable signal that Britain was getting out of the butlering business.

By this stage of the book, you will probably not be too surprised to discover all did not go as the optimists wished.

Ownership of the properties involved—two houses and two apartments—was disguised behind two Panamanian foundations, a foundation registered on the Dutch island of Curaçao and a shell company registered on the obscure British island of Anguilla. The UWOs, therefore, were directed at these shell structures plus the solicitor who appeared to run the foundations rather than at any named tycoon, but the NCA's supporting documents made clear its investigators suspected the properties had been bought with Aliyev's cash. Shortly after a court agreed to issue the UWOs, however, the NCA received a 268-page letter from the famously potent London law firm Mishcon de Reya (tagline: "It's business. But it's personal.") informing them that the properties had not been owned by Rakhat Aliyev at all. Instead, both of the apartments and one of the houses belonged to his ex-wife Dariga Nazarbayeva, while the other house belonged to their son Nurali. They had purchased the properties after she and Aliyev's divorce had been finalized, the letter said, so the source of the money could not have been Aliyev.

Mishcon de Reya contested everything that the NCA was trying to do, bringing in an expert to demolish its understanding of the structure of Panamanian foundations and providing Kazakh court documents to prove that its clients' wealth was entirely independent of Aliyev's. Reading the final judgment is like reading the report of a match between Manchester City and Hereford FC: the embattled non-league side did its best, but its players were swept aside by superior skills, fitness, knowledge and resources.

"The NCA case presented at the *ex parte* hearing was flawed by inadequate investigation into some obvious lines of inquiry," the judge concluded in April 2020 in an extremely critical assessment. "Furthermore, I consider that the NCA failed to carry out a fair-minded evaluation of the new information provided." She discharged the UWOs, and thus ended any bid by the NCA to confiscate the properties. The agency said it would contest the decision, but an appeal court judge refused it permission to do so on the grounds that "the appeal has no real prospect of success and there is no other compelling reason why an appeal should be heard."

It was a total defeat, a humiliation, the kind of huge scoreline that makes you wonder if the teams were playing football or rugby, made all the worse by the fact there were so many open goals presented to the NCA, which its investigators apparently failed to notice. Even if the properties did not belong to Aliyev but to his ex-wife, it surely would have been at least worth asking how the daughter of the head of a country where the average person earns £600 a month had managed to amass enough wealth to buy a London property empire valued by some newspapers at £80 million. That certainly looks to me like wealth that needs explanation. And if she was going to rely on Kazakh court documents to show that she had no involvement in any of Aliyev's crimes, then wasn't it at least worth questioning the legitimacy of those courts' judgments, given that they came from a judicial system ultimately controlled by her dad? These are just two of many points in the judgment where I scribbled exclamation marks in the margin, but which the NCA did not seem to feel warranted further investigation.

Dariga Nazarbayeva and her son presented evidence to show they were successful self-made entrepreneurs, and the court agreed with them. It is striking how different the agency's submissions were to the responses of the FBI every time Firtash's legal team tried to have the Chicago court case dismissed: the NCA made no effort to analyze the nature of Kazakhstan's politics or economy and was almost embarrassingly reliant on the Global Witness report for information.

There is only one use of "kleptocracy" in the document the NCA laid before the court, and just two uses of "corruption." In the final judgment, "president" features more than fifty times in the context of the organizational structuring of the Panama and Curaçao foundations that owned the properties, but only once in the context of Dariga Nazarbayeva's dad. It is perhaps indicative of how little thought the NCA obliged the judge to put into this that in this single reference she spelled President Nazarbayev's name wrong.

I know one academic expert on corruption who was so bewildered by the NCA's capitulation that he speculated—not entirely in jest—that it must have been ordered from on high: perhaps senior officers received a call from Britain's embassy in Kazakhstan asking them to present a deliberately weak case? I am sure that did not happen, but the real reason for the agency's failure is even more troubling. The NCA may or may not have had a strong case against the origins of this wealth, but they had no prospect of making it. It simply doesn't have the resources to go up against a law firm like Mishcon de Reya, and neither do any of Britain's law enforcement agencies. They have been starved for so long that they are demoralized by defeat and hollowed out by the steady departure of their officers to higher-paid positions elsewhere.

In its report into Russian interference in the UK published in July 2020, a month after the NCA's request to appeal the Nazarbayeva decision was rejected, parliament's Intelligence and Security Committee quoted NCA Director General Lynne Owens as conceding that her officers might not be able to use UWOs against oligarchs at all anymore. "We are, bluntly, concerned about the impact on our budget, because these are wealthy people with access to the best lawyers," she said. "I've got a very good legal team based within the National Crime Agency but had a lot of resource dedicated out of my relatively small resource envelope on that work." Translation: Britain, a G7 country with an economy worth nearly $3 trillion, is not prepared to pay its law enforcement agencies enough to investigate dirty money. Contrast this with the FBI's approach to Dmitry Firtash, whom they investigated for five years before indicting him, and whom they have kept battling despite his retaining a ferocious US legal team that has fought every step they have taken, and you see how feeble the British agency is.

But this is not surprising, considering how little money it has. The NCA's International Corruption Unit has an annual budget of just over £4.3 million. A judge ordered it to pay half a million pounds immediately to cover the legal costs incurred by Dariga Nazarbayeva and Nurali, and it is expected to have to pay a million more before it is done. Even before paying its own costs, therefore, this case alone will cost the International Corruption Unit more than a third of its entire annual budget. The UWO is a powerful weapon, but if enforcement agencies lack the resources they need to deploy it, it will sit on a shelf gathering dust. It's like giving a hospital a powerful new scanner but not enough money to employ technicians, or like giving the navy a pair of aircraft carriers but not enough money to buy any planes. From the government's perspective, UWOs were a triumph, garnering article after article about their tough stance against kleptocrats and their kleptobrats. From Butler Britain's perspective, they were a triumph too: rich clients and their children can continue to enjoy their wealth without worrying about being disturbed. From a law enforcement perspective, however, they were a dud.

One law enforcement source told me he was so fed up he was tempted to "move to a bank and add a zero" to his pay packet. Experienced police detectives can double their salaries by crossing over into the private sector. And the National Crime Agency, which was set up in 2013 supposedly as Britain's answer to the Federal Bureau of Investigation, is in even worse shape. Its officers work alongside those from regular police forces, but their supposedly elite status is rewarded with salaries 14 percent lower than that of colleagues in local forces. In a report on staffing published in 2019 the NCA revealed that about a tenth of its workforce leaves every year, which inevitably lessens its effectiveness, and the departures largely arise because of dissatisfaction over pay.

The phenomenon is even more concentrated in the agency's Command and Control Center, which is in charge of coordinating the response to Britain's most serious crimes but which loses its entire workforce on average every three years, with many of its agents poached by banks. The NCA has effectively become a training ground for private sector compliance officers, who can instantly earn salaries 20 to 30 percent higher than in the supposedly elite crime-fighting force. "People are leaving in droves; there's just not the money or motivation to stay," one source told me.

After the collapse of the Dariga Nazarbayeva case, one NCA financial investigator told the *Mail on Sunday* it was a waste of time trying to take on oligarchs if they employ top-flight law firms, an admission that will ensure that—if there are any more UWOs like this one—that that is precisely what the oligarchs will do. But it looks unlikely that the NCA will try to take on such a wealthy adversary again. The NCA planned to bring 200 UWOs over a decade and predicted a total cost of around £1.5 million but blew more than that on this single case, which ended in a defeat that may have doomed the UK's entire anti-money-laundering strategy. Depressingly, this possibility was predicted in 2017 when Parliament debated the UWOs. An amendment tabled by Nigel Mills MP would have capped the costs that respondents could incur so they could not outgun the NCA by engaging expensive lawyers, all ultimately to be paid by the taxpayer. The government, however, rejected this idea, arguing that the prospect of being forced to pay the respondent's costs in the event of an unsuccessful UWO would be an important check on the state abusing its new powers. And so it has turned out. In fact, the prospect will stop the state using the new powers at all.

Alarmingly, this is not even the first time this has happened. In the early 2000s the British government—seeking to emulate successes overseas, particularly in Ireland and South Africa— created the Assets Recovery Agency, which would act as a single body tasked with confiscating ill-gotten gains. Launched on a wave of hype about how much it could achieve and how little it would cost, in much the same way as UWOs, it singularly failed to deliver. In 2008, after just five years in which it failed to meet punishingly unrealistic targets, the agency was abolished and its powers split between the various agencies that are failing to do much with them now. According to a paper published by the think tank RUSI in 2019, the Crown Prosecution Service— one of these agencies—used the powers it inherited just once in the eleven years that had elapsed since the collapse of the last time that Butler Britain set its enforcement agencies up to fail.

What is particularly disastrous about the continued failure to treat financial crime as seriously as it deserves is that, even when standing still, the authorities keep falling behind. The job of private sector compliance officers is to send SARs to the National Crime Agency's Financial Intelligence Unit. However, as a result of the poaching of its officers, the NCA lacks experi- enced employees able to investigate the crimes being reported. This could have been predicted, since it's a logical result of the demands placed on private companies to report ever more SARs and on ministers' failure to pay NCA officers a salary suf- ficient to keep them in their posts. This is what happens if you underpay your investigators. And it's not a secret. Parliamen- tary reports have been exposing this reality for at least a decade, and yet the government has done almost nothing to improve the situation.

Criminal wealth is reinvested, which makes criminals richer and more potent adversaries, while companies in the City poach law enforcement officers to work in their compliance departments. It's like expecting the army to fight a war against an adversary that gets stronger all the time, while its service men and women are continually lured away to work as private security contractors or, worse still, as mercenaries for their former adversaries. You don't have to be a conspiracy theorist to start wondering if there isn't something going on, because this is a system that is not working at all.

Back in 2013 the National Audit Office calculated that of every hundred pounds earned by criminals just twenty-six pence is ever confiscated. And if anything that understates the failure, because it doesn't take into account the far larger volume of illicit wealth that is stolen overseas and either imported to the UK or laundered through the British financial system on its way elsewhere. "The relatively low level of fines, and the low likelihood of being caught, means that fines for breaching anti-money-laundering rules can be seen as the cost of doing business, rather than being dissuasive," said Global Witness in a report in 2018.

The government has been promising to replace ELMER, the IT system that receives all the SARs filed, with a more modern system since at least 2015, but has so far failed to do so, perhaps because such a system would cost, according to some estimates, half a billion pounds. And there already isn't enough money to keep trained staff working in law enforcement agencies. With banks expected to spend ever more money on compliance, they need ever more compliance officers, and the best place to find them is in law enforcement agencies. "I have a theoretical headcount of forty, I have only thirty people in post. I cannot recruit and keep the right people," said the Serious Fraud Office's

Mark Thompson in 2016. "It is very difficult. If we were able to deal with that I would have the capacity to be slightly more proactive than reactive in the way we operate."

A butler's job is to help his clients get away with their misdeeds, not help their victims achieve justice. But this causes a problem: what happens if one of Butler Britain's clients is defrauded, and the perpetrator exploits the country's refusal to adequately investigate or prosecute financial crime to get away with it? In other words, what if one of Britain's clients uses its services against another?

Fortunately, Butler Britain has a solution to this problem. Of course it does.

9

"JUSTICE"

Kazakhstan's first decade of independence was tough. It had never been a country before—its borders were sketched out on a map by Soviet planners in the 1930s—and it had to simultaneously build from scratch a political culture and a capitalist economy. Fortunately for the Kazakhs they managed to avoid the open warfare or extreme dictatorship that scarred some neighboring countries, but that doesn't mean existence was easy. Life expectancy fell, hundreds of thousands of people emigrated, millions more fell into poverty, and wealth was concentrated in the hands of a tiny elite with close ties to the ruling family. In the early 2000s, however, the economy began to pick up, and prosperity became (slightly) more widely shared. Oil prices were high, and money was cheap, so banks lent freely. That caused a construction and consumption boom, which in turn drove growth in all sorts of related sectors, which is where Argyn Khassenov saw his opportunity. The owners of the big new shops and the builders of the smart new buildings wanted to protect themselves from unforeseen risks, which meant they needed insurance.

"My job was to find clients for the insurance companies, and I earned a commission from that. That's how I earned my money," he explained over the phone from Kazakhstan (we were chatting during one of the COVID lockdowns, and I'd had to cancel my plans to fly out and visit him). "At that time there was a boom, a construction surge. Everyone was earning good money."

But this caused Khassenov the same problem that had afflicted people earning significant sums of money in ex-colonies back in the 1960s: what should he do with it? He could of course deposit it in a bank, where bankers would lend it out to other people who could build new businesses. That was nice in theory, but he didn't trust the local banks, and with good cause: an overextended bank collapsed in 2006, precipitating a major crisis that forced the government to take over much of the financial system. The Kazakh government wasn't too dreadful by ex-Soviet standards, but it was still dominated by the light-fingered Nazarbayev family, and sensible people were reluctant to trust it with wealth that, fifty years before, would have been called funk money.

This is a scenario that has played out untold times over the last few decades: someone gets rich, is worried their wealth could be taken from them and looks for a safe place to put it. And that takes them to the offshore financial system that exists everywhere and nowhere at the same time, which even the best-resourced governments struggle to access. If Khassenov could get his wealth offshore, he'd never have to worry again, so he looked for someone who could help him do that. And that's how he met Andrey Kulich, a Russian living in the UK who came highly recommended by business contacts.

"I decided to take payment abroad, and for this I decided to open a company," said Khassenov. "Andrey Kulich promised to open a company in Hong Kong, to register everything there, to get all the licenses for the company."

Kulich's suggestions were quite complicated and involved creating a network of interconnected companies in Hong Kong and the UK that would in turn be owned by a company in the BVI. Via these companies, Khassenov would have a bank account at a Hong Kong branch of Standard Chartered, the London-based global bank. He would as before find clients in Kazakhstan for multinational insurance companies, but under Kulich's plan those companies would now pay him in Hong Kong, so he would no longer have to worry about the Kazakh banking system. It looked sensible, and in September 2007 Khassenov paid Kulich about £20,000 for setting it all up and booked a flight to Hong Kong, where he would meet the bankers, sign the documents and get the new venture under way.

In Hong Kong, Khassenov was met by Kulich's son Aleksandr, who at the time was studying at a Chinese university and had agreed to show his father's client around, Kulich apparently being busy with other commitments. They traveled to the Bank of China building, a renowned Hong Kong landmark, and took the lift to the twenty-fifth floor. "There were lots of people, tables everywhere. It looked very busy. I suspected nothing—it looked just like it should. We were escorted into a separate room where a representative of Standard Chartered greeted us. He gave us his business card," explained Khassenov. "Everything looked great. People came in, gave us business cards, showed us everything, explained it, brought papers to sign, all the standard procedures for opening an account."

That done, Khassenov returned home, where he awaited confirmation that his bank account was live. It took a few months, but eventually the papers came through, along with instructions for accessing the online banking portal that would let him control his money. To allow him to do that, he received a random-number generator which ensured that his money could not be accessed by anyone but the account holder. Now he could go online, enter his details, type in the number shown on the device and see the funds he had available. He tested the account by wiring $60,000 to another company he part-owned and, satisfied, gave the details to his clients, asking them in the future to pay him in Hong Kong. "Everything worked, everything was fine," Khassenov said.

He could now sit back confident that his wealth was no longer vulnerable to predators or instability in Kazakhstan, but secure in a global bank in an international financial center in a reliable hard currency. By January 2009 more than a million dollars of Khassenov's money had flowed into the Standard Chartered account, and he could see that reassuring seven-figure total every time he logged on to the website. It was great.

It is presumably obvious from the fact I'm telling this story that the situation was not in fact great. That is an understatement. He was already, without knowing it, the victim of a spectacularly elaborate fraud. If Kulich had been an ordinary conman, he would have pocketed Khassenov's £20,000, stopped replying to his emails and vanished with the cash. But he was more than that. He was an extraordinary conman, and this was an extraordinary con. In fact, the nature of the scam that Khassenov had walked into is so remarkable that I still slightly struggle to accept that it really happened.

"I don't know how much detail Argyn's given you, but anyone would have fallen for it," said Ian Horrocks, a veteran ex-Metropolitan Police detective who we'll meet again in a few paragraphs. "I would have done, and I'm the most suspicious person in the world. It's the most sophisticated online fraud I've ever seen, or that anyone has seen who I've spoken to."

In early 2009 Khassenov decided he wanted to use some of the money, which is when he began to realize he had a problem. For some reason he could not move money out of the account, no matter how hard he tried. He asked Kulich to explain what was happening, and Kulich replied that Standard Chartered's compliance department had concerns that he could be involved in money laundering and had frozen his funds. In order to resolve the issue, Khassenov needed to provide proof of the provenance of his wealth. Khassenov's clients wrote letters explaining where it came from, which should have solved the problem but did not. On the contrary, he received a new message telling him that he was likely to be charged with facilitating money laundering and financing terrorist activities. The FBI, it said, would be seeking his extradition. None of this made sense to Khassenov. He was an insurance agent. He worked with legitimate international companies. He had done nothing wrong. This was clearly a misunderstanding, and he was determined to go and explain it to the nice account manager he had met on the twenty-fifth floor of the Hong Kong skyscraper.

"I said to Andrey Kulich, 'Let's fly to Hong Kong—you go and I'll go—and let's sort this out on the spot. I've got nothing to fear,'" Khassenov told me. "But he replied that I shouldn't go there: 'If you go there, they'll arrest you, put you in jail— you'll do time.'"

Khassenov went anyway, arriving in August 2009. He was surprised to discover that there was no branch of Standard Chartered in the Bank of China skyscraper, but he found a translator and went to another of its offices. There he showed his passport, explained who he was, gave the name of his company, handed over his documentation and said that he wanted to understand the accusations being made against him. The bank employee took his documents, checked his computer terminal, and then came the blow. "He looked in the system, and said, 'Yes, there is that company, but you have no connection to it.' That was when I started to worry."

Over the next few days and weeks, with the aid of a local lawyer, Khassenov unpicked what had happened to him, and every discovery was worse than the one before. There was not, nor had there ever been, a branch of Standard Chartered in the Bank of China building. Those bustling premises on the twenty-fifth floor had been fake, a stage set created to fool people into parting with their money. The account manager, with his convincing manners and authentic-looking business card, had been fake too, as was the accountant who'd helped with the incorporation. The web portal—www.standardchartered-online.org—was false. The random-number security device he'd used to log into his account was fraudulent. The documents for the companies that he thought he owned, they'd been falsified. The various documents showing that these companies were certified by the UK's Financial Services Authority, that the companies had "good standing" and that everything had been agreed with Hong Kong's tax authorities were forged. The suggestions that he was suspected of involvement in money laundering were lies intended to scare him into keeping away from the authorities. Everything was false, from beginning to end. The only thing that was legitimate was the bank account his clients had been paying money into, and he had no control over that.

When Khassenov's lawyer described this scam to me, it initially reminded me of the 1968 film *Only When I Larf*, in which Richard Attenborough and a team of fraudsters create a fake bank branch to fool their victim out of a large check. But as she explained further, I realized that wasn't nearly ambitious enough. This was more like *The Sting*, in which characters played by Paul Newman and Robert Redford create a whole fake betting shop, as well as an elaborate law enforcement charade around it, in order to defraud a Chicago mobster. This was a sting updated for the internet age.

And the worst thing of all—the money was gone. That reassuring banking portal, which had shown him that he still had more than a million dollars in his account, was lying to him. In reality the account now contained a grand total of $63.78. All his money had been stolen. It had been transferred to accounts controlled by a shell company called Billion Bright Trading Limited, and thence had disappeared.

Khassenov confronted Kulich about what had happened. Kulich initially offered to help him find the money in return for more payments and then disappeared altogether. "He stopped calling and didn't reappear. When I sent him text messages, he always said he was ill, that he'd gone to America, that he had some business." Khassenov was on his own, but he was furious and determined to get his money back.

At first he focused on Hong Kong, where he took his plight to the police. Officers investigated for two years, but eventually prosecutors told him there was nothing they could do because the suspect was outside their jurisdiction. He traveled to China in pursuit of Kulich's son but got no more joy from the mainland police than he'd received in Hong Kong. "They said, 'You're a citizen of Kazakhstan, he lives somewhere in England, we know nothing about whatever happened in Hong Kong.' Yes, they kicked me out nicely."

And so in 2012 Khassenov took his campaign to the UK, where he forced the butler to confront the difficult dilemma laid out at the end of the last chapter. Kulich was living in the Midlands and so was already making use of Britain's butlering services: he hid his scams behind its under-regulated financial system, knowing he was safe from its poorly resourced law enforcement system. But Khassenov was a wealthy potential client seeking to employ the same butler. How was Butler Britain to prioritize between the conflicting interests of two warring clients? It is a difficult dilemma but it has, as we shall see, an elegant solution.

Khassenov's first instinct had been to sue Kulich for damages, so he found himself a lawyer. The lawyer told him, however, that the scam sounded more like a criminal matter and advised him to employ a private detective to help him understand exactly what had happened. That led him to Horrocks, the ex-police detective, who was now employed by BGP, a private investigations agency. Horrocks sounds just like a London detective should: committed, rough, cockney-accented, suitably cynical and consistently appalled by what criminals get up to.

"It was without a doubt, the most comprehensive—if that's the right word—complicated cybercrime set-up I'd ever seen," Horrocks told me. "I don't know about a film, but you could make a mini-series on it—it would make *McMafia* look like amateur hour."

Horrocks tried to interest British law enforcement in the crime. First he took the story to the National Crime Agency, which seemed the obvious place, but its agents declined to look into it—according to Horrocks, they blamed lack of resources. Then he called Action Fraud, the central helpline that receives reports of financial crime on behalf of the police and distributes them to the relevant force. Action Fraud referred him to West Midlands Police, where Kulich lived, but its officers didn't want the case either ("too big for them"). After that he tried the City of London Police, which has a role overseeing the financial system of the whole country, but they were no more interested than their colleagues in Birmingham had been ("outside their remit"). It looked like Britain had no more intention of helping than Hong Kong or China had. "It just went into everyone's 'too difficult' tray," Horrocks said. He had to break the news to Khassenov, which wasn't fun.

"At that moment I got a bit cross," Khassenov told me. "I thought, crap, is it really not possible to find justice?"

There was one option left, however, the option that Butler Britain reserves for its wealthiest clients. If the police won't investigate, and if the Crown Prosecution Service won't prosecute, clients can do it for themselves, and that is what Khassenov decided to do. He retained Horrocks's services as an investigator, hired a specialist lawyer and availed himself of his right to bring a private prosecution—a fast-growing but still surprisingly obscure phenomenon, which effectively constitutes a special form of justice reserved for very rich people.

Before I describe the case, I'm going to pause and explain where private prosecutions come from, because they are strange and rather counterintuitive, and before I start I should point out this legal peculiarity exists only in England and Wales; Scotland has a far more sensible system.

The first point to make is that Khassenov was not suing Kulich for damages. Disputes between two individuals are often settled in civil proceedings, when one party sues the other, but that is for relatively minor issues like breach of contract or defamation. If the offense is one sufficiently serious to be deemed a crime against society, it is tried in the criminal courts, which can impose severe punishments but require a far higher standard of proof than civil proceedings. In these cases the police normally investigate and the Crown Prosecution Service prosecute. It is frustrating when they refuse to do so, but buried in the ancient practices of common law is an alternative system.

It is a founding principle of common law that all criminal

offenses are crimes against the Crown since, as one commentator put it in the days before we had a queen, "all offenses are either against the King's peace, or his crown and dignity." It is also a founding principle of common law that anyone can bring a prosecution for a criminal offense and thereby act on behalf of the Crown. Indeed, for many hundreds of years there was no state prosecution authority at all. If someone committed a crime against you, and you wanted justice, you did the prosecution yourself.

It was up to the victim to find witnesses, to bring them to court and to keep them fed; he had to pay the constable to arrest the suspect, he had to pay lawyers and he had to pay court fees for the judge. This was expensive, and the expense naturally made people reluctant to prosecute crimes. Occasionally the government would tinker with the system to try to encourage more victims of crime to come forward, but these largely made things worse. If payments were brought in for witnesses, their testimony was distrusted. If rewards were provided for prosecutors, then juries doubted their motives. "Eighteenth-century England viewed a system of professional police and prosecutors, government-paid and -appointed, as potentially tyrannical and, worse still, French," as one academic writer explains.

In the absence of government, the market came up with some fascinating ways to fight crime, including prosecution associations, whose members pledged to prosecute any crime committed against any one of them, but even that only worked for certain kinds of crime (related to property), and for certain kinds of people (rich ones). Basically, from the criminal's perspective, as long as you avoided targeting extremely wealthy people, you got away with it. The criminal justice system was a blunt and inefficient instrument.

Eventually, in the nineteenth century British politicians came to accept that perhaps it was better to follow the lead of the French than tolerate high levels of murder and theft. If they wanted to fight crime, it was better to pay people to do the job well than rely on amateurs who did the job badly. London gained a professional police force in 1829, and from there the idea spread to the rest of the country. A director of public prosecutions followed half a century later. The investigation and prosecution of crime became professionalized, and the old ways withered away. If you wanted justice, you reported the crime to the police then relied on the state to do the rest for you. Prosecutions became public.

However, this is Britain, where politicians like to add layers to the constitution without mucking out the old ones, so they did not abolish the original system when they created the new one. Private prosecutions remained possible, and a small number continued, often brought by charities like the Royal Society for the Protection of Animals or the National Society for the Prevention of Cruelty to Children. No one gave this too much thought, and when they did, tended to approve of it as a relic of ancient liberties, a reminder that the English are born free (unlike, say, the French). The idea that it is tyrannical to give the authorities a monopoly on criminal prosecution has deep roots, and private prosecutions were considered "a useful constitutional safeguard against capricious, corrupt or biased failure or refusal of those authorities to prosecute offenders against the criminal law," as one judge put it. Private prosecutions were basically a harmless anachronism, like the royal family or Channel 5.

However, after the 2007–8 financial crisis the government decided the country needed "austerity" and cut public expenditure to try to save money. One area that ministers decided was ripe for cuts was prosecuting crime. This was politically easy; the government would be saving money on lawyers, who are—according to stereotype—already well paid. Why should these fat cats gain money from the state when the rest of us are tightening our belts?

Depriving the criminal justice system of money had immediate and far-reaching negative consequences, however. Police forces stopped showing interest in cases of financial crime, which were complex, resource-intensive and lacked the urgency of the kind of crimes reported in the tabloids. In the years after 2010 the Crown Prosecution Service increasingly blamed lack of resources for its failure to bring cases, particularly with regard to fraud. What resources there were tended to go into investigating and prosecuting the crimes with the most public resonance, which meant violent crime. So, just as the spread of online banking and payments made fraud easier than it had ever been, the government abdicated responsibility for prosecuting it. According to academic research, 98.5 percent of fraud cases go unreported to the police, and of the few that are reported only 0.4 percent result in a criminal sanction.

Ever more complaints have flowed into Action Fraud, the central hotline, but it has come to function—just as the SARs database has—more as a filing system than as a launchpad for investigations. Its managers have even admitted—as with SARS— that they don't read all the reports that come in. According to Horrocks, who still has contacts with police officers and sees what they're prepared to investigate when he takes his clients' cases to them, the authorities only get involved in a case if it will earn them good press coverage. "If there's a celebrity involved, Simon Cowell or whatever-her-name-is Ecclestone, the police are all over it," he said, "but if old Mrs. Smith gets defrauded on a phone scam, and every penny to her name has gone, which might be only a few thousand quid but which has destroyed her life, no one looks at that."

This is clearly great news for many of Butler Britain's clients. If UK law enforcement had been adequately resourced, perhaps Dmitry Firtash would not have had such a comfortable few years as a philanthropist in Knightsbridge and assorted lawyers and accountants might be less ready to launder money for the world's crooks. But it is bad news for Britain's other clients if they find themselves preyed upon by fraudsters, who have nowhere to turn for justice.

And that explains the remarkable rebirth of the private prosecution.

With the prospect of publicly funded investigations and prosecutions receding, wealthy individuals have taken to funding their own proceedings, as they did in the eighteenth century. And often that means they turn to Edmonds Marshall McMahon (EMM), a niche law firm set up in 2012 as a direct response to austerity with a deliberate and specific focus on private prosecutions. Its three founders are experienced prosecutors who previously worked for the Department of Health, the Crown Prosecution Service and the Serious Fraud Office. "I worked as a government prosecutor for many years, and I know what it was like when I first started. We had resources to do the job properly," Tamlyn Edmonds, one of those founders, told me. "I had the time to work on big cases that I could dedicate myself to, and then suddenly that was taken away—there was more and more work piled on prosecutors. People become demoralized. It didn't work."

If state bodies wouldn't investigate and prosecute financial crime, then EMM would. And so, after Horrocks failed to interest any of the state bodies in Argyn Khassenov's predicament, it was to EMM that he turned.

"I wouldn't place too much weight on the reasons given by the police for not investigating," said Edmonds, whose brisk and open approach to discussing financial crime was refreshing after months trying and largely failing to extract information from the harried employees of the state judicial system. "My experience of fraud cases is that they will always try and get them off their desk. They will come up with all sorts of different reasons why they won't take a case on if it looks like it falls into the 'too difficult' box."

The fact that investigating Khassenov's case involved cooperating with the authorities in Hong Kong and finding witnesses in Kazakhstan and Russia were reasons for the police to turn it down. For Edmonds, however, these were reasons to ask Horrocks to get on a plane. Horrocks visited the fake office in Hong Kong and used the local courts to extract account details from Standard Chartered. He was able to compare emails between Khassenov and Kulich with specific transactions shown on bank statements and thus build up a picture of what had really happened to the lost million dollars.

Horrocks wasn't able to do everything that police officers could have done, of course. He had no search warrant, so he couldn't seize Kulich's computer or question him under caution. But he was remarkably resourceful. When Kulich denied having ever met Khassenov, despite them having held a meeting in Budapest, Horrocks tracked down the vendor of a particular T-shirt Kulich had given as a gift and scoured Kulich's bank statement until he found the specific transaction.

The case came to court, and in December 2017 the jury returned its unanimous verdict: Kulich was guilty. The judge sentenced him to five years' imprisonment with asset confiscation to follow. "This was a sophisticated, well planned and extremely well executed fraud . . . The offense falls into the highest category of culpability," said Judge Francis Laird. Khassenov was delighted. Justice had been done, and the butler had seen his client right at last.

It had been an impressive feat of investigation by Horrocks, of case building by Edmonds and of perseverance by Khassenov, and I am grateful to all of them for taking the time to talk me through it. I decided to write to Kulich as well, though, just to check if there were any aspects of the case that I had not thought of or which the others were not telling me about. I discovered what prison he was serving his sentence in and wrote him a letter with eleven questions covering everything from how he had first come into contact with Khassenov, to the nature of the fake website, to his opinion of the legal process that had convicted him, to whether there were other victims of the fraud as well as Khassenov. I did this more out of a desire for completeness than anything else. I never thought he would reply.

I was wrong. The following week the postman delivered a dauntingly thick A4-sized envelope that contained multiple documents as well as twenty pages covered on both sides with dense handwriting. My questions had been detailed and specific because I was trying to check the accuracy of the allegations that Khassenov had made. But Kulich was not interested in my questions. Instead, he wanted to re-litigate the whole case.

Many of his claims were wild. He claimed to have been working with Russia's financial intelligence unit and only to have come into contact with Khassenov because one of the Kazakh's associates was a money launderer. We can be pretty confident that these claims can be safely discounted because he aired them, along with allegations that the lawyers on both sides were corrupt, that the witnesses were lying and that the evidence was forged, when he attempted to appeal against his conviction. The judge was so unimpressed by his arguments that she added an extra eight weeks to his sentence for having made an application that was "wholly unmeritorious."

Other claims that he made are the kind to be expected from any thief who gets caught when he thought he'd escaped with his loot. He wrote at length about how Khassenov was the real fraudster because he had received payment offshore in defiance of Kazakh regulations. "Khassenov is an idiot. He does things which are expensive, make no economic sense, but the reason he does them is because he wants to save money," he wrote.

Kulich also wrote at length about how he had lost all his money and how his children miss him. And that is of course very sad, but it is also entirely his own fault, so I struggled to be sympathetic. He then spent pages accusing Britain of being too enthusiastic in welcoming money from the former Soviet Union and doing too little to investigate the laundering of Russian cash, all of which was fair comment but also a bit rich coming from a UK-based Russian serving a lengthy sentence for defrauding a citizen of the former Soviet Union.

But there was one paragraph that jumped out at me, not in his handwritten letter but in an appeal to the prime minister that he had also written but never sent. "I had a legal aid barrister representing me in the trial . . . against a million-pound strong army of lawyers, private detectives and countless solicitors and their secretaries," he wrote. "This case was dealt with by Ms. Tamlyn Edmonds . . . With her it is not just a matter of money. She will not just confiscate—she will devastate all that the unfortunate targeted person has—Tamlyn Edmonds on behalf of her extremely vindictive clients is unforgiving. She will make sure you lose everything."

This claim was hidden in page after page of accusations and conspiracies so was easy to overlook, but actually there is an important point here. If we pretend for a minute that Kulich was in fact what he says he was—an innocent wealth planner, working in a freelance capacity to help the Russian authorities fight money laundering, who'd been targeted by criminals as a result—would he have stood a chance? If he had in fact been privately prosecuted in the UK by a deep-pocketed and vindictive opponent, what would have happened to him?

This is a hypothetical question, but nonetheless the answer is alarming. Under measures introduced in the post-2010 austerity agenda, defendants like Kulich have no prospect of reclaiming their expenses from public funds if they are convicted. Even if they're acquitted, they can only get their expenses back if a request for legal aid has previously been turned down. And had he been prosecuted as a company rather than an individual, he wouldn't have been able to claim back his expenses at all. Meanwhile, private prosecutors—whether individuals or companies—can claim back all reasonable expenses even if they lose. Financially speaking, a private prosecution is a one-way bet. As long as you can afford the upfront cost of bankrolling the case, you'll get your money back because under common law you are acting on behalf of the Crown.

It is sometimes said that if you want to change the world, you just have to find a way for lawyers to make money out of it. And, well, here we are.

"I know from personal discussions with private prosecutors that the low costs risk is viewed as an economic incentive to bring a private prosecution. This imbalance in the costs regime is disgraceful and has opened up the risk of abuse by large corporations with deep pockets," wrote Jamas Hodivala, a barrister, in evidence to a parliamentary committee in 2020. He was speaking from experience, having defended two clients against a private prosecution brought by Apple, which despite ending in their acquittal left them impoverished. "This is a complete shambles at the moment," he wrote.

The situation is deeply illogical. Private prosecutions are far more expensive than those brought by the government, often costing three times as much, because the lawyers involved charge a full commercial rate for their time, which can be five times higher than that paid by the Crown Prosecution Service. In order to save money back in 2010, the government slashed funding to the police, meaning officers are able to investigate fewer crimes; as a result, private prosecutors do it instead and then present the government with a huge bill.

We do not have statistics on the number of private prosecutions being brought, although judges and lawyers alike agree that the number is rising fast. We can, however, see how much money is being spent out of legal-aid funds to compensate private prosecutors for the expenses they have incurred, and it is soaring. In 2014–15 the total came to just £360,000. By 2019–20 it had risen to £12.3 million. At that rate of increase it won't be long before expenditure on private prosecutions wipes out the entire saving made by the cuts to police and court budgets after 2010.

And this isn't the only way the funding system is skewed toward private prosecutors. If the state's prosecutors win a case, they rarely seek more than a relatively modest sum from defendants in compensation for their costs, but there is nothing to stop private prosecutors seeking considerably more or to stop courts from supporting them in doing so. This means defendants face financial ruin if they lose. Even if they have insurance to cover their own legal costs, the insurer won't cover the prosecutor's expenses. This inevitably skews the risk calculation for defendants: even if they're not guilty, it might be worth saying they are to avoid the risk of bankruptcy. In short, private prosecutors get to take a one-way punt at public expense, while their opponents not only have to fund their own defense but face the prospect of losing everything if convicted.

This alarming situation has pretty much entirely escaped public notice. Where private prosecutions do catch the media's attention, it tends to be when they are crowdsourced. In one case EMM acted for a cycling charity in an (unsuccessful) attempt to prosecute a driver over a cyclist's death. In another case a man raised £300,000 to privately prosecute Boris Johnson for lying during the Brexit campaign. A judge threw that case out before it even came to trial, but it gained enough publicity to give the impression that private prosecutions are a useful tool for campaigners looking to find justice. But examples like these are unrepresentative. Almost all private prosecutions are brought by large companies or wealthy individuals for a crime against their property, just as they were in the eighteenth century.

The romantic idea that private prosecutions are an ancient constitutional safeguard for the powerless, a legacy of Anglo-Saxon freedoms, is misleading; in reality they are the opposite, a powerful tool available only to the very wealthy. "An individual is poorly placed to bring a successful prosecution: the cost is prohibitive and legal aid is not available," parliament's Justice Committee said in 2020. "The right is largely used by organizations that have the means to employ the necessary investigative and legal expertise." As a result of the reductions in public expenditure, Butler Britain is providing a two-tier justice system. Wealthy individuals or companies can buy justice in a way that ordinary people cannot.

"This scenario gives rise to very real concerns about unfairness resulting from inequality of arms," wrote Vivienne Tanchel, a barrister fresh from defending a client in a private prosecution in 2018. Her client was guilty of a particularly nasty fraud and does not deserve much sympathy, but the principle of the rich being able to use the criminal court system as a weapon should be of concern to anyone. "What has arisen is a steady and significant erosion of the guarantee of the right to a fair trial because of an inequality between defense costs orders and those available to the private prosecutor," she wrote.

And this is only the beginning. Aggressive private prosecutors are beginning to appreciate the power inherent in bringing cases simultaneously in the criminal and the civil courts, using one proceeding to put pressure on the other. In 2020 the Russian oligarch Oleg Deripaska, stung by defeat in an arbitration hearing against another wealthy Russian, attempted to bring a private prosecution against him. State prosecutors stepped in to block it, but it was an alarming sign of what may be coming.

If private prosecutions are routinely used as an adjunct to civil cases, this will mean poorer defendants will have to give up without a fight. Few individuals or small companies can afford to fight on one legal front, let alone two simultaneously. I found many lawyers willing to talk enthusiastically about private prosecutions as an efficient technique for bringing justice in complex and multi-jurisdictional crimes, which undoubtedly they are. It is good that Andrey Kulich is in prison, and that would not have happened if Khassenov had not been able to act boldly in a way UK state agencies would not. I could not, however, find many lawyers willing to speak on the record about the risks inherent in subcontracting justice to rich individuals—empowering them as investigator, litigator, witness, victim and minister of justice all at the same time. However, privately I found several lawyers concerned about the direction Butler Britain is taking.

"I've just been chatting to someone today about an ethical problem that's arisen as a result of exactly this—where a commercial dispute has gone sour, and the loser in the commercial dispute is seeking to bring a private prosecution, not necessarily because he or she is particularly fussed about the interests of justice, but simply because they want revenge," said one lawyer.

"If you remove the objectivity, which is what you get when being prosecuted by the state, then it's a race to the bottom, or a race to the bottom of the pockets anyway. We are on that trajectory. It raises the startling prospect of two Russian oligarchs slugging it out in the commercial courts, and then one of them deciding suddenly he's going to bring a private prosecution against the other. Once that happens, all gloves are off."

If you think this sounds too far-fetched, think back to the previous chapters in this book. If you had told someone in the 1970s that the British Virgin Islands—"Where?"—would become the world's leading financial secrecy jurisdiction, they would have laughed. If you had told someone in the 1980s that Gibraltar—"The naval base?"—would provide a safe haven for merciless gambling operators preying on vulnerable people, they would have thought you were mad. If in the 1990s you had explained to someone that a legal structure primarily used for Scottish agricultural tenancies would shortly become the getaway vehicle for hundreds of billions of pounds of stolen wealth—"A Scottish limited what?"—and that the government would do nothing to stop it, it would have sounded like a plot rejected by a third-rate thriller writer.

Likewise, if you had told somebody in the early 2000s that a Ukrainian tycoon who considered it necessary to deny links to the world's most notorious mobster would move to the UK and within a few years meet the Queen's husband and the Speaker of the House of Commons, open trading on the London Stock Exchange and give advice to the Foreign Office, they would have written you off as an unbalanced conspiracist.

Yet all those inglorious tales are true, as are many others

so complex and involved they would take thousands of pages to tell. And the lesson is that there is pretty much nothing that Butler Britain won't do to earn a fee. If the UK thinks it could bring in extra cash by turning its criminal courts into a weapon of vengeance for the world's oligarchs, do you really think it wouldn't?

That is the UK's trajectory and has been for much of the last hundred years, but it doesn't have to be that way; money doesn't have to be the highest priority in British life. In the last chapter, therefore, I'm going to look into what has been done already and what could be done in the future to help Britain discover a new— and better—way to earn a living.

10

THE END?

In the late 1970s Eurodollars pioneer and City grandee Robert Renny St. John—"John"—Barkshire expanded into the United States, taking over a foreign exchange broker called Lasser Bros. Described by a historian as "visionary, formidably energetic and a superb networker," Barkshire was—among many other things during his career—colonel of the City of London's Territorial Army regiment, chairman of London's main futures market and a justice of the peace. In his spare time he and his wife farmed 300 acres in East Sussex. His company, Mercantile House, was a major player in an internationalizing foreign exchange market and as such wanted a presence in New York, but for Barkshire everything about the place came as a shock.

"It's difficult to put one's finger on any individual thing, but the whole of the way that the New York market operated. I suppose the Mafia element, the ethnic element, the junk food, the no lunches, the no alcohol, all of those sorts of things were operating in a totally different way. It was a much rougher market," he told an interviewer for the *City Lives* project. The man who ran Lassers, the company that Mercantile House took over, was called Anthony—"Tony"—Aloi, and he epitomized the differences between the two countries. Whereas Barkshire grew up with rugby and prep at an English private school before following his father into the City, the young Aloi had taken over a children's street gang in the Bronx by slamming the previous leader's fingers in a car door, and risen from there. He was a tough boss and a good colleague, but hugely overweight, thanks to a largely hamburger-based diet. He died of a heart attack within eighteen months of Barkshire taking over, which obliged the Englishman to fly over for the funeral.

"There were a dozen limos with black windows, and I mean quite extraordinarily, chaps with black shirts and white ties and dark glasses and black hats stepped out," he recalled.

> I sort of had a private audition with his wife and the body, and one had to go up and kiss this dead body, which was different, and I can't say that I had done it before. But there he was, dressed in his blue suit lying in an open coffin with his face made up, and it was again something of a shock, with half a dozen female relatives pouring their hearts out before you . . . And then the funeral the next day, again with people chucking themselves on the grave, and these chaps with dark glasses standing all around, and their retainers standing there with their hands inside their shirt, looking as though they were about to pull a gun at any minute.

Was he not worried that he might have essentially gone into business with the Mafia, the interviewer asked. "His connections were personal and not business," Barkshire replied with commendable wit.

I would like to see that partnership dramatized—the slim Englishman and the spherical New Yorker meeting each other, working together and gradually becoming friends, all culminating in the culture clash of the funeral. It would be like a real life version of the Hugh Grant film *Micky Blue Eyes*, in which a posh British auctioneer gets entangled with the mob, but good. Even more than that, however, I would like to hear about their encounter from the opposite perspective. It is funny and instructive to hear an Englishman's description of the folkways of Italian-Americans on Wall Street, but it would be fascinating to hear what a New Yorker made of the folkways of City gentlemen: their strange mode of speaking, their reserve, their peculiar sense of humor, their particular education and their tight-knit brotherhood.

Throughout this book men like Barkshire have cracked open the world, gone out and persuaded people to hire them as butlers. If he'd been born a generation before, he would have pumped money through the plumbing of the British empire, but as the empire died, it was his generation that launched Britain into the butlering business, making the compromises and judgments that have transformed everything. "We were rebels from the top downward, and I suppose to an extent I happily fitted into that—only marginally rebellious, I mean nobody was very rebellious in the City in those days—but into that marginally rebellious atmosphere, and it suited me very well," said Barkshire.

Throughout this book I have tried to show the damage that Britain's business model has done, using as examples the grand corruption in Tanzania and elsewhere and unrestricted gambling in the UK itself, but such stories are hard to research and difficult to tell, thanks to a paucity of primary material. It's not hard to see why Tony Aloi didn't commit his thoughts on Barkshire to paper: he barely had time to leave the office to grab a meal, let alone write his memoirs; besides, he doesn't seem like the analytical type. And it's equally easy to see why many of Butler Britain's clients, whether kleptocrats, money launderers, oligarchs or tax evaders, have been hesitant about leaving material for historians or journalists to analyze, since that material would be as useful to law enforcement agents as it would be to people like me.

As a result, we consistently see the behavior of Butler Britain through British eyes. We see the New York funeral through the surprised eyes of a City grandee confronting Italian-American culture, not through the eyes of a New Yorker marveling at a buttoned-up Brit who doesn't realize he needs to kiss the corpse. This not only skews our perspective on the encounters the butlers have, it also skews our assessment of those encounters' outcomes. In Britain butlering is almost invariably regarded as a source of jobs and wealth, because it is seen from the butlers' perspective rather than that of their clients or their victims. If Bertie Wooster's mishaps were described exclusively through the eyes of Jeeves—or, better still, through the eyes of one of Bertie's aunts—the P. G. Wodehouse stories would look very different. Britain no longer has an empire and is no longer in the business of stripping resources from the rest of the world so as to enrich itself. But it is in the business of using the skills it learned while running an empire in order to help others do what it used to do, and earning a nice income from doing so. And it entered into this business knowingly, without any illusions about what it was up to.

In the United Kingdom itself, this was done secretly, with the spread of the Eurodollar—a financial instrument that both was and wasn't a dollar, something so peculiar that it is still hard to understand—among banks and brokerages that felt no need to explain what they were doing to politicians or the public. The Bank of England was more than happy to obscure what they were up to, since its leaders largely disagreed with the country's political direction anyway—all that "socialist nonsense," as Lord Cromer described it—and ordinary politicians were busy with other things, so didn't notice until it was too late.

In smaller British overseas territories, however, the decision to turn to butlering to pay the bills was far more obvious, as was the lack of concern for the consequences elsewhere.

An early example of this were the Cayman Islands, a remote Caribbean colony that Britain kept because Jamaica didn't want it. The archipelago's 8,000 or so inhabitants traditionally survived by providing crews for sailing ships and fishing for turtles, but both these livelihoods were threatened in the immediate postwar years, and the future looked bleak. Attempts to attract tourists were only partially successful, thanks to the islands being both remote and mosquito-plagued, with poor communications. A 1950s advertising brochure was winningly honest: "You must console yourself with the thought that life anywhere is impossible without a little healthy frustration." Needing to generate revenue, the governor decided to undercut the regulations and taxes of the islands' neighbors, to attract funk money and drive development. "It didn't have any income tax, for a very good reason: they didn't have any income," Milton Grundy, a City lawyer and expert in trusts, told me. "There was nothing to tax. It was a wasteland."

Grundy arrived in the Cayman Islands in 1966, about a decade after the islands gained their first bank branch. He was there to meet a client and experienced first hand how determined the local administration was to expand its services. The governor cornered him, and asked him to write a trust law, so the islands could attract more business to the small handful of lawyers they possessed. "The governor said, 'We don't have a trust industry here; we have the makings of it because we have no income tax. People in different places have trusts, what we need is a law to govern trusts,'" Grundy remembered. Grundy obligingly created a bespoke trust law for the islands, adding some elements that were more akin to structures in continental

Europe, and a new financial product was born. The money poured in. It was boom time.

Five years later the Foreign Office dispatched Lord Asquith—not the same one as lobbied for Dmitry Firtash, but his father—to look over the place, and he was amazed by what had already been achieved, thanks to an annual economic growth rate of 29 percent. "The colony's spectacular progress in the economic field has been due to external factors: foreign businessmen attracted by the tax haven and foreign tourists," Asquith wrote in his report. "Its continuance depends on external confidence in the political stability of the islands and the good faith of their government in honoring commercial undertakings. Among the Caymanians I talked to I found a widespread appreciation and acceptance of this position."

That's a lot of words to express a simple concept: the islands had come to depend on wealthy foreigners, so they couldn't afford to do anything to upset them, any more than Bertie Wooster could afford to upset his aunts. "The Foreign Office's concern was to get the expense off the books," said Grundy.

The strategy of turning three obscure islands named after a reptile on an undersea mountain range halfway between Jamaica and Cuba into a butler has been wildly successful, seen from the islands' perspective. The Caymans are now the world's leading domicile for hedge funds and the second-leading domicile for the captive insurance industry, with an economy twice as large as Britain's per head of population. Money flows seamlessly in and out with its owners' information jealously protected.

Although the islands are no longer in the business of laundering huge volumes of cash for the drug cartels, as they were in the 1980s—for reasons that we will come to—they are still ultimately reliant on helping other countries' citizens protect their wealth from scrutiny and do more of this than pretty much anywhere else. That makes the Caymans, according to the latest *Financial Secrecy Index*, a biennial publication of the Tax Justice Network, which assesses different jurisdictions by how much they "use secrecy to attract illicit and illegitimate or abusive financial flows," the single most harmful place on the planet.

"The secrecy world creates a criminogenic hothouse for multiple evils including fraud, tax cheating, escape from financial regulations, embezzlement, insider dealing, bribery, money laundering, and plenty more," the TJN said in its preamble to the 2020 *Index*. "It provides multiple ways for insiders to extract wealth at the expense of societies, creating political impunity and undermining the healthy 'no taxation without representation' bargain that has underpinned the growth of accountable modern nation states. Many poorer countries, deprived of tax and hemorrhaging capital into secrecy jurisdictions, rely on foreign aid handouts."

The Cayman Islands are of course not alone. Joining them in the top twenty of the TJN's list are the British Virgin Islands, Jersey, Guernsey and the United Kingdom itself, while further down the list are Gibraltar, the Isle of Man and Anguilla. All these British territories made the same calculation that the Caymans did: there's good money in helping wealthy foreigners get away with stuff they couldn't do at home; in being a butler.

I was speaking to Grundy in his airy, sunny office in the City of London, a short walk from both the River Thames and St. Paul's Cathedral. As far as he was concerned, if there was a problem, it was caused by excessive use of scrutiny-dodging and tax-dodging services rather than by the services themselves. A bit of naughtiness is fine; it's only when it becomes industrialized that it causes problems. "Everybody's bought a bottle of duty-free whiskey in the airport—it's neither here nor there—but when you're doing hundreds of millions and dumping them in Bermuda so as not to pay any tax in France or Britain or wherever it is, then it becomes a matter of public concern," he said. "Large American companies have taken hold of one or two very simple tax planning ideas and used them on such a huge scale that the public is scandalized."

He clearly has a point: the damage caused by Britain's butlering services is now far greater than it was in the 1950s, simply because so much more money is involved. It's like the difference between a farmer moving a single can of petrol between the Republic of Ireland and Northern Ireland to take advantage of differences in fuel duties and him creating a giant underground tank with a hatch on each side of the border so he can move fuel in bulk. But the seeds of today's situation were sown back then, so the original architects of the butlering strategy are as culpable as its current proponents. In order to enrich themselves, British officials, politicians, bankers, lawyers and others launched themselves into a business that has done a huge amount of harm to other people. At best they didn't consider the consequences of what they were doing, at worst they didn't care.

We can see an example of this in Britain's approach to deregulating the gambling industry in the 1990s and early 2000s. Other countries also considered whether to relax restrictions, including the United States, but there Bill Clinton's administration commissioned a thorough, lengthy and rigorous investigation of the potential benefits and harms of changing the law. In Britain the investigation was cursory, and the changes were rushed through. A whole new framework was created to encourage the creation of "innovative new products" without asking whether innovation is necessarily a good thing in an industry that sells something addictive. Crack cocaine and heroin were innovative too in their time, after all. The government is now attempting to repair the damage by funding treatment for addicts and bringing taxation back onshore, but millions of families have already suffered thanks to the national predilection to help Britain's clients do whatever they like—to earn fees first and ask questions later.

This pattern—of allowing something, making money from it, then attempting to solve the problems it causes after they've occurred—has repeated itself again and again. We saw it with Cambridge University, which accepted Dmitry Firtash's wealth and then was forced to put it in a special bank account when he was arrested on an FBI warrant. We saw it with Britain's lax approach to shell companies, when it made regulation as light as possible to attract fund managers and launched an orgy of money laundering in the former Soviet Union. Again and again Butler Britain has cared about its clients' interests first, and everyone else's later if at all.

When challenged about this, politicians tend to point out that much of the bad behavior happens in other parts of the British archipelago, so they're powerless to stop it: UK politicians point to Jersey; Jersey politicians point to Gibraltar; in Gibraltar they point to the BVI; BVI politicians point back to the UK. They'd simply love to help of course, but those other jurisdictions have different laws and their own police agencies, so it's out of their hands.

This regulatory fragmentation works to the benefit of butlering services because a client's activities can be divided up between different jurisdictions, which prevents outsiders from getting a full view of what's happening. If you own a house in London via a BVI company controlled by a Jersey trust, you and your lawyer have a full overview of your affairs, but regulators, law enforcement agents or nosy outsiders like me see just fragments. And the autonomy of British jurisdictions is total but also partial. It is insisted upon when it benefits Butler Britain's clients; otherwise it's ignored, and the whole scattered collection of islands (plus Gibraltar, a peninsula) are seamless parts of a unified realm, serviced by a single tribe of lawyers, accountants and other professionals. It's rather like Bertie Wooster's approach to his family: he's hugely enthusiastic about relatives when going to dinner, because his aunt has a gifted French chef who produces delicious *Suprême de fois gras au champagne* and *Sylphides à la crème d'écrevisses*; he's extremely unenthusiastic about relatives when it involves babysitting his cousin Thomas, "England's premier fiend in human shape."

I witnessed this Woosterian approach to ties between the various British territories first hand when trying to get to the BVI in 2016. My flight from St. Kitts and Nevis was canceled, causing a wave of concern among my fellow passengers, almost all of whom were London lawyers flying into Road Town for court proceedings. It was the work of about fifteen minutes for them to find someone who owned a plane and to pay him to fly them there. They were all in court in the morning. When I finally arrived, however, I spent several days finding out nothing at all.

In the same way that Eurodollars were and weren't dollars, depending on what was profitable at the time; the BVI both are and aren't British, depending on what suits their clients. They're British when it comes to UK lawyers acting for companies; they're not when it comes to journalists investigating those companies, or indeed to UK police officers.

Two years later, in the unusual political conditions thrown up by Brexit, two astute UK politicians seized an opportunity to tackle the convenient on-off autonomy enjoyed by Britain's overseas territories. An election in 2017 had returned a minority Conservative government, and loyalties had splintered as Brits identified as much as pro- or anti-EU as they did by political party, which gave Labor's Margaret Hodge and the Conservatives' Andrew Mitchell the chance to force the UK to impose rules on its remaining colonies, so as to stop them hiding wealth. "Tax avoidance and financial crime are not trivial irritants. The problem is widespread and corrosive. If we fail to act, we are complicit in facilitating the very corruption that this government and this prime minister have told us they are determined to tackle," said Hodge. "Our overseas territories are an integral part of Britain and they should be guided by the same values as us. Clamping down on corruption and toxic wealth is morally right. We will never be a truly global Britain on the back of stolen principles."

Mitchell and Hodge proposed an amendment to a bill going through Parliament, which would oblige all parts of Britain to reveal who owned the companies registered with them, thus undermining the shell company-based business model created by the BVI and elsewhere that damaged Tanzania and so many other places. The government had long refused to do this, saying it was obliged to respect its various territories' autonomy, while the territories themselves said they would only raise their standards when all their competitors agreed to do the same. In the meantime, if they didn't take the business, somebody else would. These were the same two arguments used back in the 1960s by the City of London, still interlocked and still powerful after all these years.

Mitchell and Hodge managed to corral a cross-party coalition of MPs who rejected the fundamental premises of that argument and insisted that Britain should do the right thing regardless of other countries' rules. "Until we move, we have little chance of speeding up any response from Delaware, Panama and the other places," said veteran parliamentarian Kenneth Clarke. "It is not an overwhelming argument to say, 'Well, we should carry on having billions of pounds of criminal money flowing through our overseas territories while we wait for Panama to make a move.' That is not the strongest argument." The government conceded defeat, and the amendment went through, helping to close a loophole that tax dodgers and crooks have been enjoying for decades.

I visited the BVI shortly after Hodge and Mitchell ambushed the UK government with their amendment imposing transparent ownership on British territories' shell companies, and found local leaders who saw the situation in very different terms. They were furious that their autonomy had been violated by the government in London and nervous they were going to be bankrupted. "It's almost like you use an undemocratic means to do something that you think is essential to democracy—it's almost inherently a paradox," said Sowande Wheatley, deputy prime minister, over coffee on a Sunday morning. "We have just as much right to control our destiny as the people in the UK do."

He was concerned that the amendment would undermine all the wealth and improvements in living conditions that the islands had gained since the 1970s. "It accounts for 60 percent of the government's budget, so it's a tremendous threat to our way of life," he said. "The government's whole operation depends very heavily on the fees from the financial services, everything: schools, hospitals, roads, care for the elderly, care for persons with mental challenges."

He of course has a point. It is unreasonable for Britain, having encouraged its colonies to become self-sufficient and failing to question how they went about it, to then turn around and stop them from earning a living. But that does not mean the UK should allow the BVI and its other territories to do what they want either. There are now no good options: either London ignores local autonomy or it sits back and tolerates the enabling of massive volumes of fraud. Butlering is an intolerable way to make a living, yet butlers won't voluntarily give up butlering if they rely on butlering for their salaries. Someone needs to step in and stop them.

This paradox is one of the reasons why the UK government has done so little to clean up over so many years, despite claiming to want to, and why action was left to Hodge and Mitchell. But the limitations of action taken by backbench MPs rather than the government are obvious. Without control of the state's budget or administrative apparatus, ordinary MPs do not have the ability to boost the funding of the National Crime Agency and other law enforcement agencies or to coordinate a diplomatic push to persuade places like Panama to follow the UK's lead, and can only opportunistically exploit occasional parliamentary arithmetic to achieve isolated victories.

So what should the UK government do? For a start, it needs to do more to prevent the various bits of Britain from creating loopholes that could develop into as damaging an instrument of the butlering profession as shell companies have been. This requires far more public and political awareness of the UK's overseas territories, which are still almost entirely ignored in Britain. And the public has become no less ignorant about the BVI and the Caymans because the islands are now rich. Brits may know more about Gibraltar, but most would be surprised to hear it is anything other than a plucky military base standing guard at the gates to the Med.

When I was in Gibraltar I had a long chat with Albert Isola, minister for digital and financial services, who was surprisingly hip-looking with an open-necked shirt and multicolored thread bracelet. He was keen to talk about the peninsula's new proposal for attracting business to the Rock, which is to introduce regulations for companies that use blockchain, a mechanism by which financial or other transactions are recorded in a decentralized way and which underpins cryptocurrencies like Bitcoin.

From Gibraltar's perspective, it is acting in a nimble way to take advantage of a new business opportunity, and it is perfectly possible that the companies that submit to the peninsula's regulators will prove beneficial to the world. It is also, however, perfectly possible that this new technology will act like a twenty-first-century shell company, and help crooks and tax dodgers hide their wealth from democratic scrutiny. My concern is that Gibraltar rushed ahead and set out legislation to encourage and protect companies engaged in blockchain activities apparently without any debate or discussion of the potential downsides. This is after all exactly what happened when Gibraltar welcomed the gambling industry, and indeed Isola drew an explicit comparison between Gibraltar's approach to regulating the new technology and its early approach to gambling.

"What's our goal? To succeed in bringing quality business to Gibraltar, which is here in the long run, and which will give benefit to us by bringing economic activity, by employing people, by taking space and by paying corporate tax," he said. "That's what we did in gaming, and it worked very efficiently. In twenty-five years we hadn't had a single failure."

Isola was comparing Gibraltar with laxer jurisdictions like Malta, which issue more gambling licenses and see more companies fail as a result, but it still seems like an unfortunate way of expressing himself. Gambling has brought jobs and prosperity to the Rock, while spreading addiction and misery elsewhere.

The reason Gibraltar has not had a single failure of a gambling company is that it has exported failure to the jurisdictions where its clients live. Meanwhile, it is difficult for politicians in the UK to do anything about this for the same reason it was hard to combat shell companies—because they need to respect Gibraltar's autonomy. Could blockchain companies suck money out of the world to the benefit of Gibraltar and a handful of wealthy foreigners to the detriment of ordinary people and governments trying to provide basic services? Perhaps. We simply don't know because there has been no discussion about it in the UK, and Gibraltar has powered on regardless.

The problem was created as Britain's empire collapsed. Whereas Paris's remaining colonies are administered, taxed and represented as parts of France, Britain has never attempted to create a coherent framework for its scattered territories. Places like Gibraltar, Anguilla and the Cayman Islands did not want to be independent, but there was no mechanism whereby a colony could become part of the UK, so instead they remained in a form of jurisdictional limbo. What that has come to mean is that they are independent in ways that are profitable to the butlers and their clients, but British when it means they need UK taxpayers to fund anything costly. This was demonstrated in 2019 when Iranian forces were only prevented from seizing an oil tanker in the Arabian Gulf thanks to the intervention of a Royal Naval frigate. The tanker was identified in the media as British but was actually flying the flag of the Isle of Man, one of the many semi-detached bits of Britain. By sailing under the Manx flag, the tanker's owners could avoid paying a hefty tax bill or abiding by EU regulations. So the tanker was British enough to be protected by the UK's navy, but not so much that its owners needed to pay UK taxes to support the frigate.

The response to any criticism of such loopholes is invariably to say that if Britain didn't do it, somebody else would, and before Britain acts to stop such abuses, it needs to wait until everyone is prepared to do so, because doing otherwise wouldn't achieve anything. Surely it's better for the tanker to be registered in somewhere that is at least half-British rather than somewhere else entirely?

At the very least, Brits need to get better at questioning whether such arguments make sense. A classic example is the sale of "golden visas" to wealthy foreigners looking to move to the UK. Most people agree that selling the right to move to Britain and thus letting rich people jump the visa queue is at best morally questionable. However, other countries—the US, Canada, Australia, etc.—did this first, and so Britain joined in. Subsequently even more countries—Portugal, Greece, Italy, etc.—started selling them too, so why should Britain stop? In 2014, however, the Migration Advisory Committee, which gives expert advice to the government, examined the golden visa program and concluded that while it was hugely beneficial to its applicants, it did almost no good for Britain as a whole, while increasing inequality and thus social problems.

"Many stakeholders—major consultancy firms and wealth managers acting for the investors—claim that the UK government gains stamp duty when their clients buy houses. This is nonsense," said Professor David Metcalf, who chaired the committee. The only positive reason he could think of for retaining the program was to signal that Britain is "open and welcoming," which is something that could be done in other ways, particularly if Britain were to take into account the fact that any benefit to the UK from a program designed to attract wealthy foreigners is more than offset by harm done elsewhere. Applicants for golden visas are not coming to the UK to start businesses and create wealth, they are coming to avoid taxes and scrutiny.

The same pattern applies to the regulation of Scottish limited partnerships. When they were looking at proposed reforms, British policy makers rated the (very modest) gains that the London fund management industry could make from less regulation as far more important than the dramatic harm done by Eastern European money launderers who exploited the same loopholes. It might be too much to expect UK politicians to assess a foreign loss as being of equal value to a domestic gain, but it is surely not too much to ask them to consider their clients' victims' interests at least a bit, as well as those of their clients. Again, this is a failure of information and imagination.

Butlering thrives on loopholes. The differences between the various bits of Britain—whether the mismatch between gambling taxes in Gibraltar and the UK, the differing rules governing limited partnerships in Scotland and England or discrepancies between company regulations in the BVI and elsewhere—provide loopholes that the clever butler can use to hide his clients' assets, behavior and even existence. If there is one message I would like everyone to take from this book, it's that Britain should iron these differences out. If Gibraltar wants to be British—and, heaven knows, its politicians say often enough that they do—then their Britishness has to extend at the very least to agreeing not to undercut UK regulations and taxes. Right now Britain's territories opt into the bits of Britishness that are profitable, and out of the bits that require sacrifice. That has to stop.

Butlering also thrives on the UK's failure to enforce the rules Parliament has created, by underfunding and undermining its law enforcement agencies and regulators. It is absurd that the law agencies of such a wealthy country have to worry about whether they can afford to take on a businessman with questionable wealth. Oligarchs are rich, but they're not that rich.

It makes for good comedy when Jeeves outsmarts the village bobby, or Bertie Wooster gets away with a scam because his chum is the local magistrate, but this is no way to run a financial system. Fraud and money laundering are spreading fast, too often Britain is at the heart of them, and the only way to stop that is to give the police the powers and resources they need. A few months before the first COVID lockdown I spent a jolly evening at a policing conference drinking with a table of officers from the west of England who specialized in investigating financial crime. I had expected to hear tales of how hard they found it to obtain evidence from overseas, but that wasn't their concern at all; they were more bothered by their inability to gain usable evidence from the neighboring police force fifteen miles away. British policing is largely based around territorial forces, as if crime was still committed as it was in the nineteenth century. But financial crime works differently, it moves down wires at the speed of light, so the same scam can be committed in multiple locations simultaneously. To fight it, policing needs to be organized on a national—or better still transnational—level. One of the reasons Scottish limited partnerships were exposed as major money-laundering vehicles is that Scotland has a single police force, which could see the threat and respond strategically. In England and Wales, meanwhile, officers from dozens of local forces were still trying to work out what a limited partnership was.

And Britain needs to explore approaches used by other countries, even if they offend our delicate sensibilities. Any investigator will tell you that it's all but impossible to crack open a sophisticated fraud without an insider to explain how the money was moved, but whistleblowers put themselves in danger of retribution from their former comrades if they cooperate with investigators. In other countries whistleblowers are paid for the information they provide, yet in Britain, there remains a high-minded objection to behaving in that way. It is all very well to be high-minded, but only if you bear in mind the consequences, which in this case are that criminals get to keep the money they've stolen because Britain can't find a way to prosecute them.

Of course in the United Kingdom as in the British Virgin Islands threatening the butlering business model risks costing many influential people their livelihoods. To counteract the inevitable lobbying that will occur, those committed to getting Britain out of the butlering business need to build a lobbying operation of their own. In this they can take heart from what has happened in the United States, where committed parliamentarians devoted themselves to researching financial skulduggery, exposing the harm it did and preparing legislative responses to it. It was one such inquiry—led by Senator Carl Levin—that exposed how the Cayman Islands were responsible for laundering vast amounts of money from the United States and forced the islands' administration to step in to stop it. It was American congressmen and -women who pushed the Cayman Islands out of the shadow banking business, not British MPs. Levin and his Republican colleagues didn't just investigate, they also proposed solutions. Often those proposals came to nothing, but sometimes they were just what was needed. When new regulations for the financial system were deemed necessary after the attacks of September 11, 2001, it was an already-existing bill from Levin's committee that provided them.

The bipartisan effort from Hodge and Mitchell to impose transparency on Britain's tax havens in 2018 gave a hint of how a British equivalent might look, but it was limited by the fact that in the UK parliamentary committees have few powers and fewer resources. When Hodge ran the Public Accounts Committee between 2010 and 2015, she became famous for her work exposing tax dodging by major corporations, but she was reliant on investigative journalism for her raw material. I was delighted to have the chance in 2018 to give evidence to Parliament's Foreign Affairs Committee, but its ability to seriously interrogate the phenomenon of the Russian elite's use of Britain's butlering services was severely constrained by its inability to summon witnesses or demand documents. Just imagine what Hodge could have done if UK committees had multiple investigators working for them and could compel companies and individuals to give evidence.

And this is just the start of what needs doing to Britain's central governmental apparatus. The elevation of Russian oligarch's son Yevgeny Lebedev to the House of Lords—he is now Baron of Siberia, which sounds like a character in a sub-par Agatha Christie novel, but in reality gives him a very serious role supervising British legislation—finally demonstrated that it is time to overhaul Britain's broken second chamber. Any reform should involve empowering MPs to properly investigate both what the government is doing and what it's failing to do, and electing lords to assist them in doing so.

It will only be by imposing rational regulations and laws across the entire British archipelago, by enforcing them robustly and remorselessly and by investigating and exposing failures to do so that Brits appalled by the country's butlering industry can force it to seek a different way to earn a living. And they should not be afraid to do so. Thanks to the combined dislocations of COVID and Brexit, Britain is questioning its position in the world in ways that may not be repeated for a generation.

This is an opportunity not just for ordinary Brits harmed by the misdeeds of their rulers, but for people everywhere whose crimes are facilitated in these islands.

The last five years have heightened political divisions that often reflect fiercely different views of Britain's past. Brexiters have often referred back to 1940, when Britain stood alone and confronted a hostile Europe united against it. Some on the left harked back instead to 1945, when the war was over and Britain used the opportunity of peace to build a state that was kinder and more generous. Pro-Europeans looked to 1973, when the country accepted the loss of its empire, accepted it was an integral part of the continent and joined the predecessor to the European Union. Others had their own key moments.

Those dates all symbolize different ways of looking at the world but have one thing in common. At all of these national moments—after Dunkirk, after the war or after the crises of the 1960s—Britain made a principled decision to take a course of action not because it was profitable but because it was right. And that is the nation's idea of itself, the one it likes to put on its stamps: a country that does the right thing whatever the cost. Britain is the country that abolished slavery, that freed the colonies, that defeated the Nazis, etc. But for me the key date to understand modern Britain is not 1940, 1945 or 1973, nor any of the others I have heard. It is 1956, the year of the Suez Crisis and the year the City of London gave birth to offshore finance.

Surely whatever their differences, whichever year they see as giving birth to their Britain, all of us can reject the year that their country became a butler. Britain is better than that.

SOURCES

I recorded all the interviews I refer to in this book, and their transcripts are in my possession. When interviews were off the record, it was normally for the source's protection or occasionally because they are not authorized to talk about their work. There were also many people who talked to me at length, sharing insights important to the development of the ideas in the book but whose words I haven't used because I wanted to keep things short and pithy. To them, thank you for your time, and I hope you're not too offended.

The field of corruption studies is expanding but not as quickly as corruption, so there are always new cesspits to explore. If you're keen to start digging into one but don't know where to start, drop me a line. You can find me on Twitter and LinkedIn, or—if you've got the makings of an investigative journalist—you probably won't find it too hard to guess my email address.

I also think empire studies needs to expand too. Britain dominated—commercially, militarily or both—large tracts of the world for five centuries, and it is sad that this history is becoming a political battleground in which all nuance is stripped away. Britain is remarkable in many ways, but nothing it ever does will be as remarkable as the fact that a small island in the Atlantic used to rule a quarter of the world's surface, and I find it depressing that there isn't more curiosity among British politicians and other public figures about what that means and how it resonates in the UK today. Criticizing the empire does not automatically make you unpatriotic. As in every family, there are both heroes and villains among our ancestors, and it does us no good to pretend there aren't.

On that note, I have just read and enjoyed Sathnam Sanghera's *Empireland*, and I would recommend it to anyone interested in the consequences of empire broader than the ones I discuss in this book.

While researching *Butler to the World*, I have read hundreds of books, reports, articles and other publications, as well as watched television programs and listened to podcasts. It isn't possible for me to list every secondary source that fed into my writing, but here is a summary for each chapter of the most important books or other secondary sources I have read, with occasional suggestions for further reading.

1 The Butler Business

We know about the Ukrainian oligarchs exchanging ownership of the "grand building" on Trafalgar Square thanks to the Panama Papers. The Organized Crime and Corruption Reporting Project (OCCRP) wrote about the affair on December 15, 2017, and you can find the article online. The building housing the bookshop was the more valuable of two that were exchanged; the other was in Knightsbridge and worth £75 million.

The P. G. Wodehouse quotes and references throughout this book come from the three-volume *Jeeves Omnibus*, and I hugely enjoyed having an excuse to sit down and systematically read my way through it all.

If you're interested in becoming a literal butler (rather than a metaphorical one), there are many training schools in Britain, often with international branches. Some courses are also available online, and very reasonably priced. The British Butler Institute's website, for example, will instruct you in "how to open and close a door," "napkin presentation" or "seating a guest" for a mere £4.99 a pop.

The judge's speech was made by Sir Geoffrey Vos, chancellor of the High Court, to the Chancery Bar Association's annual conference on January 19, 2018.

2 Sun, Sand, Canal

The Suez Veterans' Association has a website—www.sunsand canal.co.uk—which contains many details of the organization. I am hugely grateful to Richard Woolley and Jeff Malone for sharing their archive of SVA newsletters with me, and for sharing their time and memories.

For the broader history of the Suez Crisis, I enjoyed Keith Kyle's *Suez* and John Darwin's *Unfinished Empire*.

3 Practical People

Richard Fry's essay is contained in a collection of speeches by George Bolton that he edited and that was published under the title *A Banker's World*; the various Bolton quotes mostly come from there as well. The trilemma idea originated in Catherine R. Schenk's *The Decline of Sterling*. She has also written interestingly about the origins of the Eurodollar market, the relationship between the City and government and much more. She took time to talk me through Eurodollars and corrected my misconceptions, for which I am very grateful, although if I've ballsed it up anyway that is of course entirely my fault.

Among other works on Eurodollars that I found useful were *Anglo-American Development, the Euromarkets, and the Deeper Origins of Neoliberal Deregulation*, by Jeremy Green, who also wrote *The Political Economy of the Special Relationship*, which develops the same themes at greater length. Gary Burn's *The State, the City, and the Euromarkets* is a classic, as is his *The Re-emergence of Global Finance*. The original investigation into the phenomenon is Geoffrey Bell's groundbreaking *The Eurodollar Market and the International Financial System*. Andrea Binder's *The Politics of the Invisible, Offshore Finance and State Power* was very useful as well.

Andrew Shonfield's *British Economic Policy Since the War* (1958) is strangely not as dated as it should be; in fact, I'd quite like someone to write a similarly approachable book about economics today. David Kynaston's *Club No More*, the fourth and final volume of his magisterial series on the City of London, has useful material on the development of offshore finance.

The *City Lives* interviews can be found on the British Library website. Many of them have been transcribed, but the original recordings are also available, and hearing the actual voices of these pioneers is fascinating. I had fun in the Bank of England archives, guided by their extremely helpful archivists, although the place is not nearly as grand as it sounds like it should be.

I'm afraid I can't remember where I read the story of the Irish farmer and the petrol tank. I've looked and asked around, but couldn't find it. If anyone knows, please drop me a line.

4 Shell Shock
Vanessa Ogle's "Funk Money, the End of Empires, the Expansion of Tax Havens, and Decolonization as an Economic and Financial Event" was published in the journal *Past & Present*. She is currently writing a history of tax havens, and frankly I wish she'd hurry up and publish it because if it's as good as that article, I'd find it extremely useful. Lewis Hunte's *Memoirs of a Caribbean Lawyer* is available online, as well as if you pop into his office. There are no book-length histories of the BVI, but there are a few useful articles in academic journals. The Chicago economist was Simon Rottenberg, who wrote about his visit in *Caribbean Quarterly*.

The Tanzanian radar scandal has been very well documented by campaigners from the Corner House and the Campaign Against the Arms Trade, and also in Andrew Feinstein's *The Shadow World*.

In the BVI, thanks to Freeman Rogers for sharing some really useful articles from the *BVI Beacon*'s archive.

5 Rock Solid
You can read a bit about my great-grandmother's serial escaper cousin Billie Stephens in Pat Reid's *The Colditz Story*, if you're so inclined. The book misses out on the best bit though. When Billie returned to London, he was locked up to await debriefing, but he wanted to

have a drink at the Ritz so he climbed out of the window. He was too drunk to shin back up the drainpipe on his return, however, and had to knock on the door to be let back in. He was a total legend, and if there is a heaven he's sure to have busted out just to have a look at the other place.

For the modern history of Gibraltar, I relied on *Fortress to Democracy, The Political Biography of Sir Joshua Hassan* by Sir William Jackson and Francis Cantos, *Rock of Contention* by George Hills and *Gibraltar: a Modern History*, by Chris Grocott and Gareth Stockey.

For issues around gambling, I relied on *Better Betting with a Decent Feller* by Carl Chinn and *Vicious Games* by Rebecca Cassidy, which is superb. Thanks to James Noyes for talking me through the issues. I found the insights in Shoshana Zuboff's *Surveillance Capitalism* very important for understanding how online gambling sucks people in. I also very much appreciated the many parliamentary reports into the betting industries, which provided useful statistics, insights and transcripts. I really like parliamentary reports, and if I was in charge I'd make sure there were more of them.

In reply to a detailed list of questions, I received a courteous email from Victor Chandler directing me to his authorized biography *Put Your Life on It: Staying at the Top in the Cut-Throat World of Gambling*, which was written by Jamie Reid and published just as I was finishing this manuscript. It is an extraordinary book, full of drama and incident far beyond the snippet I've focused on here, and someone should make it into a film. I also found his YouTube channel very useful for getting his take on how he revolutionized gambling.

In Gibraltar itself I am hugely grateful to the couple who showed me around, who I'm not going to name just in case my conclusions prove controversial. You know who you are though, and thank you very much for your kindness, insights and hospitality.

I had lots of interesting chats while I was on the peninsula, most of which I refer to in the chapter. Thanks to everyone who took the time to talk, and of those I do not quote thanks particularly to Marlene Hassan Nahon.

6 The Scottish Laundromat

The Ian Rankin novel that tackles Scottish limited partnerships and the genteel enablers of organized crime is *Rather Be the Devil*. It's great, as are all the Rebus books. The Kroll report into the Moldovan bank heist is easily discoverable online. I am very grateful to David Leask and Ian Fraser for helping me understand all this, and also to Richard Smith, who's an old co-conspirator. His blogs on Naked Capitalism are full of important insights. Graham Barrow was extremely helpful, as is his wont.

The Bellingcat/Transparency International report on SLPs—"Smash and Grab, The UK's Money Laundering Machine"—was published in 2017 and is available on both organizations' websites. There's not much written about limited partnerships, but Elspeth Perry showed me around what there is with patience and kindness. Thank you.

If I've failed to mention any of the very many scandals that SLPs have been implicated in, then my apologies; it's hard to keep track of them all.

7 Down the Tubes

I have been looking for a way to tell the story of Dmitry Firtash ever since learning he'd bought a Tube station, so this chapter is the fruit of many years of on-again off-again work. To understand the peculiarities of Ukraine, I read *Energy Dependency, Politics and Corruption in the Former Soviet Union* by Margarita Balcameda and Simon Pirani's *Ukraine's Gas Sector*. I also depended on advice from Daria Kaleniuk and her colleagues at the Anti-Corruption Action Center in Kyiv.

The lead investigator for Global Witness when it looked into Ukrainian gas was Tom Mayne, who was incredibly helpful with his time and thoughts both for this chapter and the subsequent section about unexplained wealth orders. I'm grateful to the various politicians involved with the British Ukrainian Society who did take the time to talk to me, considering there wasn't much in it for them.

Thanks also to the sources who helped me understand the legal situation in America, the Firtash links to Cambridge and his connections in UK politics.

8 Giving Evidence

I'm grateful to Tom Tugendhat MP for inviting me to give evidence to the Foreign Affairs Select Committee. He's one of the good guys when it comes to trying to ease Britain out of its butlering ways. The curious tale of the Faculty Office of the Archbishop of Canterbury began life as an article in *Prospect* magazine.

9 "Justice"

I first heard the story of Argyn Khassenov's private prosecution thanks to a presentation by EMM partner Kate McMahon at a conference. I chatted to her about it afterward, and I'm very grateful to her and her colleagues for taking so much time to talk me through it. David Clarke of the Fraud Advisory Panel helped me understand the issues around prosecuting financial crimes, and Jamas Hodivala was also generous with his time.

10 The End?

The John Barkshire quotes are from the *City Lives* project. The Tax Justice Network does excellent work investigating and exposing offshore skulduggery, and in particular I'm very grateful to John Christensen for his help. I found Elise Bean's book *Financial Exposure* very helpful in looking to understand how US congressional committees work, and I enjoyed talking to her about her work.

ACKNOWLEDGMENTS

Some parts of this book began life as articles elsewhere, so thank you to the editors who commissioned them, particularly Natalia Antelava, Sigrid Rausing and Tom Clark.

I did not do as much traveling to research this book as I originally intended because of the COVID-19 lockdown, but I was fortunate to get trips organized to the British Virgin Islands and to Gibraltar before the world shut its doors. In the BVI thank you to Aragorn Dick-Read, Frederica and family for their hospitality and the loan of their cabin, and thanks to Josie Stewart and Nick Shaxson for the introductions. In Gibraltar thank you to the couple who showed me around; you know who you are. In Bridgnorth thank you to Jeff Malone. Among the people I spoke to from my desk: huge thanks to David Leask for talking me through SLPs and to Tamsyn Edmonds for talking me through private prosecutions.

I have been lucky to accumulate a large group of friends who like talking about corruption and financial crime as much as I do, so thank you to them for letting me bounce ideas around, and in particular to: Roman Borisovich, Graham Barrow, Richard Smith, Heather Marquette, Liz David-Barrett, Sue Hawley, Peter Geoghegan and Daria Kaleniuk.

At Profile I am very lucky to work with Ed Lake, who is an understanding and encouraging editor. At Curtis Brown my agent Karolina Sutton is the big sister I never knew I needed.

Lockdown wasn't any fun obviously, but it was made incomparably better than it might have been by the fact I was stuck indoors with two such awesome sons and such a magnificent wife. I literally couldn't have done this without your support, encouragement, tolerance and occasional mockery. I owe you all ice creams/gin and tonic (delete as applicable). Thank you!

INDEX